PROJECT FIRE

Also by
STEVEN RAICHLEN

Project Smoke

The Barbecue! Bible®

Barbecue! Bible® Sauces, Rubs, and Marinades, Bastes, Butters, and Glazes, Too

How to Grill

Beer-Can Chicken

BBQ USA

Indoor Grilling

Barbecue! Bible® Best Ribs Ever

Planet Barbecue!

Man Made Meals

Miami Spice

PROJECT FIRE

CUTTING-EDGE TECHNIQUES *and* SIZZLING RECIPES *from*
THE CAVEMAN PORTERHOUSE *to* SALT SLAB BROWNIE S'MORES

STEVEN RAICHLEN

Food Photography by Matthew Benson

WORKMAN PUBLISHING
NEW YORK

Library of Congress Cataloging-in-Publication Data is available.

Paperback ISBN 978-1-5235-0276-9
Hardcover ISBN 978-1-5235-0348-3

Cover and interior design: Becky Terhune
Original photography: Matthew Benson
Food styling: Nora Singley
Prop styling: Sara Abalan
Fire wranglers: Ezra Dunn (Stokey) and Garlan Dunn (Smokey)

Additional photos: **Adobe Stock:** pp. i, ii, viii, 110, 164, 181, 223, 229 (fire); p. 13 (firewood); p. 121 (diagram). **Author photo:** p. v. **Photo by Nancy Loseke:** p. 45. **Courtesy Use:** Arteflame p. 8 (plancha grill); Carson Rodizio p. 8 (rotisserie grill); Char-Broil p. 4 (front-loading charcoal grill); Grill Works p. 6 (asado-style grill); Hōmdoor p. 8 (tandoor); Kalamazoo p. 7 (multi-fuel grill); KettlePizza p. 17 (pizza oven); Komodo Kamado p. 4 (kamado-style (ceramic) grill); Lodge p. 4 (hibachi); Meadow Creek p. 4 (table grill); Memphis p. 6 (pellet grill); Pit Barrel Cooker Co. p. 7 (upright barrel grill); Smoke N Fire Inc. p. 8 (smoker grill); Tec p. 6 (infrared grill); Weber p. 4 (kettle grill), p. 6 (gas grill).

Steven Raichlen is available for select speaking engagements. Please contact speakersbureau@workman.com.

Workman books are available at special discounts when purchased in bulk for premiums and sales promotions as well as for fund-raising or educational use. Special editions or book excerpts can also be created to specification. For details, contact the Special Sales Director at the address below or send an email to specialmarkets@workman.com.

Workman Publishing Company, Inc.
225 Varick Street
New York, NY 10014-4381

workman.com

Printed in the United States of America
First printing April 2018

10 9 8 7 6 5 4 3 2 1

In loving memory of my father
Sonny Raichlen
1929–2016

ACKNOWLEDGMENTS

Project Fire is my 31st book, and, as always, one of the great pleasures in completing it is thanking the people who helped make it possible.

But this time that pleasure is tempered with sadness, for it is my last book with my longtime editor and friend, Suzanne Rafer. For 43 years, Suzanne has polished the prose of her authors at Workman Publishing, turning their books into international bestsellers. I thank her for her expert editing, unerring counsel, and relentless pursuit of excellence. I wish her well in her retirement and will never forget how hard she has worked to make my books worthy of the name Workman Publishing on the spine.

Equally heartfelt are my thanks to my assistant, Nancy Loseke, who handles any task I throw at her—from research to recipe testing to proofreading, editing, and blogging—with an aplomb surpassed only by her enthusiasm and dedication.

The idea for *Project Fire* originated on the set of my *Project Smoke* TV show, so it's only fitting that I thank Matt Cohen, Gwenn Williams, Chris Lynch, Richard Dallett, and the many cameramen, engineers, editors, chefs, and PAs who make it possible. (That would be Bob, Dan, Dave, David, Emily, Haley, Jacob, Jillian, Joe, John, Jonathan, Jordan, Joseph, Kevin, Lauren, Michael, Paul, Rob, Ryan, Tony, and Vicki). Tip o' the hat to Steven Schupak, Stuart Kazanow, Frank Batavick, Jay Parikh, Phillip Guthrie, and Donna Hunt at Maryland Public Television.

When it came time for the photography for *Project Fire*, I had the great fortune to work again with photographer Matthew Benson, food stylist Nora Singley, and her assistants Kris Kurek and Pearl Jones, photo director Anne Kerman, prop stylist Sara Abalan, and fire wranglers Ezra Dunn (Stokey) and Garlan Dunn (Smokey).

Providing grill gear and product photos were: Arteflame, Carson Rodizio, Char-Broil, The Companion Group, Grillworks, Homdoor, Kalamazoo, Komodo Kamado, Lodge, Matsushima, Maverick, Memphis Grills, Pit Barrel Cooker Co., Safecid, Smoke 'n' Fire Inc., TEC Infrared Grills, and Weber.

Thanks, too, to Francois de Melogue (Foods in Season) and The Green Grape Provisions.

Becky Terhune designed this handsome book. Kate Karol, Carol White, Lily Kiralla, and Barbara Peragine ushered it into production, and publicity director Rebecca Carlyle and head publicist Chloe Puton will make sure people know about it. I will miss former publicity director Selina Meere, and wish her well in California. Molly Kay Upton, Erin Kibby, and Moira Kerrigan keep the barbecuebible.com website humming. (Sign up for our *Up in Smoke* newsletter if you haven't already.) Orchestrating all this are CEO Dan Reynolds, publisher Suzie Bolotin, and Workman's president, Carolan Workman. I only wish that the visionary Peter Workman were still alive to see another Raichlen book join the Workman library.

A HUGE thanks to my family: Betsy, Jake, those three rascals, Ella, Mia, and Julian, and above all, my wife of 28 years, Barbara Raichlen. Consigliere and best friend, Barbara has a hand in all the good things that happen to me, and believe me, keeping me on track is no easy task.

Last, but certainly not least, I would like to thank *you*, dear readers, for allowing me to have the greatest job on the planet. Thanks to you, I look forward to each new day, with all the new adventures and discoveries it brings.

Steven Raichlen

CONTENTS

INTRODUCTION
WHY PROJECT FIRE?

After thirty books, seven TV series, two decades of Barbecue University classes, hundreds of articles in publications ranging from the *New York Times* to *Esquire*, and literally thousands of radio and TV interviews, what more could I possibly have to say about grilling?

As it turns out, a lot.

When *How to Grill* came out in 2002, few people understood such fundamentals as indirect grilling or smoking. Today grillers debate the intricacies of dry brines and reverse-searing, of salt slab grilling and sous vide the way scientists argue the fine points of quantum physics.

Which is to say that like all else in cuisine and culture, grilling continues to evolve. Never in history have more people grilled a more diverse repertory of foods on a more sophisticated array of grills and cookers. Never have people used a wider range of grilling and smoking techniques to derive more pleasure from the ancient art of live-fire cooking. Men do it. Women do it. These days, even kids compete in barbecue competitions.

So what's new in *Project Fire*? Just about everything.

- New grills, from kamados to pellet grills, from plancha grills to hybrid wood burners.

- New tools, from remote digital thermometers to high-tech rotisseries.

- Revolutionary new techniques, from salt slab grilling to smoke-roasting, from ember-grilling to fire-heated iron.

- And of course, new foods, from alternative steaks to eco-friendly seafood, and new twists on popular classics, such as breakfast on the grill and wood-fired desserts.

Think of *Project Fire* as the companion to *Project Smoke*—my book on smoking—picking up where my previous books leave off. You have some killer grill sessions to look forward to.

THE SEVEN STEPS TO GRILLING NIRVANA

Grilling is the world's oldest and most universal cooking method, practiced in virtually every country and culture on six continents (seven if you consider the cookouts staged by grill-obsessed scientists in Antarctica). But ancient and universal don't automatically mean simple.

Today's grillers face a staggering selection of grills, from inexpensive hibachis to $20,000 supergrills. As for grilling accessories, the indispensable tongs and grill brushes are now joined by sophisticated digital thermometers and temperature controllers that communicate with your smartphone.

The once ubiquitous briquette has given way to specialty charcoals from as far away as Paraguay, Japan, and Indonesia. Then there's wood—used for adding a smoke flavor and as a grilling fuel in its own right. Which wood you use and how you add it has an enormous impact on the flavor of your food.

If you think grilling means searing a steak or burger over a hot fire, know that there are actually *five* different grilling methods—each with its own unique cooking properties for an equally unique roster of foods. And that's before you get to specialized grilling techniques, such as plancha grilling and rotisserie smoking.

Of course, you need to know about the rubs, marinades, brines, bastes, glazes, and other flavorings that transform simple grilled foods into live-fire masterpieces. How and when to apply them does much to determine the ultimate deliciousness of your final dish.

Finally, you need to know how to manage the food on the grill and cook it to the desired degree of doneness. When to take it off the grill and how to carve and serve it. How to clean and maintain your grill so it's ready for the next grill session. And some basic safety practices to keep you and your guests coming back for more.

In other words, there's a *lot* more to grilling than throwing that steak or chop on the grill.

Don't worry: I've got you covered. In the following pages, I'll walk you through the Seven Steps to Grilling Nirvana. Along the way, you'll get a refresher course on the basics and learn the new techniques and technologies needed to make you a grilling force of nature.

And now, ladies and gentlemen, fire up your grills!

STEP 1
CHOOSE YOUR GRILL

"Which grill should I buy?" is one of the questions I hear most. I wish I could give you a one-size-fits-all answer. I can't. A charcoal kettle grill offers great versatility (it's suitable for all five grilling methods—see page 19). But a convenience-minded gas griller or diehard wood griller wants a different sort of live-fire experience. Here are the basic types of grills. Smoker grills are discussed in this book; straight smokers are covered in my book *Project Smoke*.

CHARCOAL GRILLS

Charcoal grills use lump charcoal or briquettes as their primary fuel. (Some come with a propane igniter to light the charcoal.) If you love the sport of grilling—building and maintaining a fire, waltzing foods from hot spots to cooler spots—a charcoal grill is for you. Charcoal grills burn hot (up to 800°F), which is great for direct grilling, and many are well suited to indirect grilling and smoking. They tend to be less expensive and more portable than gas grills and take up less room on your patio.

Kettle grill: The charcoal kettle is a near-perfect grill. Simple to use for beginners, it's sufficiently powerful and versatile to handle just about any food you want to grill. Works for all methods of live-fire cooking.

Front-loading charcoal grill: Modeled on the *mangal* grills used

across so much of Planet Barbecue, the front-loader is a rectangular metal box with a door in the front through which you can add charcoal, wood chunks, and logs. Suitable for direct and indirect grilling and smoking.

Hibachi: Born in Japan (like me!), hibachi-style grills are used throughout Asia. Imagine a small metal (or, in some cases, stone) shoebox-like firebox with sliding vents at the bottom for heat control and a grate on top for the food. Designed for direct grilling.

Table grill: Put a large shallow rectangular metal box with a grate on legs and you've got a table grill. Some models (especially those sold or rented in Greek neighborhoods) come with rotisseries. Some models burn gas instead of charcoal. Designed for direct grilling.

Kamado-style (ceramic) grill: A large, egg-shaped ceramic grill/cooker originally from Japan—the first one being the popular Big Green Egg. Today, dozens of manufacturers make these versatile grills: most ceramic, a few metal (like the Weber Summit), others gorgeously decorated with mosaic tiles (like the Komodo Kamado). All have great thermodynamics thanks

WHAT TO LOOK FOR WHEN BUYING A GAS GRILL

There are hundreds of different gas grill models. So which is the right one for you? Price is a major factor and so are size, construction, and the warranty. Here's what to look for:

1. Burners: You want at least two burners (so you can shut one off for indirect grilling), preferably three or four. In inexpensive gas grills, the burner tubes are made from a cheap stamped metal alloy—often in a single piece shaped like an H. They burn and rust out in a couple of years. In better gas grills, the burner tubes are made of stainless steel or brass, one tube per burner. They last longer and burn better.

2. Igniters: Many gas grills have a battery-powered igniter that produces an audible click and a spark. Higher-end grills, like the Weber Summit, build the igniter right into the burner control knob. (Weber also has a Snap-Jet individual burner ignition system that gives you a whoosh of flame as each burner ignites—visual confirmation that the burner is actually lit.)

Grill grates and more, from top left clockwise: plancha; hinged grate for charcoal grill; Tuscan grill grate with legs; stainless steel gas grill grate; laser cut stainless steel grate for seafood.

3. Grate: The place where you do the actual grilling. (In fact, our word *grill* comes from the Latin *craticula*, "gridiron.") There are various types of grill grates; my personal preference is cast-iron grates with ¼-inch bars—these give you the best grill marks.

4. Grease collection system: Ducks or pork shoulders put out a lot of fat as they grill, and you want that grease funneled to and collected in a deep receptacle that's easy to access and empty. Beware of the large flat, shallow metal trays (some only ¼ inch deep) that come with some high-end gas grills; they're murder to empty.

5. Side burners: Useful for warming sauces, pan- and deep-frying, etc. I use my grill's side burner when I want to keep the spattering fat outside.

6. Cart/side tables: You can never have enough workspace, so side tables are a big plus in my book. Likewise, an enclosed cart for holding some of your grilling accessories in addition to the propane cylinder.

7. Built-in gas gauge: You need one to monitor how much gas remains in the tank. If your grill lacks one, buy a freestanding gauge like a Flame King (see page 16).

8. Built-in thermometer: Usually mounted in the lid, it indicates the *approximate* temperature in the firebox. (Remember: This is the temperature at the tip of the probe, not necessarily at the level of the grill grate.) You'll also want to get a grate-level thermometer (page 17) to tell you the temperature where you're doing the actual cooking.

9. Overall construction: Does the grill look and feel well-constructed and solid, or cheap and flimsy? Are there plenty of tool hooks and ample storage? Does it come pre-assembled? If not, are the assembly instructions clear and can you reach customer service if you need to? If you bought this book, I assume you, like me, will be spending a lot of time with your grill. Buy a grill built to last and buy more grill than you think you need: You'll grow into it.

10. Warranty: A grill has to withstand high heat, extreme weather (especially if you live up north), and a salt air environment if you live near the ocean. In other words, it undergoes a lot of stress. Buy a grill with a long, comprehensive warranty.

to their thick ceramic walls (or in some cases, insulated metal) and hyper-efficient venting: They cook low and slow (at 225°F for smoking), hot and fiery (700°F for direct grilling), and everywhere in between.

> **GRILLING HACK:** Kamado-style grills burn extremely efficiently, using very little oxygen during the cook. So sometimes when you open them, air rushes in, erupting in a potentially dangerous burst of flame called a **flashback**. To avoid this, "burp" the cooker, that is, open the lid just a little a few times to bring air into the cook chamber *before* opening it all the way.

GAS GRILLS

The gas grill came on the American outdoor cooking scene in the 1950s. It's been a complicated relationship ever since. We love the convenience—the push-button ignition and the turn-of-a-knob heat control has led some 64 percent of American families who grill (according to the Hearth, Patio, and Barbecue Association) to adopt gas as their primary grill. But purists deplore the lack of direct interaction with smoke and fire. Well, the good news is that gas grills are getting better. They're burning hotter, and many give you the opportunity to introduce wood, smoke, and even charcoal to the grilling process. If it makes you feel better, while I love grilling

over charcoal and wood, I also own gas grills and use them on busy weeknights. Suitable for direct and indirect grilling and spit-roasting. Less effective for smoking.

INFRARED GRILLS

In 1980, the Thermal Engineering Corporation (today known as TEC) introduced the first infrared grill. Here was a radical new technology that delivered an intense heat in a very short time. In 2000, TEC's patent expired and many grill companies began incorporating infrared technology into their grills—often in the form of sear stations. This gives you the option to sear your steak over the infrared burner, then move it over a conventional burner to finish cooking. Especially effective for direct grilling.

WOOD-BURNING GRILLS

In the beginning and for most of human history, grilling was done over a wood fire. It still is in grill-obsessed cultures as diverse as Argentina and Uruguay, Germany and France, and Mexico and the United States. (In Asian markets, they prefer charcoal.) Charcoal and gas give you heat, but only wood delivers a smoke flavor. If you love building and tending a fire, if you're mesmerized by the sight of flickering flames, if you relish the flavor of wood smoke, even if you love the way your clothes smell

after sitting around a campfire, a wood-burning grill is for you. Intended for direct grilling.

Asado-style grill: This is the quintessential wood-burner from South America (especially Argentina and Uruguay), and it has inspired a new generation of grills. Picture a sloping grooved metal grate (the V-shaped grooves channel away the dripping fat) over a firebox (often open in the front), with a flywheel to raise or lower the grate. More elaborate models have a burn basket in the center where you burn whole logs down to embers, which you then rake under the grill grate. Intended for direct grilling.

Pellet grills: At first glance, these grills offer the best of both gas and wood-burning grills: electric ignition and turn-of-a-knob heat control while burning real wood (or at least hardwood sawdust pellets). But when you look more closely, most pellet grills are really outdoor ovens—unsuitable for direct grilling. They work better as smokers, especially when run at lower temperatures. Determined to overcome this shortcoming, a new generation of pellet grills, like the Memphis Wood Fire Grill, have removable burn chamber covers so you can direct grill over the wood pellet fire.

BTUs: WHAT ARE THEY AND DO THEY MATTER?

Say you're shopping for a new grill. You've probably seen banners screaming "30,000 BTUs" and "1,000 square inches of grilling area!" Sounds impressive, right? But what do these numbers actually mean? And how much should they influence your decision to buy one grill or another?

BTUs—British Thermal Units—are a traditional English measure of heat: specifically, the amount of energy it takes to raise the temperature of 1 pound of water by 1°F. With grills they refer to a complex formula that uses the fuel consumption of all burners to measure the heat output. (Liquid propane, for instance, has a rating of 21,600 BTUs per pound.)

The total number of BTUs doesn't mean much: What you really want to know is how many BTUs the grill delivers for each square inch of cooking surface. That's actual cooking surface, not warming racks or the grate space over any infrared burners, although many manufacturers include this additional space in their total square inch count.

To calculate this, divide the total BTUs by the total square inches of cooking surface. In general, you're looking for at least 80 to 100 BTUs per square inch.

But BTUs are only part of the story. Many other factors affect the heat output and total performance of your grill, including:

- The distance between the burners and the heat diffuser (it should be about 2 inches).

- The distance between the heat diffuser and grill grate (it should be about 3 inches).

- The size and weight of the grate.

- How tightly the lid fits; the gap between the lid and the cook chamber.

- The overall construction of the grill, the tightness of the welds, etc.

Bottom line: Don't buy a grill based on its BTUs.

GRILLING HACK: To grill or sear on a pellet grill, install a plancha, a cast-iron skillet, or raised rail grill grates in the cook chamber. Heat your pellet grill as high as it will go. Then add the food and sear it on the hot metal.

MULTI-FUEL GRILLS

Can't decide among charcoal, gas, or wood? You don't have to. Several manufacturers make tri-fuel and dual-fuel models. Check out the high-end Kalamazoo Hybrid and the American Muscle Grill, which burn all three fuels; less expensive models include the Dyna-Glo Dual Fuel and Char-Broil Gas2Coal Hybrid Grill.

SPECIALTY GRILLS

This brings us to a few specialty grills that are quite unlike any of the charcoal or gas grills most of us grew up with.

Upright barrel grills (aka drum grills): Typically made from steel

drums, these grills combine the virtues of grills and smokers. Thanks to their singular thermodynamics, you can grill a rack of ribs vertically, with one end hanging just an inch above the coals. (Amazingly, the meat closest to the fire doesn't burn.) You build a charcoal fire in the bottom. The food sits on a grate at the top or hangs from rods stretched from side to side. With the lid off or ajar, you can use these drums for direct grilling. With the

SQUARE INCHES—HOW MANY ARE ENOUGH?

Square inches of cook surface are another selling point used by grill manufacturers, and this, too, can be misleading. First of all, a square inch—the size of a typical postage stamp—isn't very much. One hundred square inches represents a 10-by-10-inch area of grill space, which is about what you need to cook a single porterhouse steak.

You also need to know what's included in those square inches. You can't cook on a warming rack, but manufacturers often include that in the total. Nor should you count the grate area directly over an infrared sear burner.

As a rough rule, figure on about 100 square inches (the size of a large dinner plate) for each person you'll be grilling for. And remember: You always want to leave at least a quarter of your grill food-free as a safety zone.

---

lid on, use them for indirect grilling and smoking. An adjustable damper at the bottom and small vent holes at the top maintain consistent temperatures for smoking and grilling. One popular model is the Pit Barrel Cooker.

Smoker grills:
A hybrid grill of a different sort that allows you to direct grill over a hot charcoal or wood fire in the firebox section or smoke low and slow in an adjacent smoke chamber. Like a conventional offset smoker, it has a large firebox and a smoke chamber. But the firebox has a grate for grilling and dampers and a lid to manage the heat.

Plancha grills/ pedestal grills:
Cross a plancha (fire-heated metal slab—page 16) with a wood-burning grill, add a

touch of sculptural artistry, and you get a grill like the Arteflame. A wide ring-shaped steel plancha surmounts a bowl-shaped firebox. There's a heavy steel grate in the center for direct grilling over a wood fire.

Rotisserie grills: These are grills designed primarily or exclusively for spit-roasting. You light a charcoal or wood fire in the firebox. Skewer the food on the rotisserie spit(s), securing it with prongs as needed. Attach the motor, insert the end of the spit in the socket, and switch it on. The gentle rotation ensures even cooking. Especially well suited for whole birds and roasts. The cool brand here is Carson.

Tandoor: This urn-shaped clay oven is India's version of a barbecue pit, developed more than 5,000 years ago to cook flatbread. You light a charcoal fire at the bottom. The food roasts on vertical metal rods. You run it at high; you don't really vary the heat. One good model for home use is the Homdoor.

ELECTRIC GRILLS

Think of them as underpowered upside-down broilers. Don't think of them as grills. Enough said.

STEP 2
SELECT YOUR FUEL

In 1952, Illinois metalworker George Stephens created the charcoal-buring Weber kettle grill. Two years later, the Chicago Combustion Company introduced the first gas grill, the portable propane-burning "Lazy Man." A "grate" debate has raged ever since as to which is the better fuel for grilling: charcoal or gas.

Then there's the original—and to my mind, the best—wood. Master these three basic fuels, and you can grill anything, anywhere, on any type of grill.

CHARCOAL

There are many types of charcoal made by manufacturers all over the world, but you can boil them down to two main categories: lump and briquettes. Regardless of the variety, charcoal packs more energy than wood or gas: A charcoal fire can achieve temperatures of 800°F or more. Gas typically burns at 450° to 600°F.

Lump charcoal: Pure wood that is partially burned without oxygen, then broken into chunks. Common source woods include oak, apple, maple, and mesquite—each with its own subtle grilling properties—but pretty much interchangeable. Mesquite charcoal burns the hottest and has an intimidating (or thrilling, depending on your perspective) tendency to crackle and throw off hot sparks. Lump is my go-to charcoal for grilling.

Four types of charcoal (clockwise from top right): lump charcoal; briquettes; *quebracho* from South America; *binchotan* from Japan.

Pluses and minuses of lump charcoal:

- Lump charcoal contains no additives, so it burns cleaner than briquettes, producing less ash.

GRILLING HACKS

- Use scissors or a knife to open a bag of charcoal, making a clean cut at the top. Many guys (and it's usually we guys who do this) rip the top open, often resulting in a tear the length of the bag that makes it impossible to reseal.
- Store charcoal in an airtight container like a metal trash can. When it becomes wet, it becomes crumbly and moldy. And once it becomes moldy, it tastes moldy—even when burned.
- When handling charcoal, slip a plastic bag over your hand to keep your fingers clean. I learned this trick in Vietnam.

- Lump charcoal burns down more quickly than briquettes. So for long grill sessions, you need to refuel more often.

GRILLING HACKS

- Beware of "lump" charcoal that has square corners and ruler straight edges. It began as scrap lumber.
- When buying lump charcoal, look for brands that sell evenly sized pieces. Avoid brands with large amounts of pulverized pieces or dust at the bottom of the bag.

CHARCOAL GRILLING MATH

- One standard chimney starter holds about 100 briquettes. Lump charcoal varies too widely in size to give an accurate count or weight.
- One chimney full of lump charcoal is enough to fuel one 22-inch kettle grill for 30 to 40 minutes of direct grilling or 40 to 50 minutes of indirect grilling.
- One chimney full of charcoal briquettes is enough to fuel one 22-inch kettle grill for 1 hour of direct or indirect grilling.

SPECIALTY CHARCOALS

- **Binchotan:** A clean, hard, slow-lighting, super-hot burning charcoal traditionally made from oak in the Wakayama Prefecture in Japan. Due to its high cost, some Japanese grill masters use binchotan-style charcoal from China or Vietnam.

- **Quebracho:** A hard, clean- and hot-burning lump charcoal from South America. Three good brands are Fogo, Jealous Devil, and Kalamazoo.

- **Coconut charcoal (extruded):** Made from pulverized coconut shells, wood, and starch binders, then extruded into rods, cubes, or miniature logs—often with a hole in the center for better airflow. Coconut charcoal burns hot and clean, producing little ash. Note: There's also a coconut shell lump charcoal used widely in Southeast Asia.

Charcoal briquettes: For many years, charcoal briquettes were the go-to fuel for American cookouts, and while more and more grillers are using lump charcoal, briquettes remain the preferred fuel on the competition barbecue circuit, from Memphis in May to the American Royal in Kansas City.

Briquettes come in many varieties, including:

- **Self-lighting briquettes:** Impregnated with lighter fluid or other accelerant to help them light quickly and evenly. Some people like their convenience; others (me among them) would rather keep petroleum-based accelerants away from their food.

- **Wood-studded briquettes:** Contain tiny bits of hickory, apple, mesquite, or other hardwoods. Whatever wood flavor you get is subtle— blindfolded, I'm not sure you could detect their presence.

- **"Natural" or petroleum-free briquettes:** Held together with vegetable starches instead of petroleum binders.

Pluses and minuses of charcoal briquettes:

- Briquettes burn longer (about 1 hour) and at a more consistent temperature than lump charcoal.

- Briquettes produce a lot more ash than lump charcoal. This can sometimes smother the fire, so stir a briquette fire from time to time to keep it well aerated. Likewise, be sure to clean out the ash after each grill session. See page 46.

- Briquettes emit an unpleasantly acrid smoke when first lit, so wait until the coals glow red and are lightly ashed over before you begin grilling.

GAS

C_3H_8 may not be a household term, but for a majority of American households, it's the grilling fuel of choice. I speak, of course, about a petroleum distillate known as **liquid propane**. The gas is commonly sold in white metal "cylinders" (cylindrical tanks) that are available (often for exchange—empties for full) at hardware stores and gas stations everywhere.

There's another gas used for grilling—a fossil fuel derived from methane called **natural gas** (CH_4). The beauty of natural gas is that it's piped right to your patio, so you don't need to lug around propane cylinders. The drawback is that not all communities provide it. Dollars per grill session, natural gas costs significantly less than propane.

So how do natural gas and propane differ? Natural gas contains less carbon than propane so it burns cooler. To reach parity in the heat output, grill manufacturers drill larger holes in the burner tubes for natural gas grills, allowing more gas to be burned. Grills fueled with natural gas need to be specially outfitted by the manufacturer. The good news is that most grill makers offer conversion kits for natural gas.

> **GRILLING HACK:** Planning an outdoor kitchen? Consider running a gas line from your home propane tank to your grill area so you don't have to change the heavy cylinders every couple of weeks.

Pluses and minuses of propane and natural gas:

- Propane and natural gas grills offer the convenience of push-button ignition and turn-of-the-knob heat control.

- Propane requires lugging around heavy metal cylinders,

> ### GRILLING HACKS
> - To transport propane cylinders from the hardware store to your home, stand them upright in a plastic milk crate. (Or buy a plastic holder, like a Camco, designed to keep the tanks from rolling around in your trunk.) Store propane cylinders away from your grill and in an upright position outdoors.
> - Few things are worse than running out of propane during a grill session. (Yeah, it has happened to me, too.) Keep an extra full propane cylinder on hand as a backup.

while natural gas requires special plumbing and gas lines. You always seem to run out of propane during an important grill session.

- Gas burns cooler and wetter than charcoal so, historically, the sear is not quite as good. The growing presence of infrared sear burners on gas grills more than makes up for this.

WOOD

For me, the ultimate grilling fuel is neither charcoal nor gas, but wood. Wood is the fuel of choice in grill cultures as diverse as Argentinean, German, and Californian, and wood-burning grills have become the focal point of a new generation of high-end fine dining restaurants.

Charcoal and gas deliver heat, but only wood flavors your food while you cook over it. That flavor is smoke, and it comes from a complex cluster of carbon compounds found in the wood, such as *guaiacol* (also found in roasted coffee) and *syringol* (an active ingredient in liquid smoke).

Wood enters the modern grilling process in two ways: as a fuel in its own right and as a smoke-generating enhancement to a charcoal or gas fire.

HOW NOT TO RUN OUT OF GAS

One of the big frustrations of grilling with propane is knowing how much gas is left in the cylinder. There are three ways to calculate how much propane remains:

1. Check the weight of the cylinder. The "tare weight" (empty weight) is generally stamped on the top of the cylinder, preceded by the letters "TW." So subtract this from the total weight of the cylinder and you'll know how many pounds of gas it contains.

2. Check the pressure in the cylinder. To do this, install a gas gauge between the cylinder valve and the regulator tube. (Two good brands are Companion Group and Shop Master.)

3. Pour very hot water over the side of the tank. The metal will feel warm where the tank is empty and cool where the propane level begins.

GAS GRILLING MATH

- One empty propane cylinder weighs 17 to 18 pounds.

- When filled with gas, it weighs 35 to 36 pounds. (Full, it contains 18 pounds of propane.)

- The amount of cooking time you get from a full tank of propane varies from grill to grill (and according to whether you're running that grill at high, medium, or low). If you're running a typical 3-burner gas grill on high (all 3 burners on high), a full cylinder of propane will last about 13 hours. That figure changes on grills with 4 or 6 burners.

- Of course, a lot of grilling (e.g., indirect grilling) doesn't require all 3 burners and those burners don't necessarily run on high. Take notes on the propane consumption of *your* grill and after a few months, you'll get a sense of how much you need.

Typical woods used for grilling: Almost any hardwood can be used for grilling and smoking, and as you grill your way around Planet Barbecue, you'll find guava and palochina wood fires in the Philippines, pimento (allspice wood) in Jamaica, and grapevine roots and trimmings in France. But most wood fire grilling and smoking is done with one of a half dozen major species.

Wood as a grilling fuel: Wood used for grilling comes in three forms.

- **Logs:** Small whole logs or large logs split lengthwise in half or quarters.

- **Chunks:** The fuel for blower-style wood-burning grills like the WoodFlame. You can also light wood chunks in a chimney starter, burning them down to embers as you would charcoal (see page 32).

- **Chips:** The most common form of wood for grilling and smoking, chips are widely available at

Different forms of wood for grilling (clockwise from left): chips, chunks, log, pellets.

supermarkets and hardware stores. Common varieties include hickory, oak, apple, cherry, and mesquite— each with its own subtle flavor. For a light wood flavor, use the chips straight from the bag (add them to the coals or your gas grill's smoker box). For a more pronounced wood flavor, soak the chips in water to cover for 30 minutes, then drain before adding to the coals.

- **Pellets:** Made from compressed hardwood sawdust. You can also use pellets for smoking. Note: Be sure to buy food-grade pellets. Furnace pellets can contain pine, binders, and other substances you wouldn't want to bring in contact with your food.

GRILLING HACKS

- Avoid softwoods, like pine and spruce, for grilling (they put out a resinous sooty smoke). Exceptions to this rule: The French grill mussels over dried pine needles and Germans like to grill bratwurst over pinecones.

- If I could pick only one wood for grilling, it would be *oak*, which is full-flavored enough to stand up to beef, yet neutral enough to grill the most delicate poultry or seafood without overpowering it.

WOODS COMMONLY USED FOR GRILLING

Note: Smoke-roasting and smoking are covered on page 21.

WOOD	WHERE USED	FOR WHAT
Oak	Everywhere	Everything
Mesquite	Texas, the American Southwest, Hawaii, and Mexico	Beef, poultry, and seafood
Hickory and pecan	The American South	Pork and poultry. Remember, in traditional North Carolina barbecue, the pork actually roasts directly over a hickory ember fire.
Alder	Pacific Northwest	Salmon and other seafood
Cherry	Michigan and the American Midwest	Works well with all meats, especially beef, poultry, and seafood
Apple	The American Midwest and New England	Works well with all meats, especially pork and poultry
Beech	Germany and Eastern Europe	Works with all meats, especially pork

STEP 3
ASSEMBLE YOUR TOOLS

A craftsman needs the right tools, and so does a serious griller. There are hundreds of grill tools and accessories—some basic, some specialized, some indispensable, and some just silly. Here are the tools you need and what you need them for.

TEN INDISPENSABLE TOOLS FOR EVERY GRILLER

1. Tongs: For turning the food, yes, but also for cleaning and oiling the grill grate. Choose long-handled tongs (to keep your arm away from the fire) that are spring-loaded (so you can open and close them with one hand).

2. Wire grill brush/wooden grill scraper (both are shown below and on page 37)**:** For cleaning your grill grate, which you should do religiously before your food goes on and after it comes off. When choosing a wire grill brush, make sure the bristles are anchored in thick twisted wire. Cheap grill brushes may shed their bristles over time, which, in rare cases, may wind up in your food. Alternatively, use a wooden grill scraper, which eliminates the risk of stray wire bristles.

3. Grill spatula: For turning burgers, fish fillets, and so on. Choose a spatula with a long handle, thin leading edge, and holes in the head to release the steam so the bottom of what you grill won't become soggy.

4. Basting brush: Essential for basting and glazing foods during and after grilling. Silicone bristle basting brushes are easier to clean than those made with natural bristles, but the latter give you a better coating. Tip: Buy natural bristle paintbrushes at your local hardware store. They're so inexpensive, you can use them a few times and throw them out.

5. Grill light: You can't grill with accuracy if you can't see what's on your grill grate. Some grill lights clip to the lid of your grill. Others come on gooseneck stems. Yet others, like my LumaTong, mount right on the arms of your tongs.

6. Grill gloves: To protect your hands. Choose thick leather or Kevlar or other aramid gloves with long sleeves to protect your arms. While you're at it, invest in a pair of insulated grill gloves for handling hot food and some latex gloves to help keep your hands clean when touching raw meat.

7. Grate-grabber: Helps you lift a hot grate for refueling and adjusting the coals.

8. Instant-read thermometer: Photo on page 17.

9. Grill baskets: The beauty of a grill basket is that you turn the basket, not the pieces of food, which makes it great for delicate items, such as fish and small foods like shrimp, okra, and mushrooms. The all-purpose basket is comprised of two flat wire

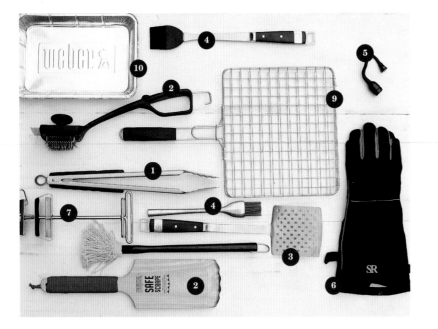

Grill baskets, grates, and woks (clockwise from top left): Herb grilling grate, fish basket, grill wok, grill basket, grilling grid.

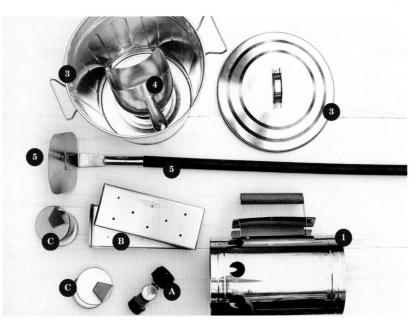

Tools for charcoal and gas grillers. Charcoal tools are numbered, this page. Gas tool descriptions are lettered in the photo and described on page 16.

panels with handles at one end and connected by a hinge at the other. There are specialized baskets for grilling whole fish, sliders, sausages, and corn.

10. Aluminum foil drip pans: While not strictly a tool, these are incredibly handy for marinating, transferring food to and from the grill, as a water pan, as a roasting pan (see pan-grilling technique on page 28), and of course, for placing under food to catch the dripping juices and fat. Buy lots in two sizes: 7½ by 5 inches and 9 by 13 inches. Restaurant supply stores and Amazon.com are good sources.

EIGHT TOOLS FOR CHARCOAL GRILLERS

1. Chimney starter: Enables you to light charcoal quickly, evenly, and without using petroleum-based lighter fluid. Instructions on how to light it on page 32.

2. Electric starter (not shown): A looped electric heating element you place under the charcoal. Especially useful for lighting kamado-style cookers.

3. Metal trash can with tight-fitting lid: Buy two: one for holding your charcoal once you've opened the bag. And one for holding hot ash and embers when you clean out your grill.

4. Charcoal scoop: Useful for shoveling coals into chimney starters or grills.

5. Grill hoe or garden hoe: Use for spreading out the lit coals to form a multi-zone fire or split fire for indirect grilling.

6. Side baskets (not shown): Use to hold the embers in neat piles for indirect grilling.

7. Airflow regulator (not shown): Use to control the airflow and thus the temperature of a kamado-style cooker or a charcoal grill or smoker. The blower unit mounts over the lower air vent with a thermocouple that clips to the grill grate. The controller increases or reduces the airflow to raise or lower the grill temperature. The best-known model is the BBQ Guru.

GRILLING HACK: There's a common misconception that stabbing meat with a barbecue fork will drain out the juices. Meat isn't a water balloon: It won't deflate. It's okay to use a barbecue fork to turn it (even though I may have advised the contrary in the past).

8. Charcoal corral: A metal insert, such as the Slow 'N Sear, corrals the coals to one side of the grill for high-heat direct grilling, creating a separate coal-free zone for indirect grilling and smoking. A V-shaped water trough between them helps keep food moist.

The Slow 'N Sear makes indirect grilling a snap.

FOUR TOOLS FOR GAS GRILLERS

1. Gas gauge (A in photo, page 15): Tells you how much propane remains in the cylinder. Higher-end gas grills have built-in gauges (often they measure the weight of the cylinder). Alternatively, attach a portable gauge, like a Charcoal Companion or Flame King, between the cylinder valve and the gas hose. Or use a propane cylinder scale, like a Grill Gauge.

2. Automatic gas shutoff valve: Have you ever forgotten to turn off the gas at the tank after a grill session? This ingenious device can be preprogrammed at 20-minute intervals for up to an hour and shuts off the gas flow accordingly. Two good brands are Fire Magic and Companion Group.

3. Under-grate smoker box (B in photo, page 15): A metal box with a perforated lid. Some models are rectangular and sit atop the heat diffuser. Other models have V-shaped bottoms to nestle between the Flavorizer Bars of a Weber gas grill. The Companion Group makes a wood pellet smoker box complete with a feed chute that rises through the bars of the grill grate.

4. Above-grate smoker boxes: Metal boxes, cylinders, mesh bags, or pucks that sit on the grill grate and emit smoke next to the food. One such device near to my heart is the **Smoke Puck** (C in photo, page 15), which I developed for the Best of Barbecue line.

SEVEN TOOLS FOR SPECIALIZED GRILLING

1. Tuscan grill: A cast-iron grill grate with short legs you position over the embers for grilling on the hearth, fireplace, or in a wood-burning oven. Elaborate versions

Tuscan grill.

have brackets so you can raise and lower the grate.

2. Plancha: A thick (typically ¼-inch-thick) sheet of cast iron you use on the grill as a griddle. (Grilltop griddles work in a similar way.) For more on plancha grilling, see page 28.

Plancha.

3. Soapstone grilling stone: Works like a plancha, but is made of nonporous stone so it won't rust or stick. One good source is Canadian Soapstone.

Top: pizza peel. Bottom: pizza stone.

4. Pizza stone: A thick, square or round, high heat-tolerant tile you place on the grate for cooking pizza. While you're at it, pick up a **pizza peel**, a large wood or metal paddle for transferring pizzas on and off the grill.

5. Pizza oven: The exploding popularity of grilled pizza has spawned a whole industry of accessories, including the KettlePizza and PizzaQue pizza kits, full-blown pizza ovens that fit atop a kettle grill.

KettlePizza.

6. Raised rail grill grates: Interlocking aluminum grill grate panels with high ridges on

Raised rail grill grate.

GRILL THERMOMETERS

Essential for monitoring your grill temperature and the doneness of your food. Yes, the pros use them too.

1. Instant-read thermometer: Insert the slender probe deep into the meat or seafood to check its internal temperature. Look for quick responding probes and backlit display panels. Two good manufacturers are Maverick and Thermapen.

> **GRILLING HACK:** When checking the internal temperature of a thin food, like a steak or chicken breast, insert the probe through the side, not the top. To check sausages, insert the probe through the narrow end toward the center.

2. Remote digital thermometer: Consists of a probe you put on the grill or in the food with a wire connected to a small transmitter you put on the side table. Plus a receiver that lets you read the temperature up to 500 feet away. Look for a model that can handle multiple probes; extra points if it communicates with your smartphone.

3. Point-and-shoot thermometer (aka infrared gun thermometer): This infrared thermometer uses a laser beam to check the surface temperature of a food, or even your grill grate, plancha, or wood-burning oven. Two good brands are Etekcity and Charcoal Companion.

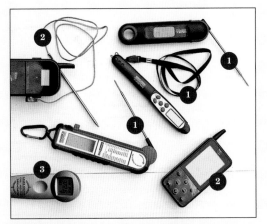

Grill thermometers including instant read (1), remote (2), and point-and-shoot (3).

a perforated base that fit atop the conventional grill grates and enhance performance by augmenting the heat, diminishing flare-ups, and channeling vaporized meat juices back to the meat. To add a smoke flavor, place wood pellets between the raised rails. The best-known brand is GrillGrates.

7. Rotisserie: For kettle grills, you'll want to buy a rotisserie collar that sits atop the kettle and accompanying spit, rotisserie prongs, and motor. (Weber makes one for its popular kettle grill; see page 26.) Higher-end gas grills often come with a rotisserie attachment that's built-in.

SIX TOOLS FOR SAFETY

1. Grill mat: A fireproof mat that goes under your grill to catch any stray embers or drips. One good manufacturer is DiversiTech.

2. Fire extinguisher: I hope you never need to use it, but have on hand a fully charged Class B dry chemical fire extinguisher to put out any fires.

3. Bucket of sand or box of kosher salt: Useful for smothering a small grease fire.

4. Color-coded cutting boards: Use one for raw meats, another for salads and vegetables, a third for cooked meats, and so on, to avoid cross contamination.

5. Nylon food tent: A foldable screen tent that keeps bugs off your food.

6. Grill cleaner: Sold in spray bottles or aerosol cans. One good brand is Safecid.

STEP 4
FLAVOR YOUR FOOD

In the beginning there was meat. Then fire. Then salt. Then wild herbs. Then mustard seeds, which turn up at Stone Age campsites. Which is to say that almost from the birth of barbecue, our prehistoric ancestors sought to enhance simple grilling by the sagacious application of seasonings, herbs, and spices.

The fourth step to achieving grilling enlightenment is flavoring your food, and while salt and pepper are indispensable (see box, this page), the flavor becomes much more complex when you introduce rubs, marinades, butters, bastes, glazes, sauces, salsas, and other

---

SALT

Salt: This simple seasoning enjoys universal popularity, but there's nothing simple about the choice of salts we have today. You can buy literally hundreds of varieties from every corner of Planet Barbecue. My personal preference is coarse **sea salt**. (*Coarse* because I like the crunch of the slow-dissolving crystals; *sea* because I like all the trace minerals found in ocean salt.) Second up would be coarse crystals of **kosher salt**. I don't particularly like fine iodized table salt, which I find has a tendency to oversalt the food.

Many grill masters and chefs sprinkle the cooked meat or seafood with coarse crystals of **finishing salt**. The ultimate finishing salt is Maldon from England, which comes in handsome pyramid-shaped crystals and possesses some of the crystalline beauty of snowflakes.

If you've watched my TV shows, you're familiar with how I raise my hand high above the meat or seafood before I sprinkle it with salt and pepper. This gives you more even dispersal of the seasoning than if you sprinkle it on an inch or two above the surface.

Want to create or reinforce a smoke flavor—even if you don't use wood chips? Make your rub or season your food with **smoked salt**.

condiments. Recipes throughout the book introduce flavorings at every stage of the cooking process—from *before* the raw meat or seafood goes on the grill to *while* the food grills to *after* it's cooked and has come off the grill.

Tools for flavoring your food (from left to right): basting brush, mister, injector, barbecue mop.

FOUR TOOLS FOR ADDING FLAVOR TO FOODS

1. Basting brush: (see page 14)

2. Barbecue mop: A miniature barbecue mop used to apply bastes and sauces. Choose one with a removable head you can place in the dishwasher.

3. Injector: An oversized hypodermic needle designed to inject marinades and other flavorful liquids deep into turkey breasts, pork shoulders, roasts, and more.

> **GRILLING HACK:** Pour injector sauces through a coffee filter or fine mesh strainer to remove any chunks of spices that could clog the injector needle.

4. Mister: Food-safe spray bottle for spraying a thin film of wine, cider, vinegar, olive oil, or other flavorful liquid over the surface of the meat during grilling.

STEP 5
CHOOSE YOUR GRILLING METHOD

Grilling is simple, right? You cook the food directly over the fire. Well, that's one method—by far the most popular. Actually, there are five major methods of live-fire

Direct grilling filets mignons.

cooking, plus other specialized methods. Each is well suited to particular foods and delivers different textures, flavors, and tastes. Master them and you can grill anything. Really.

DIRECT GRILLING

This is the simplest, most straightforward, and widely practiced method of grilling, and it's what most people on Planet Barbecue use when they fire up the grill. In a nutshell, you cook small, tender, quick-cooking foods directly over a hot fire.

Setup: Position the food on the grill grate or on skewers or in a grill basket directly over a hot fire.

Temperature: Most direct grilling is done over high or medium-high heat. (See the temperature chart on page 36.) Larger or fattier pieces of meat (chicken legs, for example) might be direct grilled over a medium fire. As a general rule, the smaller or thinner the meat, the hotter the fire.

Grilling time: Brief. Generally 3 to 6 minutes per side, depending on the cut of meat.

Well suited to: Steaks, chops, burgers, shish kebabs, chicken breasts, fish steaks or fillets, small high-moisture-content vegetables such as peppers, mushrooms, corn, asparagus, and onions (quartered or sliced), fruit (small or sliced), bread and pizza, as well as cake and other desserts.

TO ENHANCE PERFORMANCE

- To control the heat in direct grilling, work over a tiered fire (page 34). This gives you a hot zone for searing, a medium zone for cooking, and a cool or safety zone for warming and for dodging flare-ups. To control the heat, move the food back and forth over the different zones.

- When direct grilling small pieces of food like shrimp or bread, there's no need to cover the grill—they require only a couple minutes per side. For thick steaks and chops, lower the lid to hold in the heat and speed up the grilling process.

> **GRILLING HACK:** Follow the "rule of palm." If the food is thinner than the palm of your hand (¾ inch), leave the grill lid up. If thicker than the palm of your hand, lower the lid.

INDIRECT GRILLING

Direct grilling works great for small, tender, quick-cooking foods, but what about larger cuts, like whole chickens or pork loins, or fatty cuts, like whole ducks or pork shoulders? Enter indirect grilling, in which you cook the food next to—not directly over—the fire, or between two fires. Indirect grilling is almost always done with the lid closed.

Setup:

- On a charcoal grill, rake the coals into 2 mounds at opposite sides

SETTING UP A GRILL FOR INDIRECT GRILLING

1. Install the coal baskets, if using, on opposite sides.

2. Place an aluminum foil drip pan in the center.

3. Pour the hot charcoal into the coal baskets or rake them into 2 mounds opposite each other.

4. Install the grill grate with the hinged panels over the coals.

of the grill and cook the food in the center. This works great for relatively slender foods, like pork loin, turkey breast, chicken pieces, sausages, whole and planked fish, and more.

- Place an aluminum foil drip pan under the food to catch the dripping fat. This also helps you corral the fire.

- To set up a 2-burner gas grill for indirect grilling, light one side and do the indirect grilling on the other side. On a 3-burner gas grill, light the outside or front and back burners and do the indirect grilling in the center. On a 4- to 6-burner gas grill, light the outside burners and do the indirect grilling in the center.

- On a kamado-style cooker, build the fire in the bottom. Install the heat diffuser under the grate to shield the food from direct exposure to the fire.

- Pellet grills are, by their very design, set up for indirect grilling, although some can be converted to direct grilling.

Temperature: Generally done at medium or medium-high heat.

Grilling time: Longer than direct grilling. Thirty to 45 minutes for chicken pieces and sausages. One to 1½ hours for whole chickens and pork loins. Two to 4 hours for pork shoulders and rib roasts.

Well suited to: Large or fatty foods, such as whole chickens, ducks, and turkeys; pork, lamb, and beef roasts; whole fish; large or dense vegetables, such as cabbages, beets, whole potatoes, and whole onions.

TO ENHANCE PERFORMANCE

- When indirect grilling on charcoal, some people mound the coals on one side of the grill only and do the indirect grilling on the opposite side. (Rotate the food 180 degrees halfway through so it cooks evenly.) This method works well for larger cuts of meat and whole turkeys.

- As a rule, you need a grill with a lid for indirect grilling. However, you can achieve a sort of indirect grilling on a lidless grill by positioning the food very

Three forms of wood for smoking (top to bottom): dried chips, soaked chips, chunks.

high (18 to 24 inches) above the fire. This is how the Charlie Vergos Rendezvous in Memphis, Tennessee, traditionally cooks its ribs.

SMOKING

Add hardwood (in the form of chunks, chips, or logs) to the fire and you're smoking. Sometimes you smoke at medium or high heat—a process I call **smoke-roasting**. True barbecue (like Kansas City ribs or Texas brisket), as well as bacon, jerky, smoked salmon, and other fish, are smoked "low and slow" (at a low temperature for a long time). Slow smoking and dishes you use it for (like spareribs and brisket) are covered in depth in the companion book to this one, *Project Smoke*.

There are many ways you can smoke on a grill—while you're direct grilling, indirect grilling, spit-roasting, even while grilling on a plancha. Note: It's difficult

Adding wood chunks to the fire.

to smoke on a gas grill, and you'll never get the pronounced smoke flavor you get with charcoal. That's because gas grills have a wide gap between the lid and the cook chamber to release excess hot air, so the grill doesn't overheat. Most of the smoke you generate exits through this gap before it has a chance to add much flavor.

Setup:

- **When direct grilling on a charcoal grill:** Add hardwood chunks or chips to the fire (you'll need 2 chunks or 1½ cups chips). You can also place a small log on the fire.

- **When indirect grilling and spit-roasting on a charcoal grill:** Set up your grill for indirect grilling following the instructions on page 20. Place ¾ cup wood chips or 1 large or 2 small chunks of wood on each mound of coals.

- **When direct grilling on a gas grill:** Many gas grills come with a smoker box (a slender metal drawer with a dedicated burner beneath it). To be honest, while some of these put out a fair amount of smoke, they rarely produce a significant smoke flavor (again, on account of the gap between the cook chamber and the lid). Instead, place wood chunks directly on the heat diffuser (or between the inverted V-shaped Flavorizer Bars of a Weber gas grill), under the grate and under the food, then grill the latter directly over the wood.

- **When indirect grilling on a gas grill:** Set up your grill for indirect grilling. Place wood chips in the smoker box or on the heat diffuser as described above, or make a **foil smoking pouch** (see facing page) and place it over one or more burners under the grate. Again, you won't get nearly as much of a smoke flavor

HOW TO DIRECT GRILL ON A PELLET GRILL

1. Add pellets to the hopper.

2. Remove the burn chamber cover.

3. Burning wood pellets in the burn chamber.

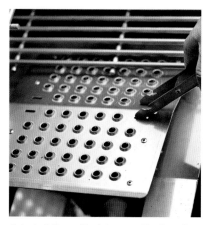

4. Install the grill plate over the burning pellets.

as you would on a charcoal grill, but this is better than nothing.

- **How to smoke on a kamado-style cooker:** Most manufacturers call for interspersing unlit charcoal with wood chunks or chips, then lighting the coals from the top down. Follow the manufacturer's instructions.

- **How to smoke when plancha grilling** (page 28)**:** Build a charcoal fire in the grill (direct or indirect, depending on how hot you want the plancha). Add wood chips, chunks, or logs to the fire. Close the lid for part of the time while the food is on the plancha to trap the smoke.

HOW TO MAKE A SMOKER POUCH

This is one of the most effective ways to smoke on a gas grill, and it costs mere pennies. Start with a 12-by-18-inch piece of heavy-duty aluminum foil arranged on the counter, narrow end toward you. (Don't have heavy-duty foil? Double up on regular foil.) Place a handful of wood chips in the center of the half closest to you. (For a quick smoke, don't soak the chips; for a slower smoke, do.) Fold the top half over it. Pleat the side and bottom seams several times to make a seal. Using a sharp implement, like the tip of an instant-read thermometer probe, make a series of holes in the top of the pouch to release the smoke.

Heat your gas grill to high. Place the smoker pouch under the grate directly over the burner. (A grate grabber—page 14—comes in handy for lifting the grate.) Once smoke starts to rise from the pouch, you can lower the heat of the grill as needed. For maximum smoke flavor, place the food on the grate directly over the pouch. For longer smoke sessions, prepare multiple smoker pouches and add them as needed.

1. Mound the wood chips in the center of the lower half of a sheet of aluminum foil.

2. Fold the foil over to make a rectangular packet.

3. Pleat the edges of the packet to make a tight seal.

4. Poke holes in the top of the packet with a sharp implement to release the smoke.

SPECIALIZED SMOKING TECHNIQUES

Most smoking is done with wood, but there are a number of techniques that use nontraditional fuels to impart an aromatic smoke flavor.

Smoking on a cedar plank: Tradition calls for soaking cedar and other wood planks in water prior to grilling to keep them from catching fire. In *Project Fire*, you'll do just the opposite: You'll char the plank to the point of smoking before adding the food. This gives you a light smoke flavor and it looks as dramatic as all get-out. (Check out the Planked Figs on page 70 or Cedar Planked Striped Bass with Miso Glaze on page 247.)

Smoking with hay, straw, pine, or spruce: Grasses and leaves can be used for smoking. Place them on the grate or in a grill basket or grill wok over a hot fire with the food right on top of them. As the grasses or leaves burn, the food smokes and cooks. (Check out the Hay-Grilled Mussels on page 231.)

Smoking with herbs and spices: Similarly, you can lay fresh herbs directly on the grill grate and smoke-roast fish, poultry, and other foods right on top of them. Or use a special herb grilling basket. Alternatively, toss bunches of fresh or dried herbs directly on the fire. Or even blowtorch fresh herbs atop a grilled chop or steak. (Shown is the Rosemary Smoked Veal Chops recipe on page 139.) When I make Jamaican jerk, I add a handful of allspice berries to the fire.

Smoking with vegetable skins: Grill corn in the husk or whole eggplants, peppers, onions, sweet potatoes, and other vegetables directly in the embers. (See Caveman Grilling—page 27.) As the skin burns, the smoke is driven into the flesh and flavors the vegetables. (Check out the Ember-Grilled Sugar Snap Peas with Fresh Mint on page 281.)

- **How to smoke on a pellet grill:** By their very construction and nature, pellet grills are smokers. (Many aren't really even grills—see page 6.) Follow the manufacturer's instructions. Note: Pellet grills smoke best when run at lower temperatures.

Temperature: Smoke-roasting is generally done at a medium heat (325° to 350°F) or medium-high heat (375° to 400°F). True barbecue is smoked at a low to medium-low heat (225° to 275°F).

Grilling time: Similar to indirect grilling times: 30 to 40 minutes for chicken pieces and sausages. One to 1½ hours for whole chickens and pork loins. Two to 4 hours for pork shoulders and rib roasts.

Well suited to: Chicken; turkey; pork loin and shoulder; rib roast and beef long ribs; whole fish; whole vegetables; tofu.

TO ENHANCE PERFORMANCE

- Use seasoned (dried) wood. It burns more efficiently than green (fresh cut) wood, producing cleaner, better-tasting smoke.

- Depending on your wood and fuel source, one load of chips (soaked) or chunks will give you 20 to 40 minutes of smoking—enough for a light smoke flavor. For larger cuts of meat, you'll need to replenish the coals and the wood—do the latter when the smoke stops rising from the top vent.

- For a slow, steady smoke, soak the chips in water to cover for 30 minutes before adding them to the coals. For a quick smoke (for desserts and ice cream, for example), add unsoaked chips to the fire.

- Foods absorb smoke best when they're cold and moist. Start with refrigerator-cold meat or seafood (which you should anyway). Spray with flavorful liquids, like cider or wine, and/or keep a water pan in the cook chamber.

SPIT-ROASTING (ROTISSERIE GRILLING)

Spit-roasting is one of the oldest methods of live-fire cooking. (There's a terrific description of an ancient Roman rotisserie hog in the *Satyricon* by Petronius.) It combines the virtue of direct grilling (direct exposure to the fire) with that of indirect grilling (cooking next to, not directly over, the fire, so you don't get flare-ups). The gentle rotation helps the food cook evenly. The result: large cuts of meat with a savory seared surface and an extraordinarily moist interior. Another advantage of this method: Spit-roasting bastes the meat both inside (with the internal meat juices) and outside (with the dripping fat).

Setup:

- For a kettle grill, set up the grill for indirect grilling. Place the rotisserie collar on the kettle and attach the motor to the mounting bracket. Install the spit, securing the end in the socket, and switch the motor on.

- For a gas grill, light the rear rotisserie burner (a feature on many high-end gas grills). Install the rotisserie motor and spit following the manufacturer's instructions.

- Some kamado-style cookers, like the Excalibur, come with a rotisserie attachment. Follow the manufacturer's instructions.

> **GRILLING HACK:** If your grill lacks a rotisserie burner, set it up for indirect grilling and make sure the food turns over the drip pan (on a charcoal grill) or over an unlit burner (on a gas grill). If you have a 3-burner gas grill with burners running front to back, spit-roast with the rear burner lit.

Temperature: Like indirect grilling, spit-roasting is generally done using medium to medium-high heat.

Grilling time: Similar to indirect grilling, but spit-roasting goes a little faster: 30 to 40 minutes for chicken pieces and sausages. One to 1¼ hours for whole chickens and pork loins. Two to 3 hours for pork shoulders and rib roasts.

Well suited to: Cylindrical or football-shaped foods, like whole chickens and ducks; pork shoulders and loins; rib roasts and so on. Good for whole fish, fish steaks, and large fillets. (You'll need to spit-roast these in a rotisserie basket.)

HOW TO SPIT-ROAST A PRIME RIB

1. Run the spit through the meat.

2. Use a fork to tighten the set screw on the rotisserie prong.

3. Insert the spit with the roast in the rotisserie collar.

4. Use an instant-read thermometer to check the roast for doneness.

5. A rotisserie prime rib in all its spit-roasted glory.

6. Hold the meat steady with a carving fork as you pull out the spit.

TO ENHANCE PERFORMANCE

- Often gas grill rotisserie burners are infrared, requiring you to depress the fuel button or burner knob for a full 10 seconds during ignition to keep the gas flowing and make sure the burner stays lit.

- When spit-roasting on a charcoal grill, you can place hardwood chips or chunks on the coals, adding smoke flavor to the benefits of rotisserie grilling. I call this technique **rotisserie-smoking**.

- When spit-roasting whole chickens, spit them from side to side so they sit perpendicular, not parallel, to the rotisserie spit. I can't explain the physics behind why this works, but that's how the vast majority of grillers around Planet Barbecue roast chicken, and birds roasted this way seem to have crispier skin and moister meat.

- To spit-roast whole fish, fish steaks, lobster tails, and other seafood, use a flat rotisserie basket. Two manufacturers are Grill Shop and OneGrill BBQ Products.

- Outside-the-box spit-roasting: Poultry and roasts are the obvious candidates, but you can also spit-roast many foods you wouldn't normally associate with the rotisserie, from onions and cauliflower to whole pineapples.

- To spit-roast in front of a fireplace or campfire, get a SpitJack rotisserie.

CAVEMAN GRILLING (GRILLING IN THE EMBERS)

This is it—the original grilling method—pioneered nearly 2 million years ago by a human ancestor called *Homo erectus*. Flash forward to the 1950s when President Dwight D. Eisenhower would grill "dirty steak" (sirloin roasted directly on the embers) at the White House to the horror of onlookers. (See the Caveman Porterhouse on page 127.) This theatrical method requires no grill grate. You grill the food directly on the coals. Although similar to direct grilling, caveman grilling gives you a crustier exterior and smokier flavor—the result of varying heat zones and micro-charring of the meat.

Setup: Build a charcoal fire and rake the embers out in a single layer with a grill hoe or garden hoe. Fan the fire with a fan, folded newspaper, or hair dryer to dislodge any loose ash. Lay the food directly on the embers.

Temperature: Comparable to that of direct grilling, that is, hot (500° to 700°F). Paradoxically, it's not quite as hot as you'd think, because the charcoal acts as an insulator where it comes in direct contact with the meat. (In part, this is what enables firewalkers to walk barefoot on beds of embers.)

Grilling time: Quick—3 to 6 minutes per side for most foods.

Well suited to: Steak is the obvious candidate for caveman grilling, but vegetables are awesome grilled this way. (The short list includes sweet potatoes, onions, bell peppers, eggplant, and squash.) Less expected, but no less delectable, are ember-roasted shellfish (try the Caveman Lobster with Absinthe Butter on page 237) and ember-roasted flatbread (drape the pizza dough on page 88 directly on the embers).

TO ENHANCE PERFORMANCE

- For the best results, build your fire with lump charcoal, not briquettes. The latter put out a lot of ash, some of which winds up on your food.

- Caveman grilling puts you closer to the fire than any other grilling method. Wear long-sleeved insulated grill gloves to protect your arms and use long-handled tongs.

- Related to ember grilling is **ash grilling** (*rescaldo* in Spanish; *alle cenere* in Italian)—in which you roast foods not directly on the embers, but buried in hot or warm ashes. Ash grilling is well suited to dense root vegetables, such as beets and potatoes. The Jews of Thessaloniki, Greece, traditionally roasted eggs in the ashes to make a Sephardic specialty called *huevos haminados*.

- Sweet potatoes are well suited to caveman grilling; baking potatoes do better cooked in the ashes.

- To caveman grill small vegetables, like asparagus or snap peas, place them in a wire grill basket and set directly on the hot coals.

SPECIALIZED GRILLING METHODS

CAMPFIRE GRILLING

Anyone who's ever fire-roasted a marshmallow to make a s'more knows the gustatory pleasure (not to mention the unabashed joy) of grilling over a campfire. Campfire grilling reenacts a ritual as old as humankind itself—cooking and eating around a communal fire. Plus, the food tastes better because you're cooking over the one fuel that actually delivers a flavor dividend: wood.

Setup: Build a fire with hardwood logs using one of the methods outlined on page 34. Some people like to cook over the flames, which gives you more charring and a more pronounced smoke flavor. (This is great for those marshmallows.) For more control, let the fire (or at least part of it) burn down to embers, and grill over these as you would over charcoal. Use a Tuscan grill (page 16) or freestanding grate for your grill grate.

Temperature: Medium to high

Grilling time: Varies according to the size and density of what you're grilling. Marshmallows burn in minutes; a whole lamb might take half a day.

Well suited to: Everything.

To enhance performance: There are many ways to cook over a campfire.

- Impale small foods (think hotdogs or marshmallows) on a green stick or a skewer, which you hold over the fire.

- Spit chickens, turkeys, roasts, and other large foods on large sticks or small saplings, position them on upright Y-shaped branches, and roast them, rotisserie style, over the fire. The Grizzly Spit Campfire Rotisserie System features a motor to turn the spit for you.

- Pinion whole lambs and hogs (butterflied) or whole racks of ribs or prime ribs on vertical spits that you stand upright next to the fire. (Gas grill rotisserie spits work well for this.) Argentineans call this *asado gaucho*; Brazilians, *fogo de chao*.

- Position a Tuscan-style grill grate over the embers and direct grill as you would over charcoal.

- You can grill the food directly on the embers or buried in the ashes (see Caveman Grilling on page 27).

PLANCHA GRILLING

Plancha is the Spanish word for a griddle (traditionally cast-iron—South Americans call it a *champa*). So what's it doing in a book on grilling? Traditionally, you heat the plancha over a wood fire, which allows you to sear, sauté, and pan-fry as you would in a cast-iron skillet, but with a whiff of the wood smoke we associate with the best live-fire cooking. I call this technique plancha grilling, and it allows you to expand your grilling repertory to foods not customarily grilled.

Temperature: Medium-high to high.

Grilling time: Brief—3 to 10 minutes per side.

Well suited to: Delicate foods that would fall apart on the grill, like flounder and sole; small foods, like bay scallops or snap peas that would fall through the bars of the grate; or foods you wouldn't normally grill, like fried eggs.

TO ENHANCE PERFORMANCE

- For the best results, combine plancha grilling with smoke-roasting (page 21), that is, heat

Grilling duck breasts on a plancha.

the plancha over a wood or charcoal fire, and then add wood chips or chunks to generate wood smoke. Cover the grill to hold in the smoke.

- Oil the plancha with an oiling towel or chunk of bacon fat before the food goes on. When you flip pieces of food, move them to a fresh section of the plancha where you still have oil to keep the food from sticking.

- The best planchas are made of cast iron, so you'll need to season them as you would a cast-iron skillet.

- Don't have a plancha? Use a large cast-iron skillet or stovetop griddle.

PAN GRILLING/DRIP PAN GRILLING

What do the Peruvian Potato Salad on page 106, the Smoke-Roasted Carrots on page 266, and the Smoke-Roasted Potatoes on page 278 have in common? All are cooked in an aluminum foil roasting pan or cast-iron skillet using a combination of direct and indirect grilling. Pan-grilling is great for small or dense vegetables that require a little extra olive oil or butter to sizzle the crust and keep them moist. I also use this technique for small or fragile foods.

Setup: Set up your grill for indirect grilling. Add wood chips or chunks to the fire to generate wood smoke. Place the food in the pan and drizzle with olive oil or melted butter and season well with salt and pepper or your favorite barbecue rub. Indirect grill until almost tender, stirring several times so the food browns evenly. Move the pan directly over the fire the last few minutes to sizzle and caramelize the food surfaces.

Temperature: Typically done at medium-high or high.

Grilling time: 30 to 60 minutes, or as needed.

Well suited to: Root vegetables, such as new potatoes and carrots. Dense vegetables, such as brussels sprouts and beets. Broccolini and broccoli florets taste great pan-grilled. Ditto for seafood, such as shrimp and scallops, and delicate fish fillets.

TO ENHANCE PERFORMANCE

- One great application for pan-grilling is to fill an aluminum foil drip pan with 1-inch chunks of root vegetables and place it under a spit-roasting chicken or rib roast. The dripping fat flavors the vegetables, and you get to cook a complete meal on the grill. (Stir the veggies from time to time so they cook evenly.)

- Want to speed up the process (and your adrenaline flow)? Try pan-grilling directly over the fire. You'll get better browning and a crustier exterior, but you have to pay constant attention, or you'll burn the food.

SALT-SLAB GRILLING

Salt slabs are newcomers to the world grill scene, but we've embraced them with gusto. I use these thick rectangles of pink salt from Pakistan often—as a plancha, grilling plank, grill press, resting platform, and even as a serving platter. The porosity of salt slabs enables them to absorb and impart flavors; up to 80 trace minerals enhance their salty taste. The surface is mercifully nonstick. The striking color and theatrical presentation speak for themselves.

Setup: Set up your grill for indirect grilling and preheat to medium-high to high. Heat the salt slab along with it.

Temperature: Medium to high (350° to 500°F).

Grilling time: Typically 30 to 60 minutes.

Well suited to: Salt-roasting whole fish (page 251) and squash

A Salt Slab Chocolate Brownie S'more (page 303).

(page 283); for resting grilled steaks and chops; even as a grill press for grilling *pollo al mattone* (Italian chicken under a brick—page 204). On page 303 you'll find an amazing dessert: Salt Slab Chocolate Brownie S'mores.

TO ENHANCE PERFORMANCE

- Heat your salt slab gradually—20 to 30 minutes or more. Rapid heating may cause it to crack.

- You can reuse your salt slab many times. Simply scrape it clean with a putty knife or metal scraper when hot, then let it cool to room temperature.

- The real enemy to salt slabs is humidity. Once the salt slab has cooled to room temperature, store it in a large, heavy-duty resealable plastic bag.

- Do not cook on salt slabs in cold weather! Hot slabs can crack or explode when exposed to cold air.

PLANK GRILLING

When the first Europeans settled in Connecticut, they encountered Native Americans grilling shad fillets on upright boards around a bonfire. (An annual shad bake continues in Essex, Connecticut, to this day.) Which is to say, that while plank grilling may seem new, it isn't. What *is* new is the way we grill—charring the plank without soaking it first—and some of the unexpected foods we now grill on a plank—from French toast to Camembert cheese. Whichever your method or whatever you cook on it, know that plank grilling delivers a protected grilling environment (less mercurial than direct grilling) and a uniquely aromatic flavor.

Setup: Set up your grill for indirect grilling. Char one side of the plank directly over the fire. Arrange the food to be planked on the charred side. Set the plank on the indirect section of the grill. Lower the lid and indirect grill.

Temperature: Planking is typically done at medium-high to high heat.

Grilling time: As short as 10 minutes (for cheese); as long as 40 minutes (for whole fish).

Well suited to: Cheese, shrimp, salmon, trout and other fish, and fruit.

TO ENHANCE PERFORMANCE

- Cedar is the most common wood for plank grilling, but you can

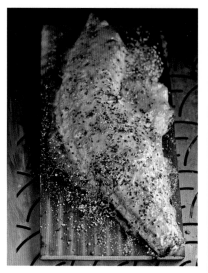

Cedar-Planked Striped Bass with Miso Glaze (page 247).

now buy cherry, oak, and hickory planks—each with a subtly different flavor.

- Can grilling planks be reused? Yes, if they're not too charred. Scrape clean with a putty knife, then scrub clean with a plastic scrubber and soapy water. Rinse well and dry. Once the plank is too charred to use for planking, you can add it to the fire to generate wood smoke.

- Feeling brave? For the ultimate smoke flavor, try *direct* grilling on a plank. Char one side and place the fish on it. Place the plank, uncharred side down, directly over the heat (work over a medium to medium-hot fire). Lower the lid and cook until the fish is done. This will be quicker than with indirect grilling, with a lot more smoke, fire, and drama. Use a squirt gun or water-filled mister to extinguish any flames at the edges.

LEAF GRILLING

Long before there were grill grates (and possibly even skewers and spits), people wrapped foods in banana, squash, grape, and other leaves and cooked them in a campfire. Gonzalo Fernández de Oviedo y Valdés (the Spanish explorer who introduced us to West Indian *barbacoa*) describes such a process for cooking corn bread in the fire in his 1526 *Natural History of the West Indies*. More recently, Malaysians delight in *ota ota*—spiced seafood mousse grilled in banana leaves. Leaf grilling introduces an inimitable herbaceous smoke flavor to any food (often seafood) cooked inside of it. Note: For an interesting variation on leaf grilling, wrap the food in cedar grilling paper and char over a hot fire. Cedar paper is available from Amazon.com.

Setup: Wrap the food in edible leaves, then direct grill on a grate or in the embers.

Sardines Grilled in Grape Leaves (page 253).

Temperature: Medium-high to high heat.

Grilling time: Brief—generally 4 to 8 minutes per side.

Well suited to: Seafood and cheese.

TO ENHANCE PERFORMANCE

- Never use leaves that have been sprayed with pesticides.

- To make banana leaves pliable, grill them for 15 seconds per side to soften them, let cool, then do the wrapping.

- Jarred grape leaves are great for wrapping and grilling, adding a briny pickled flavor as well as a smoke flavor.

HAY, STRAW, PINE NEEDLE, AND SPRUCE NEEDLE GRILLING

In this singular method, you grill seafood, meats, and even cheese in burning hay, straw, or pine or spruce needles instead of (or in addition to) charcoal or wood. The French, for example, use this method to prepare *éclade* (mussels grilled with dried pine needles—a specialty of the Île de Ré on the Atlantic Coast). What results is an intensely aromatic smoke flavor quite unlike that of wood smoke. On page 231, you'll find a recipe for mussels grilled in hay.

Setup: Fill a perforated grill wok or perforated pan with dried hay, straw, or pine or spruce needles. Place the food to be grilled on top and place the whole shebang on a hot grill set up for direct grilling. The hay will

Preparing mussels to grill in a nest of hay.

start to smolder, but you may need to touch a match to it to set it afire.

Temperature: This is a high-heat method.

Grilling time: Quick (as with most direct grilling).

Well suited to: Shellfish, seafood, and steaks.

TO ENHANCE PERFORMANCE

- You can grill directly in a hay, straw, or pine or spruce needle fire, but the heat and smoke are easier to control if you corral the fuel in a perforated grill wok, wire grill basket, or on a vegetable grilling grate.

- For a spectacular steak or chop, lay a fresh spruce or pine branch between the meat and the grate (over the hot fire) the last 30 seconds of grilling. The heat releases the spruce oils, imparting a unique piney smoke flavor to the meat.

WOOD-BURNING OVENS

Wood-burning ovens (and their propane counterparts) are beyond the scope of this book, but I want to mention that throughout Europe (especially in Italy and France), people use them for grilling. The beauty of grilling in a wood-burning oven? The food cooks both from the top and from the bottom (useful when grilling thick steak, like a porterhouse), surrounded by wood smoke. The drawback? The size and considerable cost of the oven. To direct grill in a wood-burning oven, rake a flat pile of embers toward the mouth of the oven. Position a Tuscan-style grill over the embers and place the food on top.

OPEN-HEARTH GRILLING

For most of human history, people did their grilling (not to mention most of their cooking) on an open hearth. The method is enjoying a resurgence today at cutting-edge live-fire restaurants. Hearth cooking is beyond the scope of this book, but know that it lends itself to direct grilling, spit-roasting, and grilling in the embers and ashes.

FIREPLACE GRILLING

Fireplace grilling is also beyond the scope of this book, but there are many books on the subject. You might start with my book *Indoor Grilling*.

STEP 6
FIRE IT UP

Okay, you've selected your grill, sourced your fuel, assembled your tools, flavored your food, and selected your grilling method. Now comes the fun part: firing up and using your grill.

LIGHT THE GRILL

Lighting a grill is easy—even if you grill with charcoal. It takes 15 to 20 minutes to light charcoal in a chimney starter. It takes 10 to 15 minutes to preheat a gas grill. So if you've always shied away from charcoal grilling on account of time: no excuses. Read on.

SEVEN WAYS TO LIGHT A CHARCOAL GRILL

1. If using a chimney starter, place a crumpled sheet of newspaper in the bottom of the starter. The charcoal is in the top section.

2. Light the newspaper with a butane lighter or long-stemmed match.

1. Use a chimney starter. These upright metal tubes or boxes light coals quickly, evenly, and efficiently. Set it on your grill's lower grate or on a stone surface. Place a paraffin fire starter or crumpled newspaper in the bottom; place the coals in the top section. Light the fire starter or paper. You'll have glowing embers in 15 to 20 minutes. Lump charcoal is ready to use when the coals glow orange. Briquettes are ready when they glow orange and are lightly ashed over. This is my preferred method.

2. Use an electric starter (page 15). Place the heating coil under the coals. This is handy for kamado-style cookers.

3. Use a hot air blower, like a Looftlighter. Light the coals with a blast of super hot air.

4. Use a blowtorch or a roofing torch. The latter runs off a propane cylinder (notice I said

3. Pour the lit coals into the firebox.

> **GRILLING HACK:** When you dump the embers into the firebox, leave a few at the bottom of the chimney starter. These will light the next batch of coals. Use this hack for prolonged grill sessions where you need several chimneys of embers.

cylinder, not canister) and delivers a military-strength flame. Also good for brûléeing spit-roasted pineapple. One good brand is Roofmaster.

5. Use the built-in gas igniter if your grill has one. Weber Performer and Summit charcoal grills have propane igniters. Kalamazoo and the American Muscle Grill come with a charcoal and wood tray above the gas burners.

6. Do a top-down burn. This is especially handy for upright barrel grills and kamado-style cookers. Fill your chimney with charcoal. Pour three quarters of the unlit

SUPER AMAZING TIP—
HOW TO TURN A CHARCOAL GRILL INTO A WOOD BURNER

Want to grill over a wood fire, but you don't own a wood-burning grill? Here's a technique so effective and simple, you'll wonder why you didn't think of it earlier. Fill a chimney starter with dry wood chunks (not chips) and light as you would a chimney starter filled with charcoal. The wood will burn to glowing embers after 10 to 15 minutes. (Add wood as needed to top up the chimney.) Dump and spread these embers over the bottom of the firebox. Presto: You're grilling over wood. Note: Wood grilling this way must be done with the grill uncovered (direct grilling). Lowering the lid will make your food unbearably smoky.

Wood chunks are easy to light in a chimney starter.

coals into the firebox. Light the remaining coals in the chimney and pour them on top of the unlit coals. The fire will burn down gradually. This is good for extended indirect grilling and smoking.

7. Do an ember spread burn: Use this technique for kamado-style cookers. Place unlit lump charcoal in the bottom of the firebox as specified by the manufacturer. When a smoke flavor is desired, intersperse the coals with wood chips or chunks. Using a paraffin fire starter or blowtorch, light 3 coals in the center of the top layer. Close the lid; the fire will spread gradually outward and downward for a long, slow cook.

HOW TO LIGHT A GAS GRILL

This may seem obvious, but there's a safe and proper way to do it. Ignore these steps at your peril.

1. Raise the grill lid. This is *very* important—so you don't get a potentially explosive gas buildup before you push the igniter.

2. Open the valve at the top of the propane cylinder or natural gas connection.

3. Turn the burner knob to start the gas flowing. Note: On some grills, the burners must be lit in a particular sequence; follow the manufacturer's instructions.

4. Press the igniter button. You should hear a click as the igniter

sparks, followed by a whoosh as the gas ignites.

5. Hold your hand about 3 inches above the burner to make sure the burner is really lit. Do this again after 30 seconds to make really sure.

6. If the burner(s) fails to light, turn the burner knobs to "off" and let the grill air out for a few minutes, then try again.

Warning: *Never* light a gas grill with the lid down for the reason explained in Step 1.

GRATE DEBATE—TO SOAK OR NOT TO SOAK THE WOOD

A lot of ink has been spilled over whether or not to soak wood chips before adding them to the coals. Theory may suggest one direction; experience dictates another. When you add unsoaked wood chips to the coals, you get intense smoke for a few minutes, then they catch fire. Soaking the chips for 30 minutes in water to cover, then draining them before adding them to the coals, doubles or triples the smoking time. I have tested this repeatedly. Soak your chips.

Large wood chunks are slower to ignite, so you can add them to the fire without soaking. Ditto with logs (adding a small log to a charcoal fire is a great way to generate wood smoke).

GRILLING HACK: One easy way to soak chips for smoking is in a small aluminum foil pan or measuring cup. Or use a commercial chip soaker, like Best of Barbecue or Weber.

HOW TO LIGHT A WOOD-BURNING GRILL

A wood-burning grill delivers a terrific smoke flavor.

Charcoal method: The easiest way to light a wood-burning grill is to start with a chimney full of hot embers. Dump them into the firebox, then arrange the wood on top. Start with smaller pieces of wood (about 1 inch in diameter). Once these ignite, place larger logs on top. Note: Crisscross or shingle the logs to leave plenty of gaps between them. This gives you better airflow and hence a hotter, cleaner-burning fire.

To build a wood fire without charcoal, use the **log cabin method** (logs stacked smaller to larger in a square, as though you were building a log cabin in reverse). Or use the **tepee method** (logs stood upright smaller to larger in a tepee configuration). Crumpled newspaper in the center gets you started with both methods.

CONTROL THE HEAT

Fire is a volatile heat source—especially when you burn wood or charcoal. So as you scale the ladder of grilling enlightenment, one of the most important tasks is to learn how to control the heat.

DIRECT GRILLING
Build a tiered charcoal fire.

This is the best way to manage the heat when direct grilling on a charcoal grill. (Tip o' the hat to grilling visionary and *The Thrill of the Grill* author, Chris Schlesinger, who pioneered the concept.)

1. Dump the lit coals in your chimney starter in the firebox toward the back of your grill.

2. Using a grill hoe (page 15) or a metal spatula, rake out the coals so you have a thicker mound of coals at the back of the grill, thinning out to a single layer in the center.

3. Leave the front third of the firebox without coals to create a fire-free safety zone.

4. For high-heat searing, move the food toward the back over the thick layer of coals. For a more moderate heat, move the food to the center or toward the safety zone. For low heat or to keep the cooked food

Arrange the coals for a tiered fire.

warm, move it to the front of the grill over the safety zone.

> **GRILLING HACK:** Position the bottom grill grate so the bars run from front to back. This makes it easier to rake out the coals.

5. You can also build a tiered fire on a gas grill. Set one burner (the rear burner if your grill has one) on high, the center burner on medium, and leave the front burner off. Move the food accordingly. This is more responsive than trying to adjust the heat with the burners.

> **GRILLING HACK:** Need to accelerate a charcoal or wood fire? Use a hand-held fan or battery-powered blower, like a FiAir, to aerate the embers. Alternatively, use a hair dryer.

Establish a safety zone.
Configure the fuel so that 25 to 30 percent of your grill is fire-free.

This means an ember-free section of a charcoal grill or one of the burners off on a gas grill. Here's where you'll move the food when flare-ups occur (and they will occur—especially with fattier foods like bacon and garlic bread). Here's where the food goes once it's cooked and you want to keep it warm. Note: Many gas grills come with warming racks above the main cooking grate. You can use these as your safety zone.

Use the dampers/vents to control the heat.
Fire requires two things to burn: fuel and oxygen. To increase the heat on a charcoal or kamado-style grill, open the bottom and top dampers. Start with the bottom—that brings the air to the fire. The top damper acts as your chimney, creating the draft that will pull the heat and smoke out of your grill. To lower the heat, partially close the dampers. Remember: Greater airflow means higher heat. Less airflow means lower heat.

Raise or lower the grill grate.
On some grills (like the Char-Broil CB940X or the Grillworks), you can raise or lower the grill grate—and hence the distance to the fire and the heat. On other grills (like the Hasty-Bake), you can raise and lower the coal tray.

> **GRILLING HACK:** If you still have charcoal left after a grill session, close the top and bottom dampers. This will extinguish the fire and you can use the unburned charcoal at a future grill session. Store it in a dry place.

INDIRECT GRILLING
There are three ways to control the heat when indirect grilling.

1. Use more or less charcoal. For example, for low-heat smoke-roasting (the technique you need for ribs or brisket), use only half a chimney of charcoal (replenish as necessary to maintain the target temperature).

2. Open or close the damper vents.

3. Adjust the burner knobs of a gas grill.

HOW TO CHECK A GRILL'S TEMPERATURE
You can't grill accurately unless you know the cooking temperature. There are two important numbers here: the temperature in the cook chamber and the temperature at the grate level. The former helps you with indirect grilling, smoking, and smoke-roasting; the latter with direct grilling.

- Many grills come with thermometers built into the lid, which gives you the *approximate* temperature *at the level of* the thermometer probe—usually 6 to 10 inches above the grate. The temperature at grate level will likely be different.

Here are some other ways to take a grill's temperature:

- **The point-and-shoot method:** Buy a point-and-shoot thermometer. Point the laser beam at one of the bars of your grill grate to get a reading.

- **The "Mississippi" method:**
Hold your hand 3 inches above the grate over the zone over which you'll be grilling. Start counting "one Mississippi, two Mississippi," etc. You'll be able to keep your hand over a hot grill for 2 to 3 seconds; over a medium grill for 5 to 6 seconds; over a low heat grill for 10 to 12 seconds. Yes, I know this sounds imprecise, but much of grilling involves your sense of touch. Holding your hand over the grate will give you a definite sense of the heat.

Refueling: With most direct grilling, one chimney of charcoal or wood chunks will last 30 to 60

With the "Mississippi Method," gauge the temperature of a fire using the palm of your hand.

minutes. For a prolonged direct grill session and indirect grilling, you'll need to replenish the fire.

- When replenishing lump charcoal, add fresh lumps to the fire and leave the grill open (lid off) for 5 minutes or until the fresh coals catch fire.

- When replenishing charcoal briquettes, I like to light them separately in a chimney starter, then add them to the fire. (Adding unlit briquettes to a fire often generates an unpleasant acrid smoke.)

PREPARE THE GRATE AND YOUR GRILL AREA

Once your fire is lit, you'll need to prep the grill grate. I describe how to do this in a simple mantra,

THE BASIC GRILL TEMPERATURES AND WHAT THEY'RE USED FOR

HEAT	TEMPERATURE (IN DEGREES F)	METHOD	GOOD FOR
Low	225°–250°	Smoking/true barbecue	Brisket, ribs, pork shoulder
Medium-low	275°–300°	True barbecue/ indirect grilling	Ribs, pork shoulder
Medium	325°–350°	Direct grilling Indirect grilling/ smoke roasting	Roasts, pork loin, poultry (whole birds), whole fish, large dense vegetables
Medium-high	375°–400°	Direct grilling Indirect grilling/ smoke roasting Plancha and salt slab grilling	Chicken pieces, planked fish, large vegetables (all indirect grilled)
High	450°–600°	Direct grilling	Steak, chops, fish steaks, chicken breasts, small or high-moisture vegetables, fruit
Incendiary	650° and higher	Direct grilling and infrared grilling	Searing steaks and chops

which you've undoubtedly heard me say before:

- Keep it hot.
- Keep it clean.
- Keep it lubricated.

In a nutshell, this means to start with a **hot grill grate**.

Next, **clean** or **brush** the grate vigorously with a long-handled stiff wire brush or wooden grill scraper. To avoid the slim but documented risk of a metal bristle winding up in your food, use a brush whose bristles are anchored in a twisted wire armature. Alternatively, use a wooden scraper. (For more information on these tools, see page 14.)

Finally, **lubricate** or **oil** the grate with an oiling towel or one of the other methods listed on page 39. We just reviewed how to light and heat the grill.

Tips

- Clean your grill grate when it's *hot*. This loosens any debris much more effectively than when the grate is cold.

- Clean the grill grate before you put on the food, and again *after* you finish grilling. A lot of people forget the latter, but I promise you, last week's burnt-on salmon skin does *not* add flavor to this week's grilled chicken. At least not the flavor you want.

Clean your grill grate with a stiff wire brush.

Or scrape the grate clean with a wooden scraper.

Oiling the grate (or the food) serves three purposes. Obviously, it helps keep the food from sticking and it also helps lay on well-defined grill marks. But there's a third advantage to oiling a grate with a folded paper towel or oiling cloth; it removes any debris or grease (or stray grill brush bristles) not picked up by your grill brush.

> **GRILLING HACK:** Use an oil with a high burn point. Grapeseed oil is the gold standard, but it's relatively expensive. Common canola oil works just fine. There's no need to use expensive extra virgin olive oil. Avoid peanut oil, which leaves an oily residue on the grate.

> **GRILLING HACK:** Argentinean grill masters sometimes dip their grill brushes in a bucket of salt water before scrubbing the grate. The salt water helps cleanse the grate and, who knows, may add a microscopically thin layer of flavor. The Grill Daddy grill brush brings similar moisture (if not salt) to cleaning the grate.

GRILL THE FOOD

Once you've heated, cleaned, and oiled your grill grate, you're ready to put on the food. Here, too, there are right and wrong ways to do it.

1. Arrange the food on the grate like headstones in a military graveyard: That is, put the food on in a logical sequence: from the back of your grill to the front (so you don't have to reach over a hot grill more than you need to) and/or from left to right in neat linear rows. That way you know which items went on first, need to be turned first, and need to come off the grill first.

2. Leave at least 1 to 2 inches between pieces of food: This promotes even heat and airflow and allows the sides to cook as well as the bottom.

> **GRILLING HACK:** This is one of the most common mistakes in grilling—filling every square inch with food. Leave yourself room to maneuver so you have space to dodge eventual flare-ups.

3. Grill on the diagonal: When grilling steaks, chops, chicken breasts, or other broad flat foods, arrange them running on the diagonal to the bars of the grate. This looks more aesthetically pleasing than parallel grill marks running from top to bottom or side to side.

4. Lay on a crosshatch of grill marks: For an even handsomer presentation, give each piece of food a quarter turn on each side after a couple of minutes to create a crosshatch of grill marks. Do this on both sides—it will also help the food cook more evenly.

5. Don't overcrowd your grill: I've said it before and I'll say it again: If you cover every square inch of the grate with food, you won't have room to maneuver when you get flare-ups. (And you will get flare-ups.) Leave 25 to 30 percent of your grill food-free.

6. Cook to temperature: On page 40 you'll find some of the

Leave 1 to 2 inches between each piece of food so it grills evenly.

many clues that tell us when food is cooked perfectly. The most accurate is internal temperature. Get yourself a good instant-read thermometer and use it whenever you're grilling.

7. Take the food off just before it's done: Any food will continue cooking after it comes off the

grill. (This is called **carryover cooking**.) The larger the item, the longer it will continue cooking— as much as 5 degrees for a large piece of meat, like a roast. So take foods off just *before* they reach the desired doneness.

8. Use a wire rack: Transfer steaks, roasts, and other meats to a wire rack over a rimmed sheet pan. This lets air circulate below as well as above the meat, keeping the bottom crusty, not soggy.

9. Give it a rest: Meats and poultry will be juicier if you *don't* serve them hot off the grill. Instead, let them rest a few minutes on a wire rack before serving. This "relaxes" the meat, making it juicier. A minute or two will do it for a steak, 5 minutes or so for a roast.

> **GRILLING HACK:** When resting a large cut of meat, you may want to lay a sheet of aluminum foil *loosely* over it to keep it warm. Do not bunch the foil around the meat or you'll make the outside soggy.

NINE WAYS TO OIL YOUR GRILL GRATE OR OTHERWISE KEEP YOUR FOOD FROM STICKING

Using a folded-up paper towel.

1. Use an oiling towel: Have your oil in a small bowl grillside. Fold a paper towel into a tight pad. Holding it at the end of your tongs, dip it in the oil, then rub it across the grate. (Notice how the towel cleans the grill.) Repeat as needed.

2. Use an oiling cloth: A lot of restaurants use this technique. Cut an old white cotton towel or washcloth into 3-inch strips and tightly roll them like eggrolls. (The resulting roll should be 1 inch in diameter.) Tie crosswise at the ends and in the middle with butcher's string. Dip in oil and rub across the grate with tongs.

3. Use half of an onion or lemon: This is a trick I learned in Israel. Impale a half onion (cut crosswise) slightly on the diagonal on a grill fork. Dip it in the bowl of oil and rub it across the bars of the grate.

Angle the fork on a slight diagonal.

The onion both oils and cleans the grate.

4. Use a chunk of bacon, beef, or lamb fat: This is one of the best ways to oil a grill grate—practiced across Planet Barbecue. Hold it at the end of your tongs and rub it across the bars of the grate.

5. Use spray oil: Pam and Weber both manufacture spray oils that won't flare up when you spray them at the grill grate.

6. Use a grill oiling brush: The Best of Barbecue grill oiling brush features short, hollow silicone bristles that conduct oil from a cylindrical reservoir directly onto the bars of the grill grate. Be sure to lift the oil reserve cap to start the flow of oil.

7. Brush the food with oil before it goes on the grate: This is the other popular strategy for preventing sticking and it works especially well with fish and seafood. When grilling particularly stick-prone foods like fish fillets, I oil both the grate and the fish.

8. Use a grill basket or grilling grid: Another excellent method for stick-prone foods. The beauty of a grill basket is that you turn it without disturbing the pieces of food. Remember to oil the basket before adding the food.

9. Use a silicone grill mat: These flexible nonstick grill mats prevent foods like shrimp or small vegetables from sticking to the grill grate or falling between the bars. One brand, the gridlike Frogmats, allows smoke to reach the food. Check the manufacturer's maximum heat rating; Frogmats can support heat up to 550°F.

Rest grilled meat on a wire rack set over a sheet pan so the crust on the bottom doesn't get soggy.

10. Brush or scrape your grate clean after grilling: I told you that already, but a reminder never hurts.

WHAT TO DO IF YOUR GRILL CATCHES FIRE

Whenever you deal with open flames and animal fat or vegetable oil, you run the risk of a grill fire. Flare-ups are a normal part of the grilling process, but serious grill fires can harm you and your grill.

Commonplace flare-ups: Simply move the food away from the flames to your safety zone—remember the safety zone (see page 35). Once the flare-up dies down, move the food back.

Grease fire: Sometimes the grease that accumulates at the bottom of your grill (in the drip pan of a charcoal grill or the grease pan of your gas grill) catches fire. First, if using a gas grill, shut off the burner knobs. Take off the food. Close the lid to smother the fire. For small grease fires, you can try smothering them with baking soda or salt.

Gas grill fire (from the regulator hose or at the cylinder): Turn off the burners, and if you can get to it safely, close the cylinder valve. Put out the fire with a Class B dry chemical fire extinguisher. (Yes, you should keep one on hand.) Call your local fire department immediately.

COOK TO DONENESS

You've spent considerable time, money, and effort putting your meal together. The final and most important step is being able to cook your food to the desired—make that perfect—doneness.

Sight: You can get a lot of information just by looking at the food: the handsome brown crust on a chop, the sizzling dark skin of a spit-roasted chicken, the black char of peppers and eggplants grilled caveman style (on the embers). The way mussels or clamshells pop open when the grilled bivalve is ready. And of course, the internal color of a steak.

Smell: Properly grilled food has a particular smell, at once smoky and caramelized. The sanguine smoky smell of red meat roasting on an open fire. The grassy, almost cannabis-like smell of grilled corn and lettuce. The sweet caramel candy smell of grilled peaches and other fruits.

Feel: Poke a steak when it's raw. Then rare. Then medium. Then well done. It has a very different feel, a different resiliency at each stage. This is how seasoned grill masters at steak houses often check the doneness of steak. There are several doneness tests that involve touch.

Poke test: Used for steaks, chops, chicken breasts and other relatively thin pieces of meat. Press the top with your index finger. See chart on page 42 for how the various degrees of doneness should feel.

Pinch test: Used to test the doneness of chunks of meat on a shish kebab, shrimp, onions, peppers, sweet potatoes, and so on. Pinch the food between your thumb and forefinger. Meat will correspond to the feel listed on page 42. Shrimp should feel firm. Veggies should feel soft and yielding.

Internal temperature: Of course, the most accurate test of doneness is internal temperature. Use an instant-read thermometer. (See facing page for where to insert it.) See page 42 for the key temperatures and various degrees of doneness.

WHERE TO POSITION THE THERMOMETER PROBE

To check the internal temperature of a steak or burger, insert the probe through the side of the meat.

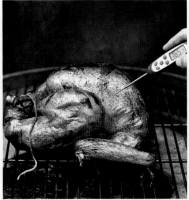

To check the internal temperature of a turkey or chicken, insert the probe in the thickest part of the breast and thigh without touching the bone.

To check the internal temperature of a sausage, insert the probe through one end to the center.

The exact location of the thermocouple (the part that measures the temperature) varies from instant-read thermometer to thermometer. So precise placement of the probe matters a lot in giving you an accurate internal temperature reading.

For a roast, leg of lamb, or other large hunk of meat: Insert it into the deepest part of the meat in several places, but try not to touch the bone. (Bone contains air, which is an insulator, unlike meat, which is mostly water.) This will measure the rarest part of the meat. Obviously, the meat will be more well done toward the surface.

Chicken and other whole birds: Insert the probe into the thickest part of the thigh and breast, but not touching the bone. Check it in several places on both sides. When the thigh is cooked to a safe temperature, the rest of the bird will be, too.

Steak: Sure, you can check the doneness by feel (see the Poke Test on facing page) and you should, but let an instant-read thermometer be the ultimate arbiter. Insert it through the side at the narrow end of the steak to the center (the probe should be parallel to the top and bottom of the steak).

Fish: For whole fish, insert the probe into the thickest part of the fish just above the bone. For fish steaks, insert the probe though one side to the center, as you would for a beefsteak.

Burgers: Insert the probe through the side of the burger to the center.

Sausages: See caption above.

JUDGING DONENESS BY FEEL

FEEL	DONENESS	FOOD	CORRESPONDING INTERNAL TEMPERATURE
Squishy	Blue (blood rare)	Steak	100°–110°F
Soft	Rare	Steak and lamb	120°–125°F
Gently yielding	Medium-rare	Steak, lamb, and veal	130°–135°F
Barely yielding	Medium	Steak, lamb, veal, and pork	140°–145°F
Firm	Medium-well to well	Steak (if you have to), lamb, veal, and pork	160°F
Soft and jiggly (I know this sounds paradoxical, but when tough, collagen-filled meats are cooked, they become soft and jiggly.)	Very well done	Brisket, beef clod (shoulder), beef plate ribs, and pork shoulder	200°–205°F

JUDGING DONENESS BY TEMPERATURE

INTERNAL TEMPERATURE	DEGREE OF DONENESS	APPROPRIATE FOR
100°–110°F	Blue (sometimes called Pittsburgh rare)	Steak, tuna
120°–125°F	Rare	Steak, lamb, tuna, duck breast
130°–135°F	Medium-rare	Steak, lamb, tuna, veal, duck breast
140°–145°F	Medium for fish	Steak and fish (other than tuna)
145°–155°F	Medium for meat	Steak, lamb, veal, and pork
165°F	Medium for poultry	Pork, chicken, and turkey
170°–175°F	Medium-well (for pork and poultry)	Pork, chicken, and turkey
175°–180°F	Well (for steaks and roasts)	Pork shoulder (for slicing) and pork ribs
200°–205°F	Very well	Brisket, beef clod (shoulder), beef plate ribs, pork shoulder for pulling

STEP 7
PUTTING IT ALL TOGETHER

So now you know how to choose your grill, source your fuel, assemble your tools, season your food, choose your grilling method, and fire it up. The last step is to put it all together and get grilling.

HOW TO COOK A WHOLE MEAL ON THE GRILL

When I was growing up, you grilled once or twice a month and it was always meat for the main course. Today we grill everything, from appetizers to vegetables, from breakfast to dessert. Which brings us to the ultimate challenge: cooking the entire meal on the grill. Actually, it's a lot easier than it sounds—in fact, it's standard operating procedure chez Raichlen.

Follow this simple strategy, and you, too, will be cooking the whole meal on the grill without breaking a sweat.

Cocktail: Sure, you could serve beer or wine—that's what everyone expects. And there's plenty of time to get to that during the meal. But why not wow with a cocktail most people have not only never experienced before, but never even conceived of? I speak, of course, about a grilled cocktail, like the citrusy Grilled Sangria on page 305 or the Grilled Peach Bellinis on page 306.

Appetizers: When people arrive at your home, they make a beeline for the grill. So you want appetizers that cook quickly and that you can serve hot off the fire. Good options in this book include Chorizo-Grilled Dates (page 65), Bruschetta Four Ways (page 80), and Greek Grilled Cheese (page 69). Better yet, grill all three.

Salad: Take a breather and choose a salad you can grill ahead and serve at room temperature. Any of the recipes in the salad chapter will work, for example: Grilled Wedge Salad with Smoked Blue Cheese Dressing (page 98); Grilled Watermelon Salad with Arugula and Queso Fresco (page 101); or Grilled BLT Salad (page 104).

Main course: For the main course, I like a large hunk of meat or whole fish. After all, everyone has gathered around the primeval fire and we're sharing a communal meal. Quite literally, because as you carve the big meat, everyone partakes. Good candidates here? The Raichlen "Cheesesteak" (page 134) or Salt Slab-Grilled Rockfish (page 251). First-Timer's Pork Shoulder (page 145) or Asian-Flavored Lamb Sliders (page 175), which have the added advantage of being able to be cooked ahead. Everybody loves sauces: Don't forget to prepare them ahead, too.

Side dishes: Buy yourself more breathing space. Serve a gorgeous platter of grilled vegetables. Grilled vegetables hold their texture and flavor well, even when grilled the day before. And they taste just fine—better than just fine—at room temperature. Case in point: Peruvian Potato Salad (page 106), Smoke-Roasted Carrots (page 266), or Sweet and Sour Grilled Onions (page 277).

Dessert: Time to perform again and leave your guests with an unforgettable finale. That means a grilled dessert—particularly one that you grill while everyone is watching. Extra points if you serve it flaming. It's hard to beat Cinnamon-Grilled Peaches (page 288), Dessert Quesadillas (page 301), or Salt Slab Chocolate Brownie S'mores (page 303).

Bottom line: Sure, you want to show off, but you also want to enjoy your party. By building our menu on a mix of dishes you grill live and that you can grill ahead, you have time both to shine and to party.

GRILLING SAFETY

Grilling routinely involves live fire, sharp knives, hot metal, and alcohol, so what could possibly go wrong?! I would be remiss if I didn't say a little about safety.

- Grill placement: Place your grill in an open, well-ventilated space in your backyard or on your patio or deck. Figure out the prevailing wind direction and, if possible, place the grill downwind. Ideally, you'll set up the lighting so it illuminates the grill and your work area at night. An outdoor sink helps with handwashing.

- For charcoal grillers: Never grill indoors or in a garage, covered patio, or breezeway. Charcoal emits odorless but deadly carbon monoxide.

- For gas grillers: Have the lid open when you light the grill. Hold your hand 3 inches over the burners once the grill is lit, and again, 30 seconds later, to make sure it's truly lit. If you smell gas, *immediately* turn the grill off, open the lid to air it out for a few minutes, then try lighting it again.

- Avoid cross contamination—especially when handling chicken and ground beef. Use separate cutting boards for cutting raw meats and salads (or any other food you plan to serve raw). Color-coded cutting boards make this a snap. Wash your hands and the knives well with soap before handling other foods.

- Likewise, never put or serve cooked meat on the same platter you used to bring out raw meat.

> **GRILLING HACK:** If you want to use the same platter for the raw meat and cooked meat, cover it with a couple of layers of plastic wrap before adding the raw meat. Once the raw meat is on the grill, discard the plastic wrap. Then you can serve the cooked meat on the same platter.

- If you want to use a marinade that came in contact with raw meat for basting or as a sauce, strain it through a fine mesh strainer into a saucepan, then boil it rapidly for at least 3 minutes to kill any potential bacteria. While you're at it, whisk in a couple tablespoons of chilled butter—it will taste better.

- Keep all meats, poultry, and seafood cold until you put them on the grill. Ditto for mayonnaise-based salads, like coleslaw. This is contrary to the advice of some to let your steaks warm to room temperature, but there isn't a decent steakhouse in the world that leaves meat out at room temperature. Remember: You grill steaks at 600°F or more, and it takes only a few seconds of grilling to warm up the meat to room temperature.

- Wear sunscreen and a hat—especially if you're grilling in the daytime. Ideally, you'll wear closed shoes, not flip flops or sandals—especially when grilling with charcoal.

- Charcoal grillers: Transfer the spent ash to a lidded *metal* trash can and let it cool for 24 hours or douse with water before transferring it to a plastic can. Yes, I too have burned out plastic trashcans with coals I thought were dead.

- Gas grillers: Remember to turn your grill off—ideally at the cylinder.

WINTER GRILLING

Quick: When it snows, what do you shovel first? The path to your car or the path to your grill? According to the Hearth, Patio, and Barbecue Association, 61 percent of Americans grill all year round, up from 30 percent ten years ago. Which is easy for guys like me, who live in Florida. Hats off to the winter warriors in Maine, Minnesota, upstate New York, and Canada who brave snow and ice to fire it up. Here are some tips to make the task easier.

Don't let this happen to you—see the game plan on this page for winter grilling.

WINTER GRILLING

- Position your grill at least 10 feet from your house, preferably in an area sheltered from the wind, and *never* under snow-laden tree branches. Never light a grill in a garage or covered breezeway; the carbon monoxide could kill you.

- Clear snow that has accumulated in and around your grill. For better traction, sprinkle the area with sidewalk salt. You don't even want to *think* about losing your footing while carrying a chimney starter full of red-hot charcoal.

- Winter days are short and dark. Make sure you have adequate lighting in the form of grill lights, overhead patio lights, or headlamps.

- Dress warmly, but avoid ultra-puffy coats, scarves, or dangling drawstrings. Replace mittens or nylon gloves with grilling gloves.

- The rubber hoses on gas grills can get brittle in cold weather; check them for leaks before heating the grill.

- Allow extra time for the grill to heat, whether charcoal, wood-burning, or gas.

- Check to make sure gas grills stay lit. Strong winds can blow out the burners.

- Allow additional cooking time (20 to 30 percent or more) for cold weather grilling. I like to light a second charcoal grill just to have an ample supply of embers.

- Stockpile extra fuel—charcoal, propane, or pellets.

- Focus on quick cooking foods, like steaks, chops, burgers, chicken breasts, fish fillets, and shrimp. While indirect grilling is possible, it can be difficult to maintain temperatures for a sustained period of time.

- Resist the temptation to peek under the grill lid too often, as heat loss will be rapid.

- Above all, don't forget that fire is hot. You may be cold, but your grill won't be. Don't burn yourself on a hot grill lid, grate, or chimney starter. (I speak from painful experience.)

SPRING CLEANING AND MAINTENANCE

If you're reading this book, you probably grill year round. But some people in extremely cold climates deep-freeze (excuse the pun) their grills during the winter. Here's how to bring them back to life.

FOR CHARCOAL GRILLS

- **Clean the grill thoroughly:** (Of course, you did that the last time you used your grill, right?) Scrape out any congealed ash at the bottom of the firebox or

GRILL CLEANING AND MAINTENANCE SCHEDULE

A practice that's essential but all too often ignored: cleaning your grill. Contrary to the belief of some, food or grease burnt on the grate from a previous grill session does not add flavor. It's gross.

Every grill session:

- Brush or scrape your grill grate conscientiously both *before* and *after* grilling.

- Hose off the exterior of the grill using a grill cleaner, or scrub with a brush and soapy water or vinegar as needed. Note: Make sure the grill is cool before you do this. Cold water against a hot grill can crack the enamel or built-in thermometer glass.

- Once the grill is cool, empty the ash that's accumulated in a charcoal grill. (Place it in a metal—not plastic—container; it may still contain some hot embers. When in doubt, douse with cold water.)

- Empty the grease trap.

Once a week or as needed:

- Using a wire brush, brush any flakes of soot ("scale") off the inside of the grill lid.

Every few months or at the end of the grill season (of course, more and more of us grill year round):

- Make sure the ash catcher and grease trap are really empty. (I know I told you to do that daily—just checking.)

- Clean off any stubborn grease inside the grill or outside, using a grill cleaner like Safecid as needed.

- Lubricate the damper vents with WD-40 so they open and close easily.

- If using a gas grill, disconnect the regulator hose from the propane cylinder. If using natural gas, shut the valve leading to the grill. Secure a plastic bag or plastic wrap around the coupling to keep it free of dust, spiders, or bugs.

- If you leave your grill outside, cover it tightly.

---

kettle bowl with a garden trowel. Empty the ash catcher (if you haven't already done so).

- **Lube the dampers:** Squirt any sticky vents with a silicone spray like WD-40.

- **Remove the rust:** Treat minor rust or dings with a high-quality heatproof paint. If rust is beginning to eat through the grill walls, it's time for a new grill, no matter how many good times you've shared with the old one.

- **Scrub the grate:** Even if you brushed and oiled your grate after the last time you used it, you'll need to do so again before your first grill session. Build a hot fire in the grill. Heat the grate, then scour it with a stiff wire brush or a wooden scraper and oil it using a tightly folded paper towel dipped in oil. (This oils the grate and removes any loose brush bristles and debris.) Repeat as needed. This usually removes light rust, too. If not, do as my assistant, Nancy Loseke,

does—she buys a new grate for her kettle grill each year for about $15.00.

> **GRILLING HACK:** Remember, the more you use the grill, the more the grate will resist rusting and sticking.

- **Check your charcoal:** If your charcoal sat in the garage or an outdoor shed all winter, it may have absorbed moisture and will not light or burn properly. Buy a fresh bag. Buy a couple so you don't run out during a grill session. Note: If you own a charcoal grill with a propane igniter, like the Weber Performer, check the igniter battery, as describe at right, and replace the small LP canister as needed.

FOR GAS GRILLS

- **Clean the grill thoroughly:** Clear out all spiders, cobwebs, and other debris from inside the manifolds, Venturi tube, connectors, and so on. Empty and clean the grease trap, lining it with a fresh aluminum foil pan or aluminum foil as required. Light the grill and build a hot fire. Brush and oil the grill grate.

Note: It's easy to clean a hot grate and almost impossible to clean a cold one.

- **Leak patrol:** Check the hoses; if they're brittle or crimped, replace them. Turn on the propane valve (with burner knobs shut). If you smell gas, make a leak detection solution by mixing equal parts liquid dish soap and water. Brush this on the hoses and couplings; if you see bubbles, you have a leak. Replace any leaking parts.

- **Clear the burner tubes:** Remove the grill grate and metal baffles or Flavorizer Bars, which keep grease away from burner tubes, and make sure flames emerge from all the holes in the burner tubes. If any look blocked, open them with a bent paperclip, straight pin, or other thin wire.

- **Igniters on:** Press the igniter button. If you fail to hear a click or see a spark, check the battery. Unscrew the lock nut at the base of the button or behind the control panel. Most igniters take a size AA battery. I replace mine every season.

- **Fuel up:** You'll want to start the grill season with a full cylinder of propane, plus have a second full tank as a spare.

BREAKFAST ON THE GRILL

It's 6 a.m. on Chappaquiddick Island, Martha's Vineyard—my favorite time of day. The sun rises, spilling golden flames over the horizon. The wind rustles the treetops, and in the distance I can hear the surf hit the shore at Norton Point. My family is still sleeping and the phones are mercifully silent. It feels like I'm the only person awake on the island. So I do what any barbecue-obsessed guy would do at daybreak. I fire up my grill. This chapter explores a grilled meal that may be new to you: breakfast. Grilled bacon and eggs. Breakfast burgers and morning quesadillas. Rise and shine and smell the wood smoke.

GRILLED BACON

YIELD: Serves 4 to 6

METHOD: Direct or indirect grilling

PREP TIME: None

GRILLING TIME: About 6 minutes (direct grilling); 15 minutes (indirect grilling)

GRILL/GEAR: Can be grilled over charcoal, wood, or gas. You also need a wire rack or a sheet pan lined with paper towels.

SHOP: Use a thick-cut (ideally ¼ inch), real wood-smoked, artisanal bacon, like Nueske's.

INSIDER TIP: There's really only one trick to grilling bacon—but it's an indispensable one—you need plenty of open grate space. It's highly possible the dripping bacon fat will cause flare-ups—especially on a charcoal grill. So you must leave plenty of maneuvering room and have a large fire-free safety zone where you can park the bacon to dodge flare-ups.

In my book *Project Smoke*, I explain how to cure and smoke bacon from scratch. Now I'm going to show you how to grill it. Wait, isn't bacon fat highly flammable and won't grilling it turn your grill into a raging inferno? Grilling is my favorite way to cook bacon, sizzling the strips, reinforcing the smoke flavor, and, above all, keeping the mess of spattering grease off your stove. (It even helps remove some of the excess bacon fat.) And as it turns out, the process isn't quite as incendiary as it might seem. But due to its high fat content, grilling bacon requires more attention than most meats.

INGREDIENTS

Vegetable oil for oiling the grill grate

1 pound thick-sliced artisanal bacon (or as much as you desire)

DIRECT GRILL METHOD

1. Set up your grill for direct grilling and heat to medium-high. Brush or scrape the grill grate clean and oil it well. Be sure you have a fire-free safety zone covering at least 30 percent of your grill.

2. Arrange the bacon strips on the grate running diagonal to the bars of the grate. Leave at least 1 inch between the strips. Direct grill the bacon until browned on the bottom, 2 to 4 minutes. If you want to lay on a crosshatch of grill marks, give each slice a quarter turn halfway through. Move the bacon to the fire-free zone if flare-ups occur, then return to the part of the grill grate that's over the fire. Turn the bacon with tongs and grill the other side the same way.

3. Transfer the bacon to a wire rack or to a paper towel-lined sheet pan to drain. (If using paper towels, blot both sides.)

INDIRECT GRILL METHOD

1. Set up your grill for indirect grilling and heat to medium-high. Brush or scrape the grill grate clean and oil it well.

2. Arrange the bacon strips on the unlit portion of the grill running diagonal to the bars of the grate. Leave at least 1 inch between the strips. Indirect grill the bacon until sizzling, browned, and crisp, 15 to 20 minutes. There is no need to rotate or turn the bacon.

3. Transfer the bacon to a wire rack or to a paper towel-lined baking sheet to drain. The bacon will crisp as it cools. (If using paper towels, blot both sides.)

CANDIED BACON

It's hard to imagine a more perfect food than bacon, but candied bacon is just that—the salty, smoky, fatty, satisfying crunch of bacon enhanced in unexpected ways by the earthy sweetness of brown sugar and maple syrup. Think of this as a bacon dish you can serve equally well for breakfast or dessert.

INGREDIENTS

Vegetable oil for oiling the grill grate and wire rack

1 pound thick-sliced artisanal bacon

½ cup pure maple syrup

1 cup packed brown sugar, dark or light

1. Set up your grill for indirect grilling and heat to medium-high. Brush or scrape the grill grate clean and oil it well.

2. Arrange the bacon strips on a lightly oiled wire rack over a sheet pan lined with parchment paper or aluminum foil to facilitate easy cleanup. (It's easier to move all bacon to the grill on a wire rack than it is to do it slice by slice.) Brush the top of each slice with maple syrup, then sprinkle generously with brown sugar, patting the sugar onto the meat.

3. Place the wire rack (reserve the prepared sheet pan) on the grill grate so the bacon is over the drip pan away from the heat.

4. Indirect grill the bacon until it is browned and crisp and the sugar is caramelized, 15 to 20 minutes. (The bacon will continue to crisp as it cools.)

5. Return the wire rack to the sheet pan and let it cool slightly before serving. (Molten sugar can burn your tongue, so test a small piece before you bite into it.)

YIELD: Serves 4 to 6

METHOD: Indirect grilling

PREP TIME: 5 minutes

GRILLING TIME: 15 to 20 minutes

GRILL/GEAR: Can be grilled over charcoal or gas. You also need a wire rack and a pastry brush.

SHOP: Use a thick-cut, real wood-smoked, artisanal bacon, like Nueske's.

INSIDER TIP: As you saw on the facing page, there are two ways to grill bacon: by direct grilling or indirect grilling. The former gives you more sear and better grill marks, and it's faster, but you greatly increase the risk of flare-ups. Indirect grilling eliminates the risk of flare-ups, but it takes longer, and it, well, deprives you of the adrenaline rush of grilling one of the world's most flammable foods. I'm a "no guts, no glory" sort of guy, so I usually direct grill my bacon. But candied bacon is different, because turning the bacon would disturb the sugar crust.

BACON AND EGG QUESADILLA

YIELD: Serves 1 and can be multiplied as desired

METHOD: Direct grilling

PREP TIME: 10 minutes

GRILLING TIME: 7 to 9 minutes

GRILL/GEAR: Can be grilled over charcoal, wood, or gas. You also need a wide-bladed spatula and 2 rimless sheet pans.

INSIDER TIP: The only remotely challenging step in this recipe is flipping the quesadilla without losing the cheese and egg. If you don't have a quesadilla grilling basket, slide a large spatula under the quesadilla and transfer it to a rimless sheet pan or the back of a rimmed sheet pan. Place another sheet pan on top, flip the quesadilla, and slide it back onto the grate. Or just take a deep breath and quickly turn it with a spatula. For even more flavor, top the quesadillas with extra sliced jalapeños, cilantro, and scallions.

For most of my life, the quesadilla has been a 5-minute lunch or a vehicle for leftovers—as Spartan or lavish as the ingredients in your refrigerator allow. And now, it's about to make an appearance at breakfast with a filling that defies physics: a "fried" egg cooked right between the tortillas. If you do it right, following the simple instructions below, the tortilla will be crisp, the cheese melted and gooey, the egg white just set, and the egg yolk still runny. To up the ante, serve it with the Ember Salsa on page 62.

INGREDIENTS

2 flour tortillas (each 8 inches in diameter)

1 tablespoon melted butter, bacon fat, or extra virgin olive oil

3 ounces (about ¾ cup) cheddar, Monterey or pepper Jack, or other cheese, coarsely grated

1 large egg (preferably farm-fresh or organic)

2 strips bacon, grilled (page 50) and slivered or crumbled, or 2 ounces smoked ham (cured or cooked), cut crosswise into thin slivers

1 jalapeño or serrano pepper, thinly sliced crosswise (optional; for a milder quesadilla, seed the chiles)

1 scallion, trimmed, white and green parts finely chopped (optional)

3 tablespoons finely chopped fresh cilantro (optional)

Vegetable oil for oiling the grate

Sour cream (optional) or Ember Salsa (optional—page 62), for serving

1. Set up your grill for direct grilling and heat to medium-high. Have one section of the grill fire-free.

2. Brush one of the tortillas with half the melted butter and place it, butter side down, on the rimless sheet pan (or on the back of a rimmed sheet pan). Sprinkle two thirds of the cheese on top in a doughnut shape (more generously around the periphery), leaving a 3-inch space in the center for the egg. Crack the egg into a ramekin (fish out any stray pieces of shell), then carefully pour it into the center of the quesadilla. Sprinkle the remaining cheese over it. Sprinkle the bacon or ham slivers on top, followed by the chile, scallion, and cilantro (if using).

3. Brush one side of the second tortilla with the remaining butter and place it, butter side up, atop the quesadilla.

4. Brush or scrape the grill grate clean and oil it well. Position the sheet pan with the quesadilla just

above the grate. Tugging from one end, gently slide the quesadilla onto the grill grate. Close the grill lid. Grill until the bottom is browned and the cheese at the edge starts to melt, 2 to 4 minutes. Reduce the heat if the quesadilla starts to burn.

5. Slide a large spatula (or a rimless sheet pan) under the quesadilla and flip it over. (See the Insider Tip, page 52, for flipping instructions.) Continue grilling until the bottom is browned and the cheese is melted, another 2 to 4 minutes. Theoretically, the cheese will be melted and the egg will be cooked by the time the tortillas are browned. If not, slide the quesadilla to the unlit part of the grill with a spatula. Close the grill lid and indirect grill until the cheese is melted and the egg is just set—a few minutes longer.

6. Transfer the quesadilla to a plate. Serve with sour cream and/or Ember Salsa, if desired. Breakfast doesn't get better than this.

GRILLED EGGS
WITH PROSCIUTTO AND PARMESAN

These grilled eggs are one of the simplest—and tastiest—breakfasts I know. They have something for everyone: creamy eggs, crusty bread crumbs, salty prosciutto, the umami flavors of Parmigiano-Reggiano—and that's before you add the richness of heavy cream. They're infinitely customizable: You could substitute Japanese panko for the bread crumbs, bacon or sausage for the prosciutto, cheddar or pepper Jack cheese for the Parmigiano-Reggiano.

YIELD: Serves 1 and can be multiplied as desired

METHOD: Indirect grilling

PREP TIME: 10 minutes

GRILLING TIME: 7 to 10 minutes

GRILL/GEAR: Can be grilled over charcoal or gas. You also need 2 hardwood chunks or 1 cup unsoaked wood chips (optional) and a small skillet or baking dish to cook the eggs. Two options come to mind: mini-cast iron skillets (available from Lodge) or *cazuelas* (shallow earthenware dishes from Mexico or Spain).

INGREDIENTS

1 thin slice prosciutto or 1 strip cooked bacon

1½ tablespoons extra virgin olive oil or melted butter

2 large eggs (preferably farm-fresh or organic)

2 tablespoons heavy (whipping) cream

1 ounce (2 tablespoons) grated Parmigiano-Reggiano or other cheese

2 tablespoons toasted bread crumbs

1 tablespoon chopped fresh chives or scallion greens

Grilled toast (optional, but desirable—page 80)

SHOP: Organic eggs; homemade bread crumbs; Parmigiano-Reggiano. Perfection lies in the details.

INSIDER TIP: Wood smoke, although not necessary, adds an interesting dimension to the eggs. There's no need to soak the chips—with 7 to 10 minutes total cooking time, you want to generate a quick blast of wood smoke. While you're grilling the eggs, grill some thin strips of toast to go with them. (Thin, so you can jab them into the yolks.) Note: This recipe makes a single portion serving, but you can quadruple it, grilling 8 eggs in a 10-inch skillet to make breakfast for 4.

1. Set up your grill for indirect grilling and heat to medium-high.

2. Lightly brush the prosciutto on both sides with a little olive oil. Place it directly over the fire and grill until crisp, 1 to 2 minutes per side. Transfer to a wire rack and let cool.

3. Grease a small heatproof skillet or baking dish with half the remaining olive oil. Crack in the eggs. Add the wood chunks or chips (if using) to the coals or place in the smoker box of your gas grill. Place the skillet with the eggs on the grill away from the heat.

4. Break the prosciutto into pieces over the eggs and cover with the cream. Sprinkle with the cheese and bread crumbs. Dot the tops of the eggs with the remaining olive oil or butter.

5. Indirect grill until the crumbs are browned and the eggs are just set, 7 to 10 minutes. (The yolks should remain a little runny in the center.) Shake the pan to check for doneness—the eggs should wiggle, not ripple. Sprinkle on the chives and serve the eggs at once with strips or slices of grilled toast.

Pour the cream over the eggs. Note how the prosciutto grills directly over the fire. You can easily cook more eggs to serve a crowd.

Sprinkle the bread crumbs over the eggs.

Add the chives before removing the skillet from the grill.

BREAKFAST "BURGERS"

Beer-can burgers rocked the barbecue blogosphere a few years ago, and while I liked the concept—molding a burger around the bottom of an oiled beer can to make a meaty cup for a filling—I don't particularly enjoy hamburgers or any ground meat smoked low and slow. (It comes out heavy and tough.) But grill these sausage burgers at high heat as described below and the meat stays moist and tender. Fill the resulting burgers with eggs and cheese and you've got a belt-loosening, soul-satisfying breakfast.

INGREDIENTS

Vegetable oil for oiling the silicone mat, beer can, and grill grate

2 pounds seasoned bulk pork sausage or sausage that's been removed from its casings, well chilled

8 strips artisanal bacon

4 large eggs (preferably farm-fresh or organic)

Coarse salt (sea or kosher) and freshly ground black pepper

8 ounces grated cheddar cheese or pepper Jack cheese

1 scallion, trimmed, white and green parts thinly sliced crosswise

4 English muffins, split and buttered, or grilled bread (page 80)

1. Line a rimmed sheet pan with a silicone mesh grill mat or aluminum foil and lightly oil it. Divide the sausage into 4 equal portions (½ pound each). Wet your hands with cold water and form the meat into 4 balls. Arrange the meat portions several inches apart on the sheet pan.

2. Oil the bottom and lower third of the beer or soda can. (Don't skip this step.) Firmly press the bottom of the beer can into one of the sausage balls to form a cup. The side of the cup should come about 1 inch up the side of the can. Carefully twist out the beer can and repeat with the rest of the meat. Use your fingers to mold the bottoms and sides of the cups into uniform thickness and to fuse any cracks in the meat. Wrap 2 bacon strips around the outside of each cup and secure with toothpicks.

3. Refrigerate the meat cups, uncovered, for 1 hour. The burgers can be prepared to this stage up to 8 hours ahead.

4. When ready to cook, set up your grill for indirect grilling and heat to medium-high. Brush or scrape the grill grate clean and oil it well. If working on a silicone mesh grill mat, simply slide it onto the grate away from the fire. Otherwise, gently pry

YIELD: Makes 4 burgers

METHOD: Smoke-roasting (indirect grilling with wood smoke)

PREP TIME: 15 minutes, plus 1 hour for chilling the burgers

GRILLING TIME: 30 to 40 minutes

GRILL/GEAR: Can be grilled over charcoal or gas. You also need 1 full can of beer or soda, well chilled; sheet pan; silicone mesh grill mat (page 39) or aluminum foil; toothpicks; and 2 hardwood chunks or 1½ cups wood chips, the latter soaked in water for 30 minutes, then drained.

SHOP: There are several options for ground meat: breakfast sausage; sweet or spicy Italian sausage; or for a Latino twist, chorizo.

INSIDER TIP: Start with very cold ground meat and oil the chilled beer or soda can well. Grilling on a silicone mesh grill mat (page 39) helps the burgers hold their shape. You can cook these burgers on a gas or charcoal grill, but you'll get a more pronounced smoke flavor with charcoal.

the burgers off the foil-lined sheet pan and transfer, open side up, to the grate away from the fire. Add the wood chunks or chips to the coals if using charcoal, or place in the smoker box of your gas grill. Lower the grill lid.

5. Indirect grill the burgers until browned and firm, 20 to 30 minutes. Using paper towels, blot any excess fat pooled in the depression made by the beer can. Crack an egg into the cup of each burger. (If this makes you nervous, crack the egg into a ramekin and carefully pour it into the cup.) Sprinkle salt, pepper, grated cheese, and chopped scallions over each egg.

6. Lower the grill lid and continue indirect grilling the breakfast burgers until the sausage meat is browned, the cheese is melted, and the eggs are cooked to taste (I like them a little runny), 8 to 12 minutes more.

7. Transfer the breakfast burgers to a platter. Grill the English muffins, cut sides down, directly over the fire, 1 to 2 minutes. Place 1 breakfast burger on the bottom of each muffin (I like to serve the burgers open-face) and get ready for one of the most outrageous breakfasts of your life.

Form a sausage cup with the oiled bottom of a beer can.

Ring the outside of each meat cup with bacon.

Secure the bacon in place with toothpicks.

STARTERS

Salsa. Poppers. Wings. These are a few of the starters pyromaniacs everywhere like to serve at the beginning of a barbecue. As you might expect, the *Project Fire* versions take you off the beaten track. Like roasting the salsa ingredients caveman-style—directly on the embers. Or spiking those poppers with Thai red curry crab or indirect grilling those wings with a sesame crust. I've also added some finger foods that may not yet be in your repertory. Such as a vegetable twist on Buffalo wings. Grilled Spanish padrón peppers. And planked fresh figs with Taleggio cheese and speck. It's common wisdom that bacon makes everything taste better, and I give edible proof with bacon- and chorizo-grilled dates and sriracha-blasted, bacon-wrapped onion rings. A simple reminder that there's no better way to start the party than by firing up your grill.

EMBER SALSA
WITH CHIVE-GRILLED TORTILLA CHIPS

YIELD: Makes 2½ to 3 cups of salsa, enough to serve 4 to 6

METHOD: Caveman grilling (in the embers)

PREP TIME: 20 minutes

GRILLING TIME: 10 minutes, plus 4 minutes for the chips

GRILL/GEAR: Must be cooked over charcoal or wood embers. A traditional chef in Mexico might grind the salsa ingredients in a *molcajete*, a lava stone mortar and pestle. You can also chop the vegetables by hand or use a food processor. A grill hoe or garden hoe is useful for raking the coals into an even layer. For the best results, use natural lump charcoal.

SHOP: The usual: Garden or farmstand produce (preferably organic) will give you the best flavor—especially if you can find tomatoes that have never seen the inside of a refrigerator.

INSIDER TIP: Sorry, gas grillers; for the full effect, you need a charcoal grill for this one. The best way to approximate the flavor of cavemanning on a gas grill is to sear the veggies on a super hot plancha (see page 16).

Salsa is the lifeblood of Mexican cuisine. This one uses a singular grilling technique—"cavemanning" (roasting in the embers) to impart a rustic char and haunting smoke flavor you just can't achieve by conventional grilling. Besides, people are always gobsmacked to see tomatoes, onions, and jalapeños grilling directly on the coals.

INGREDIENTS

1 medium-size onion, peeled and cut in half through the stem end

1 poblano pepper

8 plum tomatoes

3 large jalapeño peppers

3 limes, cut in half crosswise

1 canned chipotle chile, minced, with 1 teaspoon can juices (both optional—they reinforce the smoke flavor)

⅓ cup chopped fresh cilantro

Coarse salt (sea or kosher) and freshly ground black pepper to taste

Chive-Grilled Tortilla Chips (recipe follows)

1. Light the charcoal or wood chunks in a chimney starter. When the coals glow red, dump them into the bottom of the grill and rake them into an even layer.

2. Place the onion, poblano, tomatoes, jalapeños, and lime halves directly on the coals. Cook until charred black on the outside, 3 to 5 minutes per side (6 to 10 minutes in all) for the onion; 1 to 2 minutes per side (3 to 6 minutes in all) for the poblano and tomatoes; and 1 to 2 minutes per side (2 to 4 minutes in all) for the jalapeños and lime halves. Turn the ingredients with long-handled tongs to ensure even cooking. Transfer the charred vegetables and lime halves to an aluminum foil pan to cool.

3. Using a pastry brush, brush any ash or cinders off the vegetables. Scrape the seeds out of the jalapeños (unless you want a really fiery salsa). Scrape the burnt skin off the poblano, and then seed and core it. Don't worry about removing every last bit of burnt skin from the veggies: A few black spots add color and flavor.

4. Cut the veggies into 1-inch pieces, then grind the pieces to a coarse puree in a food processor, running the machine in short bursts. Do not overprocess. Alternatively, coarsely

Don't remove all of the burnt skin from the ember-roasted vegetables. It will add color and flavor to the salsa.

chop the salsa ingredients by hand or grind in a *molcajete* (Mexican lava stone mortar and pestle). Work in the canned chipotle chile with its juices, if using.

5. Squeeze in the juice from the charred limes, followed by the cilantro and salt and pepper to taste: The salsa should be highly seasoned. Serve with Chive-Grilled Tortilla Chips.

CHIVE-GRILLED TORTILLA CHIPS

YIELD: Makes 32 chips

Grilling produces tortilla chips with less fat and more flavor—especially when grilled with fresh chives.

INGREDIENTS

4 flour tortillas (each 8 inches in diameter)

2 to 3 tablespoons melted butter or extra virgin olive oil

4 tablespoons finely chopped fresh chives or scallion greens

Vegetable oil for oiling the grill

Coarse salt (sea or kosher)

1. Set up your grill for direct grilling and heat to medium-high.

2. Brush the flour tortillas on both sides with melted butter or olive oil. Sprinkle both sides with 2 tablespoons of the chives.

3. Brush or scrape the grill grate clean and oil it well. Arrange the chive-crusted tortillas on the grate and grill until sizzling and browned on both sides, about 2 minutes per side. (Watch carefully as they can burn easily.)

4. Transfer the tortillas to a cutting board. Sprinkle with the remaining chives and salt and cut each into 8 wedges. The chips will crisp as they cool.

CHORIZO-GRILLED DATES

I've grilled bacon-wrapped dates and prunes a hundred times, but it never occurred to me to stuff them with chorizo sausage like Micael Soares does. The Portuguese-born Quebecer runs a lively Portuguese bistro called Cervéjaria in Boucherville near Montreal. Soares blasts you with porky goodness from both sides, stuffing the dates with chorizo and grilling them wrapped in bacon—a panoply of sweet, salty, garlicky, and spicy flavors.

INGREDIENTS

24 pitted Medjool dates or other soft sweet dates

3 ounces dry-cured Spanish-style chorizo sausage, cut into 16 almond-size pieces

8 strips of bacon, gently stretched lengthwise and each cut crosswise into thirds

Vegetable oil for oiling the grill grate

1. Stuff each date with a sliver of chorizo. Wrap each date crosswise in bacon, securing the bacon with a toothpick.

2. Set up your grill for direct grilling and heat to medium-high. Brush or scrape the grill grate clean and oil it well. Be sure to have a fire-free safety zone.

3. Arrange the dates on the grate and grill until sizzling and browned on the outside and hot in the center, 2 to 3 minutes per side; 4 to 6 minutes in all. If flare-ups occur (and they usually do when you grill bacon), simply move the dates to the fire-free section of the grill until the flames die down.

4. Transfer the dates to paper towels to drain, then arrange on a plate or platter and serve while still sizzling hot.

YIELD: Makes 24, enough to serve 6 to 8 as a starter

METHOD: Direct grilling

PREP TIME: 15 minutes

GRILLING TIME: 4 to 6 minutes

GRILL/GEAR: Can be grilled over charcoal, wood, or gas. You also need toothpicks.

SHOP: A dish this simple (three ingredients) lives or dies by the quality of the dates. Look for fresh Medjool dates that feel soft, with translucent caramel-brown exteriors: sure signs that they're sweet. In the United States, fresh dates are in season the last three months of the year.

INSIDER TIP: This is the sort of finger food that lends itself to dozens of variations. Use prunes in place of dates, or Gorgonzola cheese in place of chorizo. Wrap the dates in pancetta, prosciutto, or speck instead of bacon. You get the idea.

RED CURRY CRAB POPPERS

The popper burst on the American grill scene a decade or so ago, and we've long since graduated from the classic bacon and cheese to poppers sweet with corn, smoky with pulled pork, or briny with lobster or crab. This one features what we used to call crab imperial (shellfish baked with mayonnaise) in my native Baltimore—with a twist—an electrifying jolt of red Thai chili paste.

INGREDIENTS

- 12 large jalapeño peppers with stems
- 1 to 2 tablespoons Thai red chili paste (or green or yellow curry paste), or to taste
- ½ cup mayonnaise, preferably Hellmann's or Best Foods
- 1 pound jumbo lump backfin crab meat, picked through to remove any shells
- 3 tablespoons coarsely chopped fresh cilantro or parsley
- 12 strips artisanal bacon, each cut crosswise in half
- Vegetable oil for oiling the grill grate

1. Cut each jalapeño in half lengthwise (cut through the stem, too, but leave it attached). Scrape out the seeds and ribs with a small metal spoon or a grapefruit spoon.

2. Make the filling: Place the red chili paste in a mixing bowl. Whisk in the mayonnaise. Gently fold in the crab and chopped cilantro or parsley. Spoon this mixture into the jalapeño halves. Wrap a strip of bacon around each half and secure with a toothpick.

3. Set up your grill for indirect grilling and heat to medium-high. If working on a gas grill, use the smoking techniques on page 22. Brush or scrape the grill grate clean and oil it well.

4. Arrange the poppers on the grate over the drip pan away from the heat (it helps to have them on a wire rack or grilling grid for efficient transport to and from the grill). Add the wood chunks or chips, if using, to the coals, or place in your gas grill's smoker box.

5. Indirect grill the poppers until the bacon and crab mixture is sizzling and browned and the sides of the jalapeños are soft, 20 to 30 minutes, or as needed.

6. Transfer to a platter, remove the toothpicks, and serve.

YIELD: Makes 24 halves, enough to serve 4 to 8 as a starter

METHOD: Indirect grilling

PREP TIME: 10 minutes

GRILLING TIME: 20 to 30 minutes

GRILL/GEAR: Can be grilled over charcoal or gas. You also need a wire rack or grilling grid; toothpicks; 2 hardwood chunks or 1½ cups wood chips, the latter soaked in water to cover for 30 minutes, then drained (optional).

SHOP: Look for Thai curry paste in the Asian foods section of your local supermarket, online, or, of course, at an Asian market.

INSIDER TIP: You've probably seen poppers grilled whole (often upright in special racks), but I prefer grilling them split so you can bring more smoke and fire flavor to the filling. Speaking of fillings, this Thai red curry crab is one of an infinite range of possible fillings; others might include goat cheese and wasabi, shrimp and Gouda, or shredded brisket with smoked cheddar. Note: I call for wood chips here because poppers have a natural affinity for smoke. But smoke isn't really part of the Thai flavor profile, so these poppers come out equally great without smoke on a gas grill.

GRILLED PADRON PEPPERS
WITH SESAME AND SEA SALT

YIELD: Serves 4 to 6

METHOD: Direct grilling

PREP TIME: 10 minutes

GRILLING TIME: 4 to 8 minutes

GRILL/GEAR: Can be grilled over charcoal, wood, or gas. You also need flat bamboo skewers if grilling the peppers kebab-style, or a wire mesh grill basket or grill wok.

SHOP: Once the province of ethnic markets, padrón peppers (and their Japanese cousins, shishitos) can now be found at Whole Foods and many supermarkets. Or order them online from Melissas.com or Amazon.

INSIDER TIP: The capsaicin (the heat-producing compound) level in padróns varies from pepper to pepper—even in peppers from a single plant. That's what makes them such fun to eat: You'll eat four or five mild ones, then the sixth will scorch your palate. My wife has a low tolerance for chile hellfire, so when we eat them at home or at a restaurant, I take a bite of each one to make sure it's safe for her to eat. Good husband or what?

The Spanish call them padróns. The Japanese prize a similar pepper known as shishito. For my money, these small, green, finger-shaped chiles rank among the world's best grilling peppers. Perhaps you've enjoyed them at yakitori parlors, seasoned with sesame oil and sea salt and blistered over a hot fire. Or maybe at a tapas bar, where tradition calls for deep-frying, but more and more Spanish chefs are grilling them as well. Obviously, I prefer grilling, but whatever the name or method, know you will be rewarded with a bite-size pepper you pop in your mouth with your fingers, with a rich herbaceous flavor that hints at poblano and can be bell pepper mild or serrano fiery or anywhere in between.

There are three ways to grill padrón peppers: lined up on a skewer (as with all small or slender foods, it's easier to grill five on one skewer than 25 individual peppers). Or in a grill basket (and for an interesting twist, lay the basket directly on the coals caveman-style). Or blister the peppers on a hot plancha (see page 16), which is how they'd be cooked in Spain—preferably over a hot wood fire.

INGREDIENTS

Vegetable oil for oiling the grill grate

1 pound padrón or shishito peppers (leave the stems on—they'll serve as handles when you eat them)

3 tablespoons Asian (dark) sesame oil

3 tablespoons sesame seeds

Large flat crystals of coarse sea salt, such as Maldon

1. Set up your grill for direct grilling and heat to high. Brush or scrape the grill grate clean and oil it well.

2. Skewer the peppers crosswise on bamboo skewers. Lightly brush the peppers on both sides with sesame oil and sprinkle with sesame seeds and sea salt.

3. Arrange the skewers on the grate. Grill the peppers until sizzling and browned on both sides, 2 to 4 minutes per side. Serve the peppers hot off the grill with extra salt on the side for sprinkling.

HOW TO TOAST SESAME SEEDS

Toasting sesame seeds brings out a distinctive nutty flavor. To toast sesame seeds, place them in a dry skillet over medium-high heat (or put the skillet directly on a hot grill). Cook until the seeds start to brown, 2 to 4 minutes, then transfer immediately to a bowl. (If you leave them in the hot skillet, they'll burn.)

GREEK GRILLED CHEESE
(HALLOUMI, HONEY, AND MINT)

When Cypriots and Greeks say grilled cheese, they mean it. Specifically, a cheese called halloumi, which has the genial property of being able to be direct grilled over a hot fire without melting. Made with sheep's and goat's milk and steeped in brine as part of the curing process, halloumi delivers a clean, bright, salty, cheesy flavor. (Often dried mint is added for even more taste.) In restaurants that lack grills, it's common to griddle the cheese in a two-handled pan called a *saganaki*. But you, fellow grilling fanatic, will sear the cheese directly over live fire.

YIELD: Serves 4

METHOD: Direct grilling

PREP TIME: 10 minutes

GRILLING TIME: 4 to 8 minutes

GRILL/GEAR: Can be grilled over charcoal, wood, or gas. You also need a basting brush.

SHOP: Look for halloumi at Greek or Middle Eastern markets, or at a growing number of supermarkets. Note for our friends in Quebec: You can use a similar grilling cheese from the Ile d'Orleans called Paillasson.

INSIDER TIP: Greek restaurants often serve halloumi "grilled" in a hot skillet. I prefer to sear the cheese directly over a live fire. The grill marks look awesome and give you a charred smoky flavor.

INGREDIENTS

Vegetable oil for oiling the grill grate

4 tablespoons (½ stick) unsalted butter

¼ cup fresh mint leaves, thinly slivered

1 slab (10 to 12 ounces) halloumi cheese

1 lemon, cut in half widthwise and seeded

Honey, warmed, for drizzling

Pita bread, grilled, for serving (see Note)

1. Set up your grill for direct grilling and heat to high. Brush or scrape the grill grate clean and oil it well.

2. Melt the butter in a skillet over high heat. Stir in the mint leaves and fry until crisp, 2 minutes. Set the mixture aside.

3. Cut the cheese through the narrow side into 4 broad flat slices. Brush the cheese on both sides with some of the mint butter.

4. Arrange the cheese on the grate and grill until sizzling and browned on both sides, 2 to 4 minutes per side. Give each a quarter turn halfway through to lay on a crosshatch of grill marks. While you're at it, grill the lemon until darkly browned on the cut side.

5. To serve, transfer the grilled cheese to a platter. Pour the remaining mint butter over it and drizzle with honey. Serve with grilled lemon and grilled pita bread.

NOTE: To grill pita, lightly brush both sides with melted butter or extra virgin olive oil. Grill until toasted (golden brown), 1 to 2 minutes per side. Figure on ½ to 1 pita bread per person.

PLANKED FIGS
WITH TALEGGIO CHEESE AND SPECK

YIELD: Makes 12 halves, enough to serve 3 to 4 as a starter

METHOD: Plank grilling (direct grilling, followed by indirect grilling)

PREP TIME: 10 minutes

GRILLING TIME: 15 to 20 minutes in all

GRILL/GEAR: Can be grilled over charcoal or gas. You also need 2 cedar or other hardwood grilling planks (each at least 4 by 8 inches); toothpicks.

Maybe you've experienced the combination in Italy—sweet fresh figs wrapped in salty prosciutto to make a quintessential summer antipasto. The *Project Fire* version adds two additional flavors—the pungency of Taleggio cheese and the aromatic smoke from burning cedar. Notice I say "burning" and "smoke." In old-school grilling, you would soak the cedar plank in water to keep it from catching fire. I now advocate for the opposite: Char the plank first to get it smoking. Charred wood delivers big flavor. Gas grillers take heart: You don't need a charcoal or wood fire to generate smoke.

INGREDIENTS

6 ounces Taleggio or other cheese, cut crosswise into 12 slices

6 large ripe fresh figs, cut in half

Freshly ground black pepper

6 paper-thin slices speck, each cut in half lengthwise

Saba (grape syrup) or honey (warmed), for drizzling

1 bunch fresh thyme (optional)

1. Set up your grill for indirect grilling and heat to high.

2. Place the planks on the grate directly over one of the fires. Grill until lightly charred, 2 to 4 minutes. Don't worry if the edges catch fire: You can blow out the flames. Transfer the charred planks to a wire rack to cool.

3. Meanwhile, place a slice of cheese atop the cut side of a fig half and sprinkle with pepper. Wrap both with a slice of speck and secure with a toothpick. Repeat with the remaining figs.

4. Arrange the wrapped figs on the wooden planks, cheese sides up, 6 halves to a plank.

5. Return the planks to the grill—this time, away from the heat (not directly over the fire). Close the grill lid and indirect grill the figs until the speck browns slightly and crisps and the cheese melts, 8 to 12 minutes, or as needed. Transfer to a heatproof platter for serving. Drizzle each fig with a little saba or honey and sprinkle with fresh thyme leaves, if using.

NOTE: Place the bunch of thyme between the palms of your hands, stem end up. Roll your hands, back and forth to shake off thyme leaves.

SHOP: Fresh figs are in season in the summer and fall months: Good varieties include black mission and brown turkey. Taleggio is a pungent cow's milk cheese from Lombardy in northern Italy. Speck is a smoked prosciutto. Saba (sometimes called *musto*) is an Italian grape syrup—it's thick, sweet, and grapey, with a pleasantly acidic finish. Look for it at Italian markets or online from Amazon, or substitute honey.

INSIDER TIP: Use this recipe as a broad guide rather than a blueprint. Can't find Taleggio? Substitute goat cheese or Gorgonzola. If you prefer a non-smoked ham, use prosciutto. For a Spanish twist, top the figs with Cabrales or Manchego cheese and wrap in serrano ham instead of prosciutto.

BUFFALO BRUSSELS SPROUTS

Here's a vegetable twist on a bar food classic: buffalo brussels sprouts. It uses a technique called smoke-roasting, wherein you indirect grill brussels sprouts in an aluminum foil pan, adding wood chips to the fire to generate wood smoke. The result: crispy smoky brussels sprouts in a fiery buttery slather—without the mess of deep-frying. For a meatless version, substitute carrot slices for the bacon. Tip o' the hat to one of my favorite neighborhood restaurants, the Port Hunter in Edgartown, Martha's Vineyard, where I first experienced brussels sprouts prepared this way.

YIELD: Serves 4 as a starter or vegetable side dish

METHOD: Smoke-roasting (indirect grilling with wood smoke)

PREP TIME: 15 minutes

GRILLING TIME: 30 to 40 minutes for smoke-roasting

GRILL/GEAR: Can be grilled over charcoal or gas. You also need a large (9-by-13-inch) aluminum foil pan or large cast-iron skillet; 2 hardwood chunks or 1½ cups wood chips, the latter soaked in water to cover for 30 minutes, then drained.

SHOP: For the best results, use organic brussels sprouts and a thick-cut artisanal bacon, like Nueske's.

INSIDER TIP: There are two alternative ways to grill the brussels sprouts. You can thread them on flat bamboo skewers, alternating with bacon pieces (in which case, cut the bacon into 1-inch squares). Direct grill the resulting kebabs over a medium fire. (Baste the kebabs with some of the fire butter as they grill.) Or you can grill the brussels sprouts and bacon in a mesh grill basket, stirring often so they grill evenly. Again, baste with some of the fire butter.

INGREDIENTS

FOR THE BRUSSELS SPROUTS

2 scallions, trimmed, white and green parts thinly sliced crosswise

1 pound medium-size brussels sprouts, cut in half through the stem end

3 ounces thick-sliced bacon, cut crosswise into ¼-inch slivers

1 tablespoon extra virgin olive oil or melted butter

Coarse sea salt and freshly ground black pepper

FOR THE FIRE BUTTER

5 tablespoons unsalted butter

5 tablespoons sriracha or your favorite hot sauce

1. Set up your grill for indirect grilling and heat to medium-high.

2. Set aside 2 tablespoons of scallion greens. Place the brussels sprouts, bacon, scallion whites, and remaining greens in the aluminum foil pan. Drizzle the mixture with olive oil and season with salt and pepper, stirring to mix.

3. Place the foil pan on the grill away from the heat. Add the wood chunks or chips to the coals. Close the grill lid and indirect grill until the brussels sprouts are browned and tender (test with a bamboo skewer or toothpick) and the bacon is crisp and browned, 30 to 40 minutes, or as needed. Stir the mixture from time to time so the ingredients brown evenly. To speed up the roasting, you can do part or all of the cooking directly over the fire (but in that case, you'll have to stir more often).

4. Meanwhile, make the fire butter: Melt the butter in a small saucepan on your grill's side burner or on the stove over medium heat. Add the sriracha and bring to a boil.

5. Transfer the brussels sprouts and bacon to a serving bowl. Pour the fire butter over them and stir to mix. Sprinkle with the reserved scallion greens and dig in.

SESAME SOY CHICKEN WINGS
WITH HONEY AND HOISIN SAUCE

Travel the world's barbecue trail and chicken wings are a constant—slathered with hot sauce in Buffalo, New York; spit-roasted with garlic and lime in Brazil; marinated in beer in Australia; and salved with sesame oil and sweet soy sauce in Singapore. That's the inspiration for these wings, which bring additional crunch to the party in the form of a nutty sesame seed crust.

INGREDIENTS

FOR THE WINGS

3 pounds whole chicken wings

½ cup Asian (dark) sesame oil

½ cup soy sauce

1 tablespoon peeled (minced or grated) fresh ginger

1 clove garlic, peeled and minced

1 scallion, trimmed, white and green parts minced, but kept separate

1 teaspoon finely grated fresh lemon zest

Vegetable oil for oiling the grill grate

2 cups sesame seeds

FOR SERVING

½ cup hoisin sauce, or to taste

¼ cup honey, warmed

YIELD: Serves 4 to 6 as a starter

METHOD: Indirect grilling

PREP TIME: 20 minutes, plus 1 to 2 hours for marinating

GRILLING TIME: 30 to 40 minutes

GRILL/GEAR: Can be grilled over charcoal or gas.

SHOP: As always, buy organic chicken when possible. For sesame oil, use an Asian brand, like Kadoya from Japan. The most cost-effective way to buy sesame seeds is at an Asian or Middle Eastern market or in bulk at a natural foods store.

INSIDER TIP: Smoke isn't really part of the Asian flavor palate, so I don't call for hardwood chunks or chips here. You can certainly add them if you want to.

1. Cut each chicken wing through the joints into 3 sections. You'll use the larger section (the part that resembles a small drumstick) and the middle section. Discard the wingtips or save for stock. To turn the larger section into a drumette, make a cut in the meat to the bone around the circumference of the small end, just above the joint. Scrape the meat from this end up to the larger end to form a ball. Scrape the bone clean. You should wind up with what looks like a miniature drumstick.

2. Combine the sesame oil, soy sauce, ginger, garlic, scallion whites, and lemon zest in a large mixing bowl. Stir in the wings. Marinate in the refrigerator for 1 to 2 hours, stirring a couple times so the wings are seasoned evenly.

3. Meanwhile, set up your grill for indirect grilling and heat to medium. Brush or scrape the grill grate clean and oil it well.

4. Drain the chicken wings well, reserving the marinade. You'll boil the

marinade with hoisin sauce to make a sauce (see below). Have the sesame seeds in a shallow bowl at grillside. Dip each chicken wing in sesame seeds to coat completely and arrange the wings on the grill grate away from the heat. Close the grill lid.

5. Indirect grill the wings until the sesame seeds are browned, the skin is crisp, and the meat is cooked through to the bone (make a little slit in the largest wing to check for doneness), 30 to 40 minutes.

6. Meanwhile, make the sauce: Boil the reserved marinade for 3 full minutes. Then, whisk in the hoisin sauce, adding more as needed to taste. Let cool to room temperature.

7. Mound the wings in a shallow bowl or on a platter. Drizzle with honey and sprinkle with the reserved scallion greens. Serve the sauce in small bowls on the side for dipping.

Variations

For Vietnamese-style wings, substitute fish sauce for 2 tablespoons soy sauce in the marinade and 2 tablespoons minced lemongrass (the pale parts only) for the lemon zest in the marinade. Dip the chicken wings in finely chopped peanuts instead of sesame seeds.

For Pac-Rim buffalo wings, douse the Sesame Soy Chicken Wings with the fire butter on page 72.

Indirect grill the chicken wings skin side up. The melting fat will baste the wings.

BACON-GRILLED ONION RINGS

Bacon-grilled onion rings rocked the blogosphere a few years ago—it was love at first sight and first bite. They're based on the simple premise that bacon makes everything taste better (it does), and, yes, the salty-smoky bacon really seems to make the onions taste sweeter. The bacon serves another purpose—giving you some of the crunch associated with batter-fried onion rings. The hot sauce brings it all into focus.

YIELD: Serves 4

METHOD: Indirect grilling

PREP TIME: 15 minutes

GRILLING TIME: 20 to 30 minutes

GRILL/GEAR: Can be grilled over charcoal or gas. You also need toothpicks.

INGREDIENTS

2 large sweet onions such as Vidalias, Walla Wallas, or Texas Sweets

½ cup of your favorite hot sauce, such as sriracha or Frank's RedHot

1½ pounds thin-sliced bacon

Vegetable oil for oiling the grill grate

1. Set up your grill for indirect grilling and heat to medium-high.

2. Trim the ends off the onions and peel off the thin papery skins. Slice each onion crosswise into ½-inch-thick slices. Carefully pop the centers out of each slice, keeping the two outermost layers together. (Two layers make a sturdier foundation for the bacon.) Set aside the largest onion rings. You should have 8. Save the remaining onion pieces for another use.

3. Pour the hot sauce into a mixing bowl or shallow dish. Brush each onion ring with the sauce.

4. Spiral each onion ring with bacon, slightly overlapping each strip, until the ring is covered. (You'll need 2 to 3 strips of bacon for each onion ring.)

Use toothpicks to secure the ends of the bacon.

5. Brush or scrape the grill grate clean and oil it well.

6. Arrange the onion rings on the grill grate, away from the fire, and close the lid. Cook until the bacon is golden brown and sizzling, 20 to 30 minutes. Drain the onion rings on a wire rack spread with paper towels. Dig in.

Variations

Instead of hot sauce or barbecue sauce, brush the onion rings with melted butter and season them with your favorite barbecue rub. Or brush them with warm maple syrup and dredge the onion rings in brown sugar before wrapping them with bacon.

Tightly wrap the bacon around each onion ring, leaving no space between rounds.

BREADS AND PIZZAS

The grill was the original bread oven and toaster, and in cultures as diverse as French, Italian, and Indian, it remains indispensable for baking and serving bread. Not that you have to travel that far, for what Lone Star State barbecue would be complete without Texas toast? This chapter explores the world's great grilled breads, starting with traditional Tuscan bruschetta. Next come those newly fashionable, French-inspired open-face grilled bread sandwiches known as tartines. You'll learn to make a simple honey beer yeast dough from scratch and use it to cook pizza on a grill-top pizza stone or directly on the grill grate. If bread is the staff of life, it definitely belongs on your grill.

BRUSCHETTA FOUR WAYS

YIELD: Makes 4 slices and can be multiplied as desired

METHOD: Direct grilling

PREP TIME: 5 minutes

GRILLING TIME: Quick—
1 to 2 minutes per side

GRILL/GEAR: Can be grilled over charcoal, wood, or gas. No special gear unless you're grilling over a campfire (which I highly recommend), in which case, grill the bread slices in a grill basket.

SHOP: The traditional bread for bruschetta is *pane toscano*, a dense crumbly loaf that's remarkable for the one ingredient it lacks—salt. (Tuscans originally devised it to dodge a salt tax imposed by the Pisans.) It's weird on its own, I admit, but quite tasty when grilled and seasoned with olive oil and salt. You rarely find Tuscan bread in the United States, but you should certainly try it if you travel to Italy. Happily, any firm artisanal country loaf will work. As for salt, use a coarse sea salt, like Italian *fiori di sale*, French *fleur de sel*, or Maldon from England.

INSIDER TIP: You can certainly toast bruschetta (pronounced "broo-sketta") on a gas or charcoal grill, but to get the full effect, grill it over a wood fire to infuse the bread with wood smoke.

Bruschetta (from the Italian word for "to burn") was the original garlic bread—thick slices of saltless Tuscan bread grilled over a wood fire, then rubbed with raw garlic, drizzled with olive oil, and seasoned with crunchy crystals of sea salt. Four ingredients—that's it—yet those four ingredients were enough to make it one of the most globally beloved appetizers today.

TUSCAN BRUSCHETTA

Here's the original bruschetta, followed by a tomato- and mint-topped bruschetta from Puglia, a Catalan tomato bread, and an orange and olive bruschetta from Sparta, Greece.

INGREDIENTS

Vegetable oil for oiling the grill grate

4 slices saltless Tuscan bread (if you can find it) or Italian semolina or sesame bread (each slice should be 6 to 8 inches long, 4 inches wide, and ¾ inch thick)

2 cloves garlic, peeled and cut in half lengthwise

Best-quality extra virgin olive oil, preferably Tuscan

Coarse sea salt

1. Set up your grill for direct grilling and heat to medium-high. Be sure to have a fire-free safety zone (see page 35) in case the bread starts to burn. Brush or scrape the grill grate clean and oil it well.

2. Arrange the bread on the grate and grill until toasted, 1 to 2 minutes per side. If you're feeling fancy, give each slice a quarter turn on both sides halfway through to lay on a crosshatch of grill marks.

3. Remove the bread from the grill, and then, protecting your hand with a cloth napkin, take a hot slice of bread in one hand and rub the top with cut garlic. (The roughened, toasted crumb will act like a grater.) Drizzle with extra virgin olive oil and sprinkle generously with sea salt. If you do it right, the bread will warm the garlic and olive oil, fusing these four elemental ingredients into a wondrous whole.

TOMATO MINT BRUSCHETTA

Here's the Puglian version, topped with a simple tomato mint salad. For an even more colorful bruschetta, use a mix of red, green, and yellow tomatoes. Note that some versions substitute peppery arugula (preferably wild) for the mint.

INGREDIENTS

1 pint cherry tomatoes, halved

¼ cup thinly slivered fresh mint leaves

1 scallion, trimmed, white and green parts thinly sliced (optional)

3 tablespoons best-quality extra virgin olive oil, plus extra for the bread

1 tablespoon balsamic vinegar, or to taste

Coarse salt (sea or kosher) and freshly ground black pepper

Vegetable oil for oiling the grill grate

4 thick slices of crusty country-style bread (each slice should be 6 to 8 inches long, 4 inches wide, and ¾ inch thick)

2 cloves garlic, peeled and cut in half lengthwise

1. Combine the tomatoes, mint, scallion (if using), olive oil, and balsamic vinegar in a bowl and mix gently. Season to taste with salt and pepper. Transfer to a serving bowl and set aside.

2. Set up your grill for direct grilling and heat to medium-high. Brush or scrape the grill grate clean and oil it well. Grill the bread as described in Step 2 on page 80 and rub with garlic. Spoon the tomato salad with its juices on top and dig in.

CATALAN TOMATO BREAD

Pa amb tomàquet (pronounced "pom to mocket")—tomato bread—turns up wherever Catalonians grill, and pretty much wherever they eat. It's so simple, I'm embarrassed to include a recipe for it—except that it's so much fun to serve and satisfying to eat, I'd be remiss if I didn't. Let your guests do the work after you pull the bread off the grill.

INGREDIENTS

2 large cloves garlic, peeled and cut in half crosswise

2 plum tomatoes, cut in half crosswise

Best-quality extra virgin olive oil, preferably Spanish

Vegetable oil for oiling the grill grate

4 slices of your favorite artisanal bread (each slice should be 6 to 8 inches long, 4 inches wide, and ¾ inch thick)

Coarse salt (sea or kosher) and freshly ground black pepper

1. Place the garlic and tomatoes in small bowls or on a plate; serve the olive oil in a bottle, small pitcher, or cruet.

2. Set up your grill for direct grilling and heat to medium-high. Brush or scrape the grill grate clean and oil it well. Grill the bread as described in Step 2 on page 80.

3. Transfer the toasted bread slices to napkins. Have each eater rub the hot bread first with garlic, then tomato, mashing the latter into the bread to cover it with tomato pulp. Discard the tomato skins. Season with salt and pepper and drizzle with olive oil. It's that simple.

ORANGE AND OLIVE BRUSCHETTA

H ere's a stunningly colorful bruschetta that reflects the Greek love of bold, in-your-face flavors: bittersweet oranges, salty kalamata olives, and of course, pungent garlic and Greek oregano. Yes, you're meant to keep the rind on the oranges (you can trim it off if you don't like bitterness). Thanks to Diane Kolchilis, host of *My Greek Table* on Public Television, for the idea.

INGREDIENTS

1 orange (preferably with a thin rind)

1 cup pitted kalamata olives

3 tablespoons extra virgin olive oil, preferably Greek

1 clove garlic, peeled and thinly sliced crosswise

1 teaspoon dried oregano, preferably Greek

Vegetable oil for oiling the grill grate

4 thick slices crusty country-style bread, preferably Greek (each slice should be 6 to 8 inches long, 4 inches wide, and ¾ inch thick)

1. Cut the orange crosswise into ¼-inch-thick slices, then cut each slice into 1-inch-wide wedges. Remove and discard any seeds. Drain the olives.

2. Heat the oil in a small saucepan over medium-high heat. Add the garlic and oregano and cook until the garlic is lightly browned, 1 to 2 minutes, stirring with a wooden spoon. Do not let burn.

3. Stir in the oranges and olives and cook until warmed, about 2 minutes. Set aside and keep warm.

4. Set up your grill for direct grilling and heat to medium-high. Brush or scrape the grill grate clean and oil it well. Grill the bread as described in Step 2 on page 80.

5. Spoon the orange mixture on top and enjoy.

TEXAS TOAST
(GRILLED GARLIC BREAD)

YIELD: Makes 12 slices, enough to serve 4 to 6

METHOD: Direct grilling

PREP TIME: 10 minutes

GRILLING TIME: Quick—1 to 2 minutes per side

GRILL/GEAR: Can be grilled over charcoal, wood, or gas.

SHOP: You'll want a fresh bakery loaf for this recipe—a firm-textured, country-style white bread for traditional Texas toast. You can also make killer garlic bread with a French baguette or Italian loaf.

When I was growing up, garlic bread meant a spongy loaf of supermarket "Italian" bread doused with butter and garlic powder, wrapped in aluminum foil, and baked in the oven. It came out soft, steamy, and disgusting—a travesty of the bruschetta (page 80) that inspired it. But opt for an artisanal loaf and toast it on the grill, and you wind up with garlic bread that plays crunchiness against softness and smoke flavors against butter and garlic. In other words, garlic bread worth firing up your grill for. Consider the following recipe a rough blueprint to be customized to suit your taste.

INGREDIENTS

FOR THE GARLIC BREAD

1 loaf country-style white bread, or a baguette, or Italian bread

12 tablespoons (1½ sticks) salted butter, at room temperature

3 cloves garlic, peeled and minced so fine it will blow off your cutting board if you sneeze

3 tablespoons minced fresh flat-leaf parsley, chives, or scallions

ADDITIONAL FLAVORINGS (OPTIONAL)

3 tablespoons minced prosciutto or cooked crumbled bacon

1 cup (about 4 ounces) finely grated Parmigiano-Reggiano or Pecorino Romano cheese, or crumbled Roquefort or gorgonzola cheese, at room temperature

1 teaspoon paprika (sweet, smoked, or hot)

Vegetable oil for oiling the grill grate

INSIDER TIP: There are two ways to apply the garlic butter: Whisk the minced garlic into room temperature butter and slather it on with a spatula; or add it to melted butter and apply it with a pastry brush. I prefer the first method, as the garlic is less likely to fall off the bread.

1. If using white bread, cut it crosswise into ¾-inch-thick slices. If using a baguette, cut it sharply on the diagonal into ¾-inch-thick slices or cut the whole loaf in half lengthwise through the side. If using Italian bread, cut it crosswise into ¾-inch-thick slices. If using supermarket "Italian" bread or hoagie rolls, cut in half lengthwise through the side.

2. Place the butter in a mixing bowl. Whisk in the garlic and parsley. (You can do this in a food processor, but the parsley will turn the butter green.) Whisk in any of the other flavorings, if using. Using a palette knife or butter knife, spread the bread slices on *both* sides with a thin, even layer of garlic butter.

3. Set up your grill for direct grilling and heat to medium-high. Brush or scrape the grill grate clean and oil it well. Be sure to have a fire-free safety zone (see page 35) in case the bread starts to burn.

4. Arrange the bread slices on the grate and grill until sizzling and browned on both sides, 1 to 2 minutes per side, turning with tongs. (Give each slice a quarter turn on both sides to lay on a crosshatch of grill marks, if desired.) Serve hot off the grill.

TARTINES AND COMPANY

YIELD: Makes 4 tartines and can be multiplied as desired

METHOD: Direct grilling

PREP TIME: 5 minutes for the tartines, plus the time it takes to make the toppings

GRILLING TIME: Quick— 1 to 2 minutes per side

GRILL/GEAR: Can be grilled over charcoal, wood, or gas. No special gear unless you're grilling over a campfire (which I highly recommend), in which case, grill the bread slices in a grill basket.

SHOP: The quality of the bread makes or breaks your tartine. Start with an artisanal-style loaf from a craft bakery—a bread with a crisp, dark, thick crust, a firm but moist crumb, and the rich, soulful flavor that comes from slow fermentation.

INSIDER TIP: I like tartines made with natural sourdough bread (leavened with a starter, not granulated yeast). Bread baking is undergoing a renaissance these days, and you can find great craft bakeries in most American cities, such as Iggy's in Cambridge, the Sullivan Street Bakery in New York, Zak the Baker in Miami, Ken's Artisan Bakery in Portland, Oregon, and, of course, Tartine in San Francisco. White, rye, whole wheat, and multigrain— all make great tartines.

Tartine (pronounced "tar-teen") is French for an open-face sandwich. It has given its name to an excellent craft bakery in San Francisco, not to mention a stylish new genre of appetizers served at trendy restaurants all over the world. Italians call it bruschetta (page 80), and it serves to remind us that the grill was the first toaster. And that grilled bread—especially grilled over a wood or wood-enhanced fire—has a superior texture and taste to what pops out of your toaster. Here are three tartines that elevate toast to the level of art.

GOAT CHEESE, THYME, AND HONEY TARTINES

Tangy goat cheese and fragrant fresh thyme are timeless French flavors, here showcased on slices of grilled baguette. Tip: Use dental floss to cut the cheese neatly into slices.

INGREDIENTS

Vegetable oil for oiling the grill grate

1 French baguette, cut in half lengthwise through the side, each half cut into 5-inch-long sections

1 log (8 ounces) of your favorite soft goat cheese, cut into ¼-inch-thick slices

4 sprigs of fresh thyme

Freshly ground black pepper

Best-quality extra virgin olive oil

Honey (warm the jar in a bowl of hot water so it drizzles easily)

1. Set up your grill for direct grilling and heat to medium-high. Be sure to have a fire-free safety zone (see page 35) in case the bread starts to burn.

2. Brush or scrape the grill grate clean and oil it well. Arrange the bread slices on the grate running on the diagonal to the bars of the grate. Grill until darkly browned, 1 to 2 minutes per side, turning with tongs.

3. Transfer the toasted bread slices to a wire rack or clean dishtowel (this keeps the bottoms from getting soggy). Shingle the goat cheese slices on top and sprinkle with thyme leaves or tiny sprigs and pepper. Drizzle with olive oil and honey and serve while the toasts are still warm.

AVOCADO CHILE TARTINES

Born in Los Angeles, the avocado tartine has become the new power breakfast. Some people fire it up with chili powder, cayenne, or Espelette pepper, but I like fresh serrano chiles.

INGREDIENTS

1 to 2 serrano or jalapeño peppers, or to taste

2 ripe avocados

Vegetable oil for oiling the grill grate

4 slices of your favorite artisanal bread (each slice should be 6 to 8 inches long, 4 inches wide, and ¾ inch thick—cut the loaf on the diagonal to obtain large slices)

Extra virgin olive oil

Maldon salt or coarse salt (sea or kosher) and freshly ground black pepper

¼ cup coarsely chopped fresh cilantro

1 lime, cut into wedges for serving

1. Set up your grill for direct grilling and heat to medium-high. Be sure to have a fire-free safety zone (see page 35) in case the bread starts to burn.

2. Cut the serranos crosswise into paper-thin slices (for milder tartines, seed the chiles, then slice).

3. Meanwhile, halve the avocados, and pit, peel, and cut them lengthwise into ½-inch-wide slices. (Do this at the last minute so the avocado doesn't discolor. If you want to do this more than 10 minutes ahead of time, squeeze fresh lime juice over the avocado slices to keep them from browning.)

4. Brush or scrape the grill grate clean and oil it well. Grill the bread slices as described in Step 2 on the facing page.

5. Transfer the toasted bread slices to a wire rack or a clean dishtowel (this keeps the bottoms from getting soggy). Shingle the avocado slices on top and dot with serrano slices. Drizzle with olive oil and sprinkle with salt, pepper, and cilantro. Serve with lime wedges for squeezing.

TOMATO FETA TARTINES

Here's a tartine with piquant Greek flavors. For the best results, use heirloom tomatoes that have never seen the inside of a refrigerator.

INGREDIENTS

Vegetable oil for oiling the grill grate

4 slices Greek or other sesame seed-dotted bread or semolina bread (each slice should be 6 to 8 inches long, 4 inches wide, and ¾ inch thick—cut the loaf on the diagonal to obtain large slices)

2 luscious red ripe tomatoes, thinly sliced

Coarse salt (sea or kosher) and freshly ground black pepper

2 ounces feta cheese, drained

1 tablespoon chopped fresh oregano or 1 teaspoon dried oregano

Best-quality extra virgin olive oil, preferably Greek

1. Set up your grill for direct grilling and heat to medium-high. Be sure to have a fire-free safety zone (see page 35) in case the bread starts to burn.

2. Brush or scrape the grill grate clean and oil it well. Grill the bread slices as described in Step 2 on page 86.

3. Transfer the toasted bread slices to a wire rack or clean dishtowel (this keeps the bottoms from getting soggy). Shingle the tomatoes on the toasts and season with salt and pepper. Crumble the feta cheese on top, sprinkle with oregano, and drizzle with olive oil.

HONEY BEER PIZZA DOUGH

YIELD: Makes dough for two 12-inch pizzas

PREP TIME: 10 minutes for the dough, plus 1 to 2 hours for rising

GRILL/GEAR: Food processor

Pizza is one of the hottest growth categories in grilling, with a huge proliferation of pizza grilling accessories and grill-top pizza ovens (see pages 16–17). In the next two recipes, I'll tell you how to grill pizza on a grill-top pizza stone and directly on the grill grate. But before that, here's a simple made-from-scratch pizza dough enriched with honey and beer. (The latter serves as an additional leavening agent.) Tip o' the hat to restaurateur Michael Schwartz, who uses this dough at his Harry's Pizzeria and Fi'lia restaurants in Miami.

INGREDIENTS

¼ cup lager or other light-style beer, at room temperature

1½ tablespoons honey

1 package (2¼ teaspoons) active dry yeast

½ cup warm water (about 105°F), plus more if needed

1¾ cups bread flour, plus additional for stretching

3 tablespoons whole wheat flour

1½ teaspoons coarse salt (sea or kosher)

1½ tablespoons extra virgin olive oil, plus more for the bowl

1. Combine the beer, honey, yeast, and the ½ cup warm water in a small bowl; stir gently to dissolve. Let the mixture stand until foamy, 5 to 10 minutes.

2. Place the flours and salt in a food processor fitted with a dough blade (or metal blade) and pulse to mix. Add the oil and yeast mixture and run the processor until the dough comes away cleanly from the sides of the bowl, 3 to 5 minutes. If the dough is too dry, add water a tablespoon at a time; if too wet, add a little flour. The dough should be compact, but still a little sticky. You can also mix the dough in a mixer fitted with a dough hook, or by hand.

3. Lightly oil a bowl and set it aside. Turn the dough out onto a very lightly floured work surface and knead by hand for a minute or two to give it a human touch. Gather it into a ball and place in the prepared bowl; turn it over to coat with the oil. Cover the dough with plastic wrap, then a clean damp kitchen towel, and let it rise in a warm spot until doubled in bulk, 30 to 60 minutes.

4. Punch the dough down. Turn the dough out onto a lightly floured surface and knead gently. Cut it in half. Each half should weigh about 8 ounces. Roll each half into a ball under the palm of your hand until the top of the dough is smooth and firm. Cover the dough with plastic wrap and a damp kitchen towel and let rise until doubled in bulk, 20 to 30 minutes. The pizza dough is ready for stretching and grilling. Alternatively, wrap the dough balls in plastic wrap and refrigerate for up to 24 hours or freeze for up to 2 weeks.

5. Let the dough sit at room temperature for 20 minutes before forming the pizza crust. This makes it easier to roll. If it has been frozen, thaw the dough before proceeding with the recipe.

SHOP: Bread flour has a higher gluten content than all-purpose flour, so it's easier to stretch the dough to form the pizzas. A plus if the flour is organic.

INSIDER TIP: Okay, so not everyone has the time or patience to make pizza dough from scratch (although with a food processor, it's only a 10-minute process). A ready-made dough from your local pizza shop or food market can produce a fine pizza. But homemade dough gives you additional street cred.

PIZZA STONE PIZZA
WITH OLIVES, RICOTTA SALATA, AND BACON TOMATO SAUCE

YIELD: Makes two 12-inch pizzas

METHOD: Grilling on a pizza stone

PREP TIME: 10 minutes

GRILLING TIME: 5 to 8 minutes

GRILL/GEAR: Can be grilled over charcoal, wood, or gas. You also need a pizza stone (widely available at grill and cookware shops or on Amazon). Many manufacturers, like Big Green Egg, sell pizza stones specifically designed for their grills. If you're a gear geek, get yourself a point-and-shoot laser thermometer that tells you the surface temperature of the pizza stone. One good brand is Etekcity. You need 2 hardwood chunks or 1½ cups unsoaked wood chips (optional); pizza peel or a rimless sheet pan.

There are two ways to cook a pizza on the grill: on a pizza stone and directly on the grill grate. The first method produces the sort of pizza you'd get from a wood-burning oven—crisp crust with a chewy center topped with sizzling tomato sauce and cheese. That's the kind of pizza featured here. In the second method (described in full in the next recipe), you cook the raw pizza dough directly on the grill grate. This gives you a very different texture—simultaneously crackly and chewy, like a soft bread roll sandwiched between crackers—with some of the smoke flavor you find in grilled bread. Pizza stone pizza is easier to make and more reliable. You don't have to worry about flipping the pizza or burning the dough (unless your stone is too hot). The toppings go on before the pizza hits the grill, giving you greater ease in assembly. Get ready for big flavors in the form of olives, capers, ricotta salata, and Bacon Tomato Sauce.

INGREDIENTS

1 batch of Honey Beer Pizza Dough (page 88, through Step 5) or your favorite ready-made dough, divided into 2 balls

Flour for dusting the dough and work surface

Cornmeal for dusting the peel

1 recipe Bacon Tomato Sauce (recipe follows) or 3 cups of your favorite tomato sauce

12 ounces ricotta salata, thinly sliced or crumbled

½ cup whole oil-cured or brined black olives, drained (pitted optional)

¼ cup brined capers, drained

8 fresh basil leaves, julienned (rolled up and cut into thin slivers)

Extra virgin olive oil, for drizzling

1. Set up your grill for direct grilling. If using a gas grill, place the pizza stone on the grate while the grill is unlit. Light the grill and gradually heat it to high so that the surface of the pizza stone is about 500°F. (The stone could crack if not slowly acclimated to the heat.) Use a point-and-shoot thermometer (see page 35) to check it, or sprinkle a few drops of water on it—they should evaporate in a second or two.

2. To prepare a 12-inch pizza, dust one of the dough balls with a little flour, shake off the excess, and put the dough on a lightly floured surface. Stretch the dough with your hands, turning the ball as you press down on the center. Continue spreading the dough into a 12-inch circle or rectangle with your hands or with a rolling pin. The dough should be a little less than ¼ inch thick. Repeat with the second ball of dough.

3. Dust a pizza peel or rimless sheet pan with cornmeal and pull the pizza dough onto it (or slide it under the dough—whichever method works best). It's easier to top the pizza with the dough already on the peel.

4. Spread half the tomato sauce over the pizza. Top with ricotta salata, olives, capers, and basil. Drizzle with olive oil. Prepare the second pizza the same way.

5. Optional: To simulate the smoke of a wood-fired pizza oven, add a couple of wood chunks to the coals or place under the grate directly over the metal diffuser plate of a gas grill.

6. Slide one of the pizzas onto the pizza stone. Immediately lower the grill lid: You need to trap the heat so it cooks the pizza from the top as well as the bottom. Grill the pizza until the dough is crisp and browned on the bottom, the tomato sauce is bubbling, and the cheese is melted, 5 to 8 minutes. Transfer to a cutting board and cut into wedges or squares for serving. Cook the second pizza the same way.

SHOP: Ricotta salata is a firm, tangy, salty cousin of fresh ricotta. Look for it at Italian markets, Whole Foods, or Fresh Market, or substitute soft ricotta, fresh mozzarella, burrata, or another favorite cheese.

INSIDER TIP: Sure you can use a favorite ready-made tomato sauce, but the purist may wish to try the homemade Bacon Tomato Sauce, this page.

BACON TOMATO SAUCE

YIELD: Makes 3 cups

Bacon gives this quick tomato sauce a rich smoky flavor.

INGREDIENTS

2 tablespoons extra virgin olive oil

1 strip bacon or speck (smoked prosciutto), cut crosswise into ¼-inch strips

1 small onion, peeled and diced

1 clove garlic, peeled and minced

1 teaspoon dried oregano

1 can (28 ounces) diced tomatoes, drained and coarsely chopped (save the juice for Bloody Marys)

3 fresh basil leaves, thinly julienned (rolled up and cut into thin slivers)

Sea salt and freshly ground black pepper

Pinch of sugar (optional)

Pour the oil in the bottom of a sauté pan and warm over medium heat. Add the bacon, onion, garlic, and oregano, and cook until browned, 4 to 5 minutes, stirring often. Add the tomatoes and basil and gently simmer, stirring occasionally, until the sauce is thick and richly flavored, 6 to 10 minutes. Add salt and pepper to taste, and sugar if you like a touch of sweetness.

GRILLED PIZZA, REALLY,
WITH POTATOES, BROCCOLINI, AND ITALIAN SAUSAGE

YIELD: Makes two 12-inch pizzas

METHOD: Direct grilling

PREP TIME: 15 minutes

GRILLING TIME: 6 to 9 minutes

GRILL/GEAR: Charcoal or gas—doesn't matter. You also need tongs and a large wide-bladed spatula to help you turn the pizza.

SHOP: Sweet or hot Italian sausage, preferably from an artisanal butcher

INSIDER TIP: This pizza can be grilled on a pizza stone as in the previous recipe, just like the previous pizza can be direct grilled like this one. (If you do that, don't put the toppings on until you've grilled one side of the pizza dough and flipped it.)

Pizza grilled on a pizza stone tastes as awesome as it looks, but you pretty much get the same pie as you would baked in a hot oven. Pizza grilled directly on the grill grate delivers a totally different experience in technique, texture, and taste. When you do it right, the dough bubbles and blisters, producing a smoky, crackling crust on both sides. Direct grilled pizza demands a different set of tactics. Unlike conventional pizza, you stretch the dough in oil on a sheet pan rather than in flour. You grill the dough first to cook one side through, *then* add the toppings. These go in the reverse order of how you'd arrange them on a conventional pizza: cheese first (so it melts on the hot crust), then cooked toppings, and last of all, the sauce. The grill setup differs, too: You heat one zone to medium-high to sear the dough, leaving the other zone low to keep the crust warm while you lay on the toppings. Okay, all this sounds a lot more complicated than it really is. In keeping with the unusualness of the grilling method, I give you an equally unusual topping of potatoes, broccolini, and Italian sausage.

INGREDIENTS

1 gallon water

Coarse salt (sea or kosher)

12 ounces new or Yukon Gold potatoes, scrubbed and cut into ¼-inch dice

1 bunch broccolini, trimmed, and cut crosswise into ¼-inch pieces

12 ounces bulk sweet or hot Italian sausage

1 medium-size sweet onion, peeled and finely chopped

Vegetable oil for stretching the pizza dough and oiling the grill grate

1 batch Honey Beer Pizza Dough (page 88, through Step 5) or your favorite ready-made dough, divided into 2 balls

12 ounces cave-aged Gruyère cheese, aged provolone, or other firm cheese, coarsely grated

Extra virgin olive oil

⅓ cup freshly grated Parmigiano-Reggiano cheese

Hot red pepper flakes, to taste

1. Bring the water and 1 tablespoon of salt to a boil. Add the potatoes and boil until almost tender, 2 minutes. Transfer with a wire skimmer or slotted spoon to a colander to drain, rinse with cold water, then drain again. Set the potatoes aside in a bowl.

2. Add the broccolini to the boiling water and blanch for 2 minutes. Drain in a colander, rinse with cold water, then drain again.

3. Brown the sausage and onion in a large heavy skillet over medium heat, chopping the sausage with the blade of a spatula to break it up. This will take 5 to 8 minutes. Increase the heat to high the last 2 minutes and stir in the potatoes and broccolini. You want to brown the potatoes. Drain off the excess sausage fat and let the mixture cool to room temperature. The toppings can be prepared up to a day ahead of time if covered and refrigerated.

4. Set up your grill for direct grilling. One burner should be set on medium-high, the other on low. It doesn't hurt to have a fire-free safety zone (see page 35) in case the pizza starts to burn.

5. Generously oil a rimless sheet pan and place one of the dough balls in the center. Pat the dough flat, then stretch it out into an oval or a rectangle about 9 by 12 inches and ¼ inch thick. Generously oil the top.

6. Carry the sheet pan with the crust to the edge of the grill. Brush or scrape the grill grate clean and oil it well. Gently and carefully lift the dough by one end and drape it flat on the grate over the hot section of the grill. Grill until the top bubbles and blisters and the bottom browns, 3 to 5 minutes.

7. Slide a wide-bladed spatula under the crust, and with the aid of tongs, move it to the cooler section of the grill. Brush it with olive oil and turn it over. Spread half the grated cheese on top of the crust (on the grilled part). Arrange half the sausage mixture, potatoes, and broccolini on top. Sprinkle with half the Parmigiano-Reggiano and half the hot red pepper flakes. Drizzle with more olive oil.

8. Slide the pizza back over the hot section of the grill. Close the grill lid to concentrate the heat. Continue grilling until the cheese has melted, the toppings are sizzling, and the crust is browned on the bottom, 3 to 4 minutes. Transfer to a cutting board and cut into squares for serving. Prepare the remaining pizza the same way.

The pizza dough will bubble as it cooks on the grill. You'll need a spatula with a wide blade to flip the dough.

Pull the pizza off to the cooler section or onto the peel before adding the toppings.

SALAD HITS THE GRILL

When I acquired my barbecue chops, salad just wasn't something you grilled. Today, chefs routinely grill the lettuce for Caesar and other salads. Grilled vegetables often double as salads, and more and more of us are roasting those veggies in the embers to give them a smoke flavor you simply can't achieve by conventional grilling. In the following pages, you'll find a grilled wedge salad (complete with smoked blue cheese dressing) and a BLT sandwich deconstructed and reconstructed as salad. Beets go caveman (grilled in the embers) to create a smoky twist on a traditional Russian *zakuski*. You'll learn how to make Spain's beloved *escalivada* (an ember-roasted vegetable salad) and a Vietnamese-inspired grilled shrimp and pineapple salad. And four quintessential summer foods shine as salads: grilled watermelon and *queso fresco* salad, a Peruvian Potato Salad, and grilled asparagus and corn salad. Salads have always been served at a barbecue. They're about to become barbecue itself.

GRILLED WEDGE SALAD
WITH SMOKED BLUE CHEESE DRESSING

YIELD: Serves 4

METHOD: Direct grilling

PREP TIME: 15 minutes

GRILLING TIME: About 4 minutes

GRILL/GEAR: Can be grilled over charcoal, wood, or gas. You also need a food processor for the dressing (optional); 2 hardwood chunks or 1½ cups unsoaked wood chips (optional).

SHOP: You'll need only one special ingredient for this salad: Rogue Creamery Smokey Blue Cheese. Look for it at a store with a good cheese department or order it online from roguecreamery.com. (In a pinch, you could use Roquefort or Gorgonzola plus a drop of liquid smoke.)

INSIDER TIP: Wedge salads are often served with crisped bacon, and you can certainly add that if you want to. I've kept this one meatless for our vegetarian friends out there.

The wedge salad is an American steakhouse classic. We're about to give it the *Project Fire* treatment by—you guessed it—grilling the lettuce. The trick is to work over a very hot fire (ideally a wood or wood-enhanced fire), so you char the exterior and put some wood smoke between the leaves while leaving the heart of the lettuce raw and crunchy. The dressing gets smoked, too, thanks to an amazing smoked blue cheese made in Central Point, Oregon, by the historic Rogue Creamery.

INGREDIENTS

FOR THE DRESSING

3 ounces blue cheese, preferably Rogue Creamery Smokey Blue Cheese, at room temperature

¼ cup mayonnaise, preferably Hellmann's or Best Foods

¼ cup heavy (whipping) cream or half-and-half

1 tablespoon rice vinegar or distilled white vinegar, or to taste

Freshly ground black pepper

FOR THE SALAD

Vegetable oil for oiling the grill grate

1 head of iceberg lettuce (ideally organic), cut into quarters through the stem end

Extra virgin olive oil

3 ounces blue cheese, crumbled

½ cup toasted walnut pieces (optional; see Box, page 100)

¼ cup chopped fresh chives

1. Make the dressing: Place the 3 ounces of room temperature blue cheese in the bottom of a mixing bowl. Mash it to a paste with the back of a fork. Mash in the mayonnaise, then stir in the cream, rice vinegar, and pepper. (Alternatively, make the dressing in a food processor.) Add more vinegar or pepper to taste: The dressing should be highly seasoned. You can make it several hours ahead; cover and refrigerate.

2. Just before serving, set up your grill for direct grilling and heat to high. Brush or scrape the grill grate clean and oil it well. Add hardwood chunks to your charcoal fire or place them under the grate over the metal heat diffuser in your gas grill (see instructions on page 22), if using.

3. Lightly brush the cut sides of the lettuce with olive oil. Arrange the wedges on the grill grate, cut sides down, running diagonal to the bars of the grate. Grill until lightly browned on the bottom, about 2 minutes, giving each wedge a quarter turn after 1 minute to lay on a crosshatch of grill marks. Grill the other cut side the same way. Work quickly so the lettuce remains raw and crunchy in the center.

4. Transfer the lettuce wedges to a platter or plates. Spoon the dressing over them and sprinkle with crumbled blue cheese, walnuts (if using), and chives.

EMBER-ROASTED VEGETABLE SALAD
ESCALIVADA

The name says it all. *Escalivar* is the Spanish verb for "to roast in the embers." This sweet-smoky ember-roasted or grilled vegetable salad turns up across Spain, where it's served as a salad, a side dish, or even spooned atop toast to make tapas. True, these days most escalivada comes grilled or sautéed, but nothing beats the haunting smoke flavor of onions, eggplants, and peppers roasted directly on the embers. A simple escalivada would contain those three vegetables only; a more elaborate version might also include celery, leeks, and scallions. Hazelnuts aren't strictly traditional, but I like the nutty flavor they bring to the salad.

YIELD: Serves 4

METHOD: Caveman grilling (roasting in the embers) or direct grilling

PREP TIME: 15 minutes

GRILLING TIME: 10 minutes

GRILL/GEAR: Can be grilled over charcoal, wood, or gas. You also need long-handled tongs.

SHOP: Sherry vinegar—made from sherry wine—has a nutty sweetness you won't find in other wine vinegars. Look for it in Spanish food markets, Whole Foods, or online. If unavailable, use red wine vinegar, adding a few drops of cream sherry.

INGREDIENTS

2 medium-size onions

2 long slender eggplants (about 1 pound total)

2 red bell peppers, or 1 red pepper and 1 yellow pepper

2 ribs celery (optional)

1 bunch scallions, trimmed

2 tablespoons sherry or wine vinegar, or to taste

Coarse salt (sea or kosher) and freshly ground black pepper

3 to 4 tablespoons extra virgin olive oil, preferably Spanish, or to taste

¼ cup chopped toasted hazelnuts (optional; see Box, page 100)

¼ cup chopped flat-leaf parsley

1. Ember-roasting on a charcoal grill: Set up a charcoal grill for ember-roasting (caveman grilling—see page 27). Rake out the coals in an even layer and lay the onions, eggplants, and peppers on the embers. Roast until charred black on all sides and tender in the center (a slender metal skewer will pierce the onions and eggplants easily). You'll need 8 to 10 minutes for roasting the onions; 6 to 8 minutes for the eggplants and peppers. Turn with tongs so the veggies roast evenly. Ember-roast the celery, if using, for about 2 minutes per side; the scallions for 1 to 2 minutes.

Direct-grill method: Heat your gas or wood-burning grill as hot as it will go (600°F or more). Brush or scrape the grill grate clean and oil it well. Direct grill the veggies until charred on the outside and cooked through (follow the cooking times above). Test for doneness with a metal skewer.

2. Transfer the charred vegetables to a sheet pan and let cool. Using a paring knife, scrape off and discard the burnt skins (don't worry about removing every last bit—a few spots of black add color and flavor). Cut the vegetables into ¾-inch dice and transfer to a mixing bowl along with any vegetables from the sheet pan or the cutting board. Add any released juices to a separate bowl.

3. Make the dressing: Add the sherry vinegar and salt and pepper (about ½ teaspoon of each) to the vegetable juices in the bowl. Whisk until the salt crystals are dissolved. Whisk in the olive oil. Taste for seasoning, adding oil, vinegar, or salt to taste; the dressing should be highly seasoned.

4. Add the diced grilled vegetables to the dressing and toss to mix. To serve, mound the salad onto plates. Sprinkle each serving with hazelnuts (if using) and parsley.

HOW TO TOAST NUTS

Heat a dry cast-iron skillet over your grill's side burner or on a stove's burner over medium heat. (Do not use a nonstick pan.) Add the nuts. Toast until the nuts become fragrant and start to brown, 1 to 2 minutes, shaking the pan or stirring with a wooden spoon so they cook evenly. Immediately, transfer the toasted nuts to a heat-proof bowl.

Toasting gives nuts a smoky flavor that's infinitely more appealing than when they're raw.

To skin toasted hazelnuts, grab a small handful of the hot nuts at a time, place them in a clean tea towel, and rub them vigorously between the palms of your hands. This will loosen the skins, which you should discard.

GRILLED WATERMELON SALAD
WITH ARUGULA AND QUESO FRESCO

Watermelon has long brought a barbecue to a joyful conclusion. You're about to integrate it into your meal more fully: by turning it into a grilled salad. Picture the same moist crunch, the same refreshing sweetness. But grilling adds caramel (burnt sugar) overtones and a smoky element—especially when done over a wood or wood-enhanced fire. *Queso fresco* brings in a salty note that has an uncanny way of heightening a watermelon's sweetness. More riotous flavor comes from a ginger-lime dressing, fresh mint, and candied nuts.

INGREDIENTS

FOR THE GRILL

Vegetable oil for oiling the grill grate and basting the cheese

4 slices (each 1 inch thick) fresh red or yellow watermelon (preferably seedless)

1 chunk (8 ounces) queso fresco, blotted dry

FOR THE GINGER-LIME DRESSING

2 limes, halved crosswise

2 tablespoons honey

2 tablespoons minced candied ginger

¼ cup vegetable oil

Coarse salt (sea or kosher) and freshly ground black pepper

TO FINISH THE SALAD

1 bunch baby arugula, rinsed and spun dry

¼ cup thinly slivered fresh mint

½ cup chopped candied pecans or walnuts

YIELD: Serves 4

METHOD: Direct grilling

PREP TIME: 12 minutes

GRILLING TIME: 8 minutes (4 minutes if everything is grilled together)

GRILL/GEAR: Can be grilled over charcoal, wood, or gas. You also need 2 hardwood chunks or 1½ cups unsoaked wood chips (optional).

SHOP: *Queso fresco* ("fresh cheese" literally) is a mild sweet-salty cheese from Mexico and Central America; look for it in the dairy section of most supermarkets. Other options include halloumi (see page 69) or feta. As for the watermelon, how do you select a sweet one? I could tell you to lift and shake it (it should feel heavy) or thump it with your knuckles (it should sound hollow). The field spot (the part that rested on the ground while the melon was ripening) should be a dark yellow. But the best way is to buy it from a store that has one cut open for sampling.

1. Set up your grill for direct grilling and heat to high. Ideally, you'll be working over a wood or wood-enhanced fire. If using a charcoal grill, add the wood chunks or chips to the fire. If using a gas grill, place wood chunks under the grate directly over one of the burners to generate wood smoke. Brush or scrape the grill grate clean and oil it well.

2. Arrange the watermelon slices on the grill and grill until singed and grill-marked on both sides, but still raw in the center, 1 to 2 minutes per side. Use a large spatula and tongs to turn. Lightly brush the cheese with vegetable oil on both sides and grill until browned, 1 to 2 minutes per side. While you're at it, grill the lime halves for the dressing, cut sides down, until darkly browned, 2 to 4 minutes.

Grilled Watermelon Salad

Transfer the watermelon, cheese, and limes to a wire rack to cool.

3. Make the dressing: Squeeze the juice from the grilled limes into a large mixing bowl. Whisk in the honey, candied ginger, vegetable oil, and salt and pepper; the dressing should be highly seasoned.

4. Cut the watermelon into 1-inch squares (discard the rind and any seeds) and add it to the bowl with the salad dressing. Add the arugula and mint. Crumble in the grilled cheese. Gently toss the ingredients to mix. Sprinkle the candied nuts on top and serve at once.

EMBER-ROASTED BEET SALAD
WITH SOUR CREAM AND DILL

Beets sauced with sour cream and dill is a classic Russian *zakuski* (appetizer). In the following recipe, you'll give them a thoroughly un-Russian smoke flavor—by roasting the beets caveman style, directly on the embers. Some versions call for the beets to be grated, but I like them diced, to give you something to chew. If you like the earthy mineral flavor of beets, the crunch of walnuts and cucumbers, the silky richness of sour cream, and the aromatic sweetness of dill, prepare to experience salad nirvana.

INGREDIENTS

4 large beets (preferably yellow or orange), trimmed and scrubbed

2 scallions, trimmed

1 cup sour cream or plain Greek-style yogurt

Coarse salt (sea or kosher) and freshly ground black pepper

1 teaspoon sugar, or to taste

½ teaspoon freshly grated lemon zest

2 tablespoons chopped fresh dill, plus 4 sprigs for garnish

1 cucumber, peeled, seeded, and cut into ½-inch dice

½ cup walnut halves

YIELD: Serves 4

METHOD: Caveman grilling (in the embers) or direct grilling

PREP TIME: 15 minutes

GRILLING TIME: 20 to 30 minutes

GRILL/GEAR: Can be grilled over charcoal, wood, or gas. You also need latex gloves for handling the beets.

SHOP: Red beets are the most common, but yellow or orange beets show off the ember-roasting flavors better.

1. Ember-roasting on a charcoal grill: Set up a charcoal grill for ember-roasting (caveman grilling—see page 27). Rake out the coals in an even layer and lay the beets on top. Roast until charred black on all sides and tender in the center (a slender metal skewer will pierce the beets easily), turning often with tongs, 20 to 30 minutes. While you're at it, lay the scallions on the embers and grill until browned, 1 minute per side. Transfer the beets and scallions to a sheet pan to cool.

Direct grilling: Set up your grill for direct grilling and heat your gas or wood-burning grill as hot as it will go. Brush or scrape the grill grate clean. Direct grill the beets until charred on the outside and cooked through. Test for doneness with a metal skewer,

20 to 30 minutes. Grill the scallions until browned, 1 to 2 minutes per side. Transfer the beets and scallions to a sheet pan to cool.

2. Meanwhile, make the dressing: Place the sour cream in an attractive serving bowl. Add ½ teaspoon each of salt and pepper, as well as the sugar, lemon zest, and chopped dill, and whisk to mix. Fold in the cucumber and walnut halves with a rubber spatula.

3. Transfer the cooled beets to a cutting board. Using a paring knife, trim off the charred exterior. Cut the beets into ½-inch dice. Fold them into the salad. Correct the seasoning, adding salt or sugar to taste; the salad should be highly seasoned. Garnish with the sprigs of dill.

GRILLED BLT SALAD

YIELD: Serves 4 to 6

METHOD: Direct grilling

PREP TIME: 20 minutes

GRILLING TIME: 18 minutes or less

GRILL/GEAR: Can be grilled over charcoal, wood, or gas. You also need 2 hardwood chunks or 1½ cups unsoaked wood chips.

Here's a twist on an American classic, and if you think a BLT sandwich tastes good, wait until you try it deconstructed and reconstructed as a salad. You already know how to grill bacon (page 50). The bread in a traditional BLT becomes grilled croutons. But the real magic comes from the lettuces—grilled long enough to give them charred smoky edges, but quickly enough to leave them raw and crisp in the center. I call for a mix of lettuces—ideally, varieties sturdy enough to stand up to the heat of the grill. The only ingredient I don't grill is the tomatoes; I like them fresh and wet to counterpoint the smoke and crunch of the other ingredients.

INGREDIENTS

FOR THE DRESSING

3 tablespoons mayonnaise, preferably Hellmann's or Best Foods

3 tablespoons buttermilk, heavy (whipping) cream, or half-and-half

2 tablespoons rice vinegar or distilled white vinegar, or to taste

Coarse salt (sea or kosher) and freshly ground black pepper

FOR THE SALAD

2 Little Gem lettuces or 1 head of Boston lettuce or iceberg lettuce or 2 hearts of romaine

1 head of radicchio, or more lettuce

2 Belgian endives, or more lettuce

Extra virgin olive oil for brushing the lettuces

Vegetable oil for oiling the grill grate

4 strips thick-cut artisanal bacon

4 slices French bread, each about ½ inch thick

3 luscious ripe red tomatoes, diced

1 tablespoon chopped chives

SHOP: Take the trouble to procure thick-sliced artisanal bacon for this salad. Wisconsin's Nueske's comes to mind. For lettuces, you can go the straight iceberg or hearts of romaine route, but I like to mix up the greens with Little Gems, radicchio, and Belgian endive.

INSIDER TIP: You can prepare this salad on any type of grill, but you'll get more flavor if you grill over a wood fire, or add hardwood chunks to the charcoal or place them under the grate of your gas grill (see page 22).

1. Make the dressing: Place the mayonnaise, buttermilk, and vinegar in a large attractive serving bowl and whisk to mix, adding salt and pepper to taste.

2. Prepare the lettuces: If using Little Gem or romaine lettuces, remove any dirty or wilted exterior leaves and cut in half lengthwise. Leave the root end attached—it helps keep the leaves together. If using iceberg lettuce, cut it in quarters through the stem. Cut the radicchio the same way. If using Belgian endives, cut them in half lengthwise (in quarters if the endives are large). Lightly brush the cut edges of the lettuces with olive oil and season with salt and pepper.

3. Set up your grill for direct grilling. Have a high zone for grilling the lettuce; a medium-high zone for grilling the bacon and bread; and a fire-free safety zone in case the bacon starts to burn. Brush or scrape the grill grate clean and oil it well.

4. Grill the bacon over the medium-hot zone until browned and crisp, 2 to 4 minutes per side. Move the bacon to the safety zone if flare-ups occur. Transfer the bacon with a slotted spoon to paper towels to drain, then cut it crosswise into ½-inch strips.

5. Grill the lettuces over the hot zone to char the cut sides, 1 to 2 minutes per cut side. Don't overcook; the centers of the lettuces should remain raw. Transfer to a cutting board and let cool, then slice widthwise into ½-inch strips.

6. Lightly brush the bread slices with olive oil on both sides. Grill until browned, 1 to 2 minutes per side. Set aside.

7. Add the grilled bacon, lettuces, and tomatoes to the bowl with the salad dressing. Add the grilled bread, breaking it into 1-inch pieces. Toss just before serving and dust with the chopped chives.

PERUVIAN POTATO SALAD

YIELD: Serves 4

METHOD: Smoke-roasting (indirect grilling)

PREP TIME: 15 minutes

GRILLING TIME: 40 to 60 minutes

GRILL/GEAR: Can be grilled over charcoal or gas. You also need a disposable aluminum foil roasting pan; 2 hardwood chunks or 1½ cups wood chips (optional), the latter soaked in water to cover for 30 minutes, then drained.

Papas huancaína (named for a Peruvian city in the Andean highlands) may be the most flavorful potato salad on Planet Barbecue. In place of the traditional mayonnaise-based dressing, you use a creamy piquant cheese sauce spiked with spicy Peruvian chiles. Wood smoke adds another dimension of flavor. Don't let the exotic sound of the ingredients deter you. Most can be found at good supermarkets and the sauce can be made in 5 minutes.

INGREDIENTS

2 pounds baby fingerling potatoes (ideally a mix of red, white, and purple), scrubbed and blotted dry

2 scallions, trimmed, white parts cut crosswise into 1-inch pieces, green parts finely chopped and set aside for serving

1 tablespoon extra virgin olive oil

Coarse salt (sea or kosher) and freshly ground black pepper

Vegetable oil for oiling the grill grate

Huancaína Sauce (recipe follows)

1. Set up your grill for indirect grilling and heat to medium-high.

2. Cut any large potatoes in half or thirds so all the potatoes are the same size, that is, 1 to 1½ inches. Place the potatoes and scallion whites in a disposable aluminum foil pan large enough to hold them in a single layer. Toss with olive oil and season generously with salt and pepper.

3. Brush or scrape the grill grate clean and oil it well.

4. Place the pan with the potatoes in the center of the grill away from the heat. Add the wood chunks or chips to the coals, if using. Close the grill lid and smoke-roast the potatoes until tender, 40 to 60 minutes. (For instructions for smoking on a gas grill, see page 22.) Insert a bamboo skewer in one of the potatoes to test for doneness: The skewer should go in easily. Stir the potatoes from time to time so they roast evenly. For extra crispness, roast the potatoes (still in the pan) directly over the fire during the last 5 minutes.

5. Transfer the potatoes in their foil pan to a wire rack and let cool to room temperature. Place in an attractive mixing bowl and stir in the Huancaína Sauce. Sprinkle with the chopped scallion greens and serve.

HUANCAINA SAUCE

YIELD: Makes 1½ cups

This spicy, creamy cheese sauce is one of the wonders of Peruvian cuisine. There are work-arounds for the less familiar ingredients, like queso blanco and *aji amarillo*. Huancaína sauce is also pretty awesome on grilled chicken and seafood.

INGREDIENTS

6 ounces queso blanco, ricotta salata, or grated white cheddar cheese

1 bottled aji amarillo chile (Peruvian yellow chile), ¼ cup aji amarillo paste, 2 teaspoons aji amarillo powder, or 2 teaspoons hot paprika

1 teaspoon ground turmeric

1 tablespoon fresh lemon juice, or to taste

½ cup evaporated milk

3 tablespoons vegetable oil

Coarse salt (sea or kosher) and freshly ground black pepper

Place the ingredients for the sauce in a food processor and puree until smooth. Correct the seasoning, adding salt or lemon juice to taste; the sauce should be highly seasoned.

SHOP: I like to use a mix of fingerling potatoes: red, yellow, and of course, Peruvian purple potatoes. If unavailable locally, one good source is Melissas.com. You can also use Yukon Gold potatoes. You'll need to know about a few special ingredients for the sauce. *Queso blanco* is a soft, fresh, salty Latin American cheese. Look for it in the dairy section of many supermarkets, or substitute Italian ricotta salata or white cheddar. To be authentic, you'd use a yellow Peruvian chile called *aji amarillo*. You can order jarred chiles in brine or in paste form from Amazon. But hot paprika produces excellent Huancaína Sauce if you can't find the chiles.

INSIDER TIP: Smoke-roasting is one of my favorite ways to cook small dense vegetables, from potatoes to carrots (see page 266) to brussels sprouts (page 71). You season the veggies with olive oil and indirect grill them in a foil pan next to a fire enhanced with hardwood. Stir often so the veggies brown evenly.

GRILLED PINEAPPLE AND SHRIMP SALAD
WITH VIETNAMESE FLAVORS

YIELD: Serves 6 as a salad course; 4 as a main course

METHOD: Direct grilling

PREP TIME: 20 minutes

GRILLING TIME: 8 minutes

GRILL/GEAR: Can be grilled over charcoal, wood, or gas.

SHOP: Fish sauce is available at most supermarkets or can be purchased online. My favorite brand is Red Boat.

INSIDER TIP: This salad calls for three popular Southeast Asian herbs: cilantro, mint, and Thai basil. If you have only one—even if it's Italian basil instead of Thai—you'll still wind up with a killer salad.

*M*am *nem* is one of the most singular grilling sauces on Planet Barbecue —a sweet-salty pineapple-based Vietnamese condiment enriched with cooked shrimp and sometimes anchovies. Like many Asian sauces, it boasts soulful salty umami flavors (Asian fish sauce will do that), and enough chile hellfire to make you sit up and take notice. I couldn't help thinking that the same vibrant interplay of flavors would make an electrifying salad. Think smoky grilled shrimp, fresh Asian herbs, and fire-roasted pineapple. And don't think of letting the summer grilling season go by without trying it. I like to leave the shells on the shrimp to keep them moist and for extra flavor. Grill shrimp peeled if you prefer.

INGREDIENTS

2 pounds jumbo shrimp, shells on, or peeled and deveined

½ teaspoon coarse salt (sea or kosher)

½ cup canola or grapeseed oil, plus more for oiling the grill grate

4 cloves garlic, peeled and thinly sliced crosswise

2 shallots, peeled and thinly sliced crosswise

½ cup freshly squeezed lime juice, or to taste

⅓ cup Asian fish sauce

⅓ cup sugar, plus 1 cup sugar in a shallow bowl for dredging the pineapple

1 pineapple, peeled, cored, and cut crosswise into ¾-inch-thick slices

1 bunch cilantro, rinsed, shaken dry, and stemmed

1 bunch fresh mint, rinsed, shaken dry, and stemmed

½ cup fresh Thai basil or regular basil leaves

3 jalapeño or serrano peppers, thinly sliced

Freshly ground black pepper

½ cup chopped dry-roasted peanuts

1. Combine the shrimp and salt in a mixing bowl and toss to mix. Let marinate for 20 minutes.

2. Meanwhile, heat the oil to medium-high in a small saucepan on your stovetop or your grill's side burner. Add the garlic and fry until lightly browned and crisp, 1 to 2 minutes. Do not let it burn, or it will taste bitter. With a slotted spoon, transfer the garlic to a plate lined with paper towels to drain.

If you want impressive grill marks on your pineapple slices, give them a quarter turn after 1 minute per side.

Fry the shallots the same way. Let the oil cool to room temperature and set aside.

3. Place the lime juice, fish sauce, and the ⅓ cup sugar in a large serving bowl. Whisk until the sugar dissolves.

4. Set up your grill for direct grilling and heat to high. Brush or scrape the grill grate clean and oil it well.

5. Brush the pineapple slices on both sides with some of the reserved garlic-shallot oil. Dredge in sugar on both sides, shaking off the excess. Arrange the pineapple on the grate and grill until browned on both sides, but still raw in the center, 1 to 2 minutes per side, turning with tongs. Transfer the pineapple slices to a wire rack to cool. Add them with any pineapple juices to the bowl with the dressing.

6. Add the cilantro, mint, basil, and peppers to the pineapple, but do not toss.

7. Right before serving, brush the shrimp on both sides with some more of the garlic-shallot oil and season with salt and black pepper. Grill the shrimp until browned and cooked through, 1 to 2 minutes per side, turning with tongs. Add the shrimp and any remaining garlic-shallot oil to the salad and gently toss to mix.

8. Sprinkle the salad with the fried garlic and shallots and the peanuts and serve at once. If you've grilled the shrimp in their shells, supply plenty of napkins. You can be sure there will be at least some handwork involved in the eating of what may be the most electrifying salad you've ever tasted.

GRILLED ASPARAGUS AND CORN SALAD
WITH CHARRED LEMON VINAIGRETTE

Grilled asparagus and grilled corn are two of our favorite summer vegetables. This salad brings them together—where else?—on a hot grill. Grilling accentuates the sweetness of any vegetable by caramelizing the natural plant sugars. (It also imparts an intoxicating smoke flavor.) To reinforce those smoke flavors, you dress the salad with a sesame and charred lemon vinaigrette.

INGREDIENTS

1 pound asparagus, fibrous ends snapped off

2 ears sweet corn, husked

Asian (dark) sesame oil for basting, plus 3 tablespoons for the dressing

Coarse salt (sea or kosher) and freshly ground black pepper

Vegetables oil for oiling the grill grate

FOR THE VINAIGRETTE

1 lemon, zest finely grated (you'll need ½ teaspoon) and fruit cut in half crosswise

¼ cup sugar, in a shallow dish

2 tablespoons rice vinegar

1 tablespoon water

3 tablespoons chopped fresh cilantro or chives

1 tablespoon black or toasted white sesame seeds (see box, page 69)

1. Set up your grill for direct grilling and heat to high.

2. Pin the asparagus stalks together with bamboo skewers or toothpicks to form rafts, 4 to 5 stalks per raft. (Alternatively, arrange them in a single layer in a grill basket. Or on a preheated vegetable grilling grate on the grill.)

3. Lightly brush the asparagus and corn with sesame oil and season with salt and pepper.

4. Brush or scrape the grill grate clean and oil it well. Grill the asparagus and corn until well browned, 3 to 4 minutes per side, 6 to 8 minutes in all for the asparagus and 9 to 12 minutes in all for the corn. Transfer to a wire rack to cool. Cut the kernels off the corn cobs using long lengthwise strokes of a chef's knife.

YIELD: Serves 4

METHOD: Direct grilling

PREP TIME: 16 minutes

GRILLING TIME: 12 minutes

GRILL/GEAR: Can be grilled over charcoal, wood, or gas. You also need small bamboo skewers or toothpicks or a grill basket or vegetable grilling grate.

SHOP: When buying the asparagus, choose thick spears (they're easier to pin and grill). Choose an Asian roasted sesame oil; one good widely available brand is Kadoya. Black sesame seeds are available at Asian markets and many supermarkets—otherwise use more toasted white sesame seeds.

INSIDER TIP: The easiest way to grill asparagus is a technique I pioneered many years ago in *The Barbecue! Bible*: stalks laid side by side and pinned together to form a raft. It's a lot easier to grill and turn the rafts this way than individual stalks.

5. Meanwhile, make the vinaigrette: Dip the cut sides of the lemon halves in the sugar and place them, sugared side down, on the grill grate. Grill until darkly browned, 3 to 4 minutes.

6. Squeeze the juice from the caramelized lemon halves into a mixing bowl, discarding any seeds. Add the lemon zest, vinegar, 2 teaspoons of sugar (left over from dipping the lemon), and salt and pepper and whisk until the salt and sugar crystals are dissolved. Whisk in the 3 tablespoons of sesame oil and 1 tablespoon of water. Stir in the grilled corn, chopped cilantro, and salt and pepper to taste; the mixture should be highly seasoned.

7. Remove the skewers or toothpicks, if used, and arrange the grilled asparagus spears on a platter or plates. Spoon the grilled corn mixture over them, leaving the ends of the asparagus exposed. Dust with black sesame seeds and you're in business.

BEEF

There's no denying the cool factor of grilled appetizers, breads, and salads. But admit it: This chapter is *really* why you bought this book. To learn how to grill the perfect steak. Make that many steaks, from T-bones to tomahawks to filets mignons, using different grilling techniques, from cavemanning to dry-brining to reverse-searing. But that's not all. You also want to know how to grill the perfect prime rib (hint: use your rotisserie) and whole beef tenderloin (hint: stuff it with grilled onions, peppers, and provolone, like a Philly cheesesteak). Beef ribs? Check. Kebabs? Check. And while we're at it, I'll show you how to grill the ultimate veal chop (the process involves a blowtorch).

FIRST-TIMER'S T-BONES
(HOW TO GRILL THE PERFECT STEAK)

YIELD: Serves 4 normal people as part of a full meal or 2 *really* hungry carnivores

METHOD: Direct grilling

PREP TIME: 10 minutes

GRILLING TIME: 10 minutes

GRILL/GEAR: Can be grilled over charcoal, wood, or gas. If you like a wood smoke flavor, grill over a wood fire or add 2 hardwood chunks or 1½ cups of unsoaked wood chips to the fire following the instructions on page 21. You also need a small cast-iron skillet (6 to 8 inches) and a wire rack set over a rimmed sheet pan.

SHOP: If price is no object, buy an aged prime T-bone (see Beef Speak on page 120). If health concerns are foremost, buy a grass-fed or organic steak. If cost matters, buy "Choice," but whatever you buy, make sure your steak is 1¼ to 1½ inches thick. This gives you the best ratio of dark crust to juicy interior.

Your first time? I understand you're a little nervous. Don't worry: I'm here to walk you through it step-by-step. I guarantee you'll emerge a pro. I'm talking about grilling your first steak, and I'm so confident in your success, I've chosen a cut most of us associate with the professionals: the T-bone. It's actually two steaks in one: a New York strip and a slender section of filet mignon connected by a T-shaped bone. Here's the trick (four tricks, actually): Buy it thick; season it assertively; grill it over a hot fire—and don't forget to finish it with sizzling beef fat. Each bite will bring you the intoxicating taste of beef, fat, fire, and smoke—in short, nirvana for carnivores. And don't forget to post photos of *your* first time on reddit.com/r/BarbecueBible.

INGREDIENTS

1 chunk (about 2 inches square and 2 ounces) steak fat or beef fat, cut into ¼-inch dice, or 4 tablespoons (½ stick) unsalted butter

1 scallion, trimmed, white and green parts thinly sliced crosswise, or 3 tablespoons chopped fresh flat-leaf parsley

2 T-bone steaks (each 14 to 16 ounces, 1¼ to 1½ inches thick)

Coarse salt (sea or kosher) and cracked black peppercorns

Vegetable oil for oiling the grill grate

1. Set up your grill for direct grilling and heat to medium-high.

2. Place a small cast-iron skillet directly over the fire or on your grill's side burner or directly on the grill or on the stove. Add the diced steak fat to the skillet and cook until the fat melts and the cubes crisp, 3 to 5 minutes or as needed. Stir so the fat melts evenly. Once the fat sizzles, add the scallion and cook until it's sizzling and beginning to brown, 2 minutes. Remove the pan from the heat. If you don't have beef fat, melt and lightly brown the butter and cook the scallion.

3. Very generously season the T-bones on both sides with salt and pepper. Brush or scrape the grill grate clean and oil it well. Arrange the steaks on the grill grate running slightly on the diagonal to the bars of the grate. Grill for 2 minutes, then give each steak a quarter turn to lay on a crosshatch of grill marks.

4. When the bottom is sizzling and browned (you may see beads of blood start to form on the top), turn the steaks and grill the other side the same way. You'll need about 3 minutes per side for rare (120° to 125°F); 4 minutes per side for medium-rare (130° to 135°F); 5 minutes per side for medium (140° to 145°F). Use an instant-read thermometer inserted through the strip side of the steak to check for doneness. Alternatively, use the poke test (see page 40).

5. Transfer the steaks to a wire rack set over a sheet pan to rest for a minute or so before serving. (The wire rack keeps the bottoms of the steaks from getting soggy.) Meanwhile, reheat the beef fat.

6. Transfer the steaks to a platter or plates. Pour the sizzling beef fat over them and dig in.

INSIDER TIP: There's a good chance you've heard of the celebrated Brooklyn steakhouse Peter Luger. Besides the premium beef (raised and cut to their specifications) and the industrial-strength broiler, there's a simple technique you can use at home that gives the restaurant's steaks their extraordinary sizzling crust, luscious mouthfeel, and supernatural richness: They douse the cooked steak with melted beef fat a moment before it's served. Make friends with your butcher (or the meat cutter at the supermarket) and ask for a 2-inch chunk of steak fat or beef fat.

REVERSE-SEARED TOMAHAWK STEAKS
WITH BLUE CHEESE BUTTER

If you've fired up the grill for the first recipe in this chapter (which I hope you've done), you know how to grill a T-bone steak. Now, here's a recipe for the second of the so-called "noble" steaks—the rib steak—and in particular, in its most extravagant form: the beef tomahawk. Picture a monster 24-ounce steak cut from the rib roast with an extra long section of rib bone attached. It doesn't take much imagination to see a tomahawk. Imagine biting into beef that, on account of the veins of fat that surround it, tastes even richer and more luscious than a T-bone or filet (the third "noble" steak, see page 122). When meat is this extraordinary, you want to keep the preparation simple—good coarse salt, freshly ground black pepper, and wood smoke—with a disk of unctuous blue cheese butter melting into the meat for the ultimate richness.

YIELD: Serves 4 normal people as part of a full meal or 2 *really* hungry carnivores

METHOD: Reverse-searing (indirect grilling followed by direct grilling)

PREP TIME: 10 minutes, plus 5 minutes for the blue cheese butter and 1 hour for chilling

GRILLING TIME: 70 minutes

GRILL/GEAR: Reverse-searing can be done over charcoal or gas, but you'll get a more pronounced smoke flavor over charcoal. You also need 2 hardwood chunks or 1½ cups wood chips (the latter soaked in water to cover for 30 minutes, then drained); aluminum foil to keep the ends of the rib bones from burning; an instant-read or remote digital thermometer; and a wire rack set over a sheet pan.

SHOP: The beef tomahawk is the ultimate luxury steak—you'll likely need to special-order it from a high-end butcher or online meat company. Ask for tomahawks cut from the loin end of a rib roast—they're more tender than steaks cut from the chuck end. As for blue cheese, I'm partial to an incredible smoked blue from the Rogue Creamery in Central Point, Oregon (see page 98), but French Roquefort, Spanish Cabrales, German Cambozola, or Italian Gorgonzola make equally distinctive steak butters, too.

INSIDER TIP: One of the best ways to grill a monster-thick steak, like a beef tomahawk, is to use a technique called "reverse-searing." In a nutshell, you indirect grill the steak over low heat to cook it to an internal temperature of around 105°F, then sear it over high heat to crust the exterior. This offers two other advantages: You get to smoke the steak before grilling it, and you can serve it sizzling hot off the grill.

INGREDIENTS

FOR THE BLUE CHEESE BUTTER

2 ounces of your favorite blue cheese (see suggestions in Shop), at room temperature

5 tablespoons salted butter, at room temperature

1 tablespoon minced fresh flat-leaf parsley

FOR THE STEAKS

Vegetable oil for oiling the grill grate

2 beef "tomahawks" (bone-in rib-eyes, preferably dry-aged, each about 1½ pounds and 2 inches thick)

Coarse salt (sea or kosher) and coarsely and freshly ground black pepper

1. Make the blue cheese butter: Place the cheese in a mixing bowl and mash it to a paste with a fork. Stir in the butter and parsley. Alternatively, place the ingredients in a food processor and process until creamy and smooth.

2. Place a 12-inch-square piece of plastic wrap on your work surface and mound the butter in the center. Roll it up into a 1-inch-thick cylinder, twisting the ends of the wrap to compact the butter. Refrigerate or freeze until firm, about 1 hour. The butter will keep for at least 5 days in the refrigerator or up to 3 months in the freezer. You can prepare it ahead of time. The butter is also excellent atop burgers, asparagus, potatoes, or other grilled or smoke-roasted vegetables.

3. Set up your grill for indirect grilling and heat to medium-low. Brush or scrape the grill grate clean and oil it well. Add wood chunks or chips to the fire.

4. Generously season the steaks on both sides with salt and pepper. Arrange the tomahawks on the grill grate away from the heat. Close the lid and smoke-roast the steaks to an internal temperature of about 105°F on a digital remote thermometer or instant-read thermometer. This will take 40 to 60 minutes.

5. Transfer the steaks to a wire rack set over a sheet pan and let them rest for 10 minutes. Meanwhile, set up your grill for direct grilling and heat to high.

6. Arrange the tomahawk steaks over the hottest part of the grill grate, running diagonal to the bars. Direct grill until both sides are sizzling, browned, and crusty, 2 to 4 minutes per side. You want a final internal temperature of 120° to 125°F for rare; 130° to 135°F for medium-rare; or 140° to 145°F for medium. If the exposed parts of the rib bones start to burn, slide a folded sheet of aluminum foil under them.

7. Transfer the tomahawks to a platter or plates and top each with disks of blue cheese butter. Serve while the butter is still melting into the meat.

BEEF, VEAL, AND GAME

Some people, especially in Europe, like their steak so rare it's almost mooing, with a seared exterior and cool, bluish red center. The French call this *bleu*, "blue" literally, and at least one great American steakhouse cooks its porterhouses this way: Chi Spacca in Los Angeles. Note: Blank spaces in the grid indicate temperatures are inappropriate for this particular cut.

CUT	BLUE	RARE	MEDIUM-RARE ** my favorite	MEDIUM	MEDIUM-WELL	WELL	VERY WELL
Steak, rib roast, rib-eye, beef tenderloin	100°–110°F cool red center	120°–125°F warm red center	130°–135°F hot red center	140°–145°F hot pink center	155°–160°F hot gray center		
Tri-tip		120°–125°F warm red center	130°–135°F hot red center	140°–145°F hot pink center	155°–160°F hot gray center		
Beef long ribs						175°–185°F hot gray center	
Beef short ribs and plate ribs							200°–205°F hot gray center
Brisket and beef clod							200°–205°F hot gray center
Veal chops			130°–135°F hot red center	140°–145°F hot pink center	155°–160°F hot gray center		
Veal roast			130°–135°F hot red center	140°–145°F hot pink center	155°–160°F hot gray center		
Venison chops		120°–125°F warm red center	130°–135°F hot red center	140°–145°F hot pink center			
Venison roast		120°–125°F warm red center	130°–135°F hot red center	140°–145°F hot pink center			

BEEF SPEAK

Grass-Fed: The preferred beef of South America and of more and more carnivores in the United States. "Grass-fed" cattle forage for food on open pastureland. This is a cow's natural diet, so the animal is healthier (and lower in saturated fat than grain-fed beef), keeping us and the planet healthier, too. Grass-fed steers are typically leaner and slower to mature than grain-fed, with lean, distinctively flavored meat. Buy American grass-fed beef when possible. (Note: "Grass-fed" does not automatically mean organic. Ask your purveyor.)

Grain-Fed: Cattle raised on grain-based diets (corn, soy, and supplements) on feedlots gain weight faster than grass-fed cattle. Their meat tends to have more marbling (fat) and a richer taste with a more luscious mouthfeel. Many producers aim for the best of both worlds by raising cattle on grass for the first 6 to 12 months, then finishing them on grains before they go to market.

Prime: The USDA (at the invitation of meat packers) grades beef using a complicated and somewhat subjective system that evaluates marbling in the rib-eye muscle between the twelfth and thirteenth ribs and factors in the animal's age. Typically from young, well-fed cattle, "Prime" is the top beef grade in the United States. Less than 2 percent of American beef can be called Prime, and most of that goes to high-end restaurants, hotels, and specialty meat markets. Look for the distinctive USDA shield; it should say "Prime." Buttery-rich, juicy, and tender, Prime beef responds beautifully to grilling.

Choice: Beef that is graded "Choice" by the USDA is leaner than Prime, but still very good. Because it may come from an older animal and contain less fat, the meat might be slightly less juicy and less tender than its Prime equivalent. Choice beef is commonly sold in supermarkets. Although not as rich as Prime beef, it, too, is excellent for grilling or smoking.

Select: Another grade of beef that can be found in supermarkets and big box stores is USDA "Select." Leaner than Prime or Choice, Select meat is often a relative bargain. Marinate or mechanically tenderize (pound with a mallet or jacquard) before direct grilling, or smoke low and slow to maximize tenderness.

Certified Tender and **Very Tender:** In addition to the meat grading shields discussed previously, there are also shields that indicate relative tenderness. The USDA Tenderness Program aids the consumer by identifying beef cuts that are consistently tender when compared with other cuts of beef. These include rib-eye, strip steak, and eight other cuts.

Dry-Aged: Premium grades of beef are sometimes dry-aged under carefully controlled conditions to improve their flavor, increase tenderness, and add value. Primal and sub-primal cuts are typically aged for three to four weeks (although the drying period can be longer) during which the meat can lose up to a quarter of its original weight through evaporation. This concentrates the flavor, plus enzymes develop during the aging process that add a complex and unique flavor to the meat. The dark dried surface is trimmed off at the end before sale, adding to the cost of the meat. Most dry-aged beef is sold to restaurants or specialty meat markets. It is rarely available in supermarkets.

Wet-Aged: Beef can also be aged by enclosing it in a vacuum-sealed package called Modified Atmosphere Packaging (MAP). The meat retains its moisture, and requires only four to ten days to age; there is no loss of weight as there is with dry-aging. Wet-aging adds some flavor, although not as much as dry-aging. Though popular with producers, true beef connoisseurs profess to prefer dry-aged meat.

Wagyu: The cachet of Japanese Kobe beef in the 1980s and '90s (and the high prices it commanded) did not go unnoticed by American cattle producers, who began breeding Japanese cattle with American Angus. They appropriated the wagyu name, but the meat is sometimes sold as "American-style Kobe beef." Recognized for its superior marbling and tenderness, wagyu is widely available in the United States—at correspondingly premium prices. Its high fat content makes it an excellent choice for the grill. Unfortunately, there are no national standards for wagyu-Kobe beef that would be meaningful to consumers. Note: True "Kobe" beef comes from Kobe, Japan, only.

According to Larry Olmsted, author of *Real Food, Fake Food* (a must-read if you care about what you eat), only nine restaurants in the United States are authorized to sell genuine Kobe beef. In other words, it's extremely rare. Most of what's sold as "Kobe" beef in the United States may be wagyu, but it certainly isn't Kobe.

Purge: Packaged meat often exudes a pinkish liquid that is often mistaken for blood. It is actually water tinted with myoglobin—a muscular protein that gives meat its color—that has been released from the cells. Rinse it off, blot the meat dry, and you're ready to grill.

CUTS OF BEEF

DRY-BRINED PEPPERED FILETS MIGNONS
WITH ANCHOVY CREAM OR CUTTING BOARD SAUCE

YIELD: Serves 4

METHOD: Direct grilling

PREP TIME: 1 hour for dry-brining; plus 10 minutes for the sauce

GRILLING TIME: 8 to 10 minutes

GRILL/GEAR: Can be grilled over charcoal, wood, or gas. You also need 2 hardwood chunks or 1 cup unsoaked wood chips (optional); a small (6- to 8-inch) skillet; a wire rack set over a sheet pan; a cutting board with a well.

SHOP: See notes on buying a steak on page 120.

INSIDER TIP: This recipe uses a technique called dry-brining to give depth of flavor to a steak that's normally mild. You season the steak generously with salt an hour ahead of time. The salt draws out and mixes with some of the meat juices, creating a brine (saline solution), which, with time, is partially reabsorbed into meat. The result: added flavor and succulence.

I've always preferred richer, fattier cuts, like rib-eyes or strip steaks. But filet mignon has its partisans—people who prize its tenderness (you can virtually cut it with the side of a fork) and mild flavor—the mildest of all cuts of beef. Dry-brining gives you the best of both worlds: tenderness *and* flavor. With these filets, I give you two options for sauce: Anchovy Cream or Cutting Board Sauce. You assemble the latter right on the cutting board with the meat juices and aromatic herbs when you carve the steak.

INGREDIENTS

4 filet mignon steaks (each 6 to 8 ounces and at least 2 inches thick)

Coarse salt (sea or kosher)

Vegetable oil for oiling the grill grate

½ cup cracked black peppercorns, spread out in a shallow bowl

Anchovy Cream (recipe follows) *or* Cutting Board Sauce (recipe follows)

1. Arrange the filets mignons in a baking dish. Generously season with salt on both sides. (Tip: Sprinkle the salt from a height of 6 inches for even distribution.) Dry-brine the steaks in the refrigerator for 1 hour, uncovered, turning them once.

2. Set up your grill for direct grilling and heat to medium-high. Brush or scrape the grill grate clean and oil it well.

3. Dip each filet mignon in cracked black pepper to crust the top and bottom. Arrange the steaks on the grill grate. Grill for 1½ minutes, then give each steak a quarter turn to lay on a crosshatch of grill marks. When

the bottom is sizzling and browned (you may see beads of blood start to form on the top), turn the steaks and grill the other side the same way. Grill the steaks on the sides, too, to expose all surfaces to the heat.

4. You'll need about 3 minutes per side for rare (120° to 125°F); 4 minutes per side for medium-rare (130° to 135°F); 5 minutes per side for medium (140° to 145°F). Use an instant-read thermometer inserted through the side of the steak to check for doneness. Alternatively, use the poke test (page 40).

Filets on Cutting Board Sauce

5. Transfer the filets mignons to a wire rack set over a sheet pan to rest for a minute or so before serving. (The wire rack keeps the bottoms from getting soggy.)

6. Pool the Anchovy Cream on the bottom of a platter or individual plates. Set the filets mignons on top and serve. Or serve the steaks with Cutting Board Sauce as outlined on the facing page.

ANCHOVY CREAM

YIELD: makes ¾ cup

Anchovies and steak have a long established affinity. Don't believe me? You find anchovies in two classic steak sauces: Worcestershire and A.1. Their salty umami flavor goes great with the sanguine meatiness of the beef.

INGREDIENTS

1½ cups heavy (whipping) cream

4 oil-packed anchovy fillets, drained and blotted dry

1 clove garlic, peeled

1 tablespoon unsalted butter

Freshly ground black pepper

1. Place the cream, anchovies, and garlic in a heavy saucepan and briskly simmer over medium heat until thick and reduced by half, 8 to 12 minutes. Stir often. If the mixture starts to scorch or boil over, lower the heat.

2. Puree the mixture in a blender or food processor or use an immersion blender. Return the mixture to the pan and whisk in the butter and lots of black pepper. Keep the finished sauce warm over low heat, but do not let it boil.

CUTTING BOARD SAUCE

Tip o' the hat to chef Adam Perry Lang, who had the ingenious idea of combining the sauce ingredients with the hot meat juices right on the cutting board.

INGREDIENTS

1 clove garlic, peeled

½ cup stemmed flat-leaf parsley or other fresh herbs

2 scallions, trimmed

1 red jalapeño or serrano pepper

Coarse salt (sea or kosher) and freshly ground black pepper

⅓ cup best-quality extra virgin olive oil, in a small bowl

1. Working on a large cutting board with a well (a juice-catching groove usually around the periphery), finely chop the garlic and parsley. Thinly slice the scallions (both white and green parts) and the pepper crosswise. Season generously with salt and pepper and pour half the olive oil on top. Mix with the blade of the knife.

2. Remove the hot filets mignons from the grill and lay them directly on top of the ingredients on the cutting board. Cut each steak with downward strokes of the knife into ¼-inch-thick slices. (There is no need to let the meat rest.) Pour the remaining olive oil over the sliced steaks and toss on the board with a spoon and the blade of the knife: The idea is to coat the steak slices with herbs and oil and mix them with the meat juices. Add salt and pepper to taste. The whole process should take less than a minute. Transfer to a platter or plates and serve at once.

HANGER STEAKS
WITH MUSTARD AND CARAMELIZED ONION SAUCE

YIELD: Serves 2 and can be multiplied as desired

METHOD: Direct grilling

PREP TIME: 5 minutes for the steaks; 15 minutes for the sauce

GRILLING TIME: 8 minutes

GRILL/GEAR: Can be grilled over charcoal, wood, or gas. You also need a medium-size saucepan and an instant-read thermometer.

SHOP: Hanger steak may well require a trip to a specialty butcher, or order it online from getbutcherbox.com.

INSIDER TIP: Unlike most steaks, the hanger steak (nicknamed the "butcher's cut" because meat cutters used to keep this rich-tasting steak for themselves) does not connect to a bone. Rather, it "hangs" from the steer's underbelly in close proximity to the diaphragm. It has a minerally flavor much prized by diehard beef lovers. Like most fibrous steaks from the undercarriage (for example, skirt and flank), hanger steak should be grilled quickly and sliced thinly on a diagonal to maximize its succulence and tenderness. I can't promise you will like it cooked anything beyond medium-rare.

*O*nglet (as the French call hanger steak) was a staple of my student days in Paris. It was cheap, filling, and full of flavor. I ate it at a bistro near the rue Cler market (this was back before bistros became chic), and in lieu of sauce, it came with a little crock of Dijon mustard. Mustard proved to be the perfect condiment for this steak, with its rich beefy flavor. The following hanger steak gets a double blast of mustard flavor: first, in a light brushing of mustard on the steak itself; then in a mustard and caramelized onion sauce.

INGREDIENTS

FOR THE SAUCE

2 tablespoons butter

1 medium-size onion, peeled and finely chopped

1 cup heavy (whipping) cream

1 tablespoon coarse-grained Meaux-style mustard or Dijon mustard

Coarse salt (sea or kosher) and freshly ground black pepper

FOR THE STEAK

1 pound hanger steaks, trimmed

¼ cup Dijon mustard

Vegetable oil for oiling the grill grate

2 tablespoons minced fresh chives (optional)

1. Make the sauce: Melt the butter in a small saucepan on your grill's side burner or on the stove. Add the onion and caramelize over medium heat (cook until soft and browned), 8 to 12 minutes, stirring often. Reduce the heat as needed so the onion softens and browns without burning.

2. Whisk in the cream and increase the heat to high. Boil the cream until reduced by half (5 minutes or as needed). Whisk in the mustard and add salt and pepper to taste; the sauce should be highly seasoned. The sauce can be made up to 30 minutes ahead and kept warm.

3. Make the steaks: Using a pastry brush, brush the hanger steaks on all sides with mustard, then season generously with salt and pepper.

4. Set up your grill for direct grilling and heat to high. Brush or scrape the grill grate clean and oil it well.

5. Arrange the hanger steaks on a diagonal on the grill grate. Grill until sizzling and browned on the outside and cooked to taste, about 2 minutes per side for rare (120° to 125°F); 3 minutes per side for medium-rare (130° to 135°F). Give each steak a quarter turn after 1 minute to lay on a crosshatch of grill marks, if desired. Use an instant-read meat thermometer inserted through the side of the steak to check for doneness. Alternatively, use the poke test (page 40).

6. Transfer the steak to a cutting board and let rest for a minute or so. Meanwhile, reheat the mustard sauce, if necessary. Cut the hanger steaks on the diagonal into ½-inch-thick slices and transfer to a platter or plates. Pour the mustard sauce on top, sprinkle with chives (if using), and dig in.

CAVEMAN PORTERHOUSE
WITH PEPPER HASH

In 1953, an American general-turned-politician became the thirty-fourth president of the United States. We remember Dwight D. Eisenhower here, not for his great leadership or military genius, but for a singular method of grilling he brought to the White House. "He rubs the steak (a 4-inch-thick sirloin) with oil and garlic," wrote a reporter from the *Miami Daily News*, one Mr. Byres, "then, as the horrified guests look on, casually flings the steak into the midst of the red and glowing coals." Thus was born what I like to call "caveman" steak. (Steaks were no doubt grilled this way in prehistoric times, and likely have been ever since.) Ember-roasting gives you an exemplary crust and pronounced smoky flavor. To round out the taste, you'll top the beef with a pan-fry of poblano and bell peppers—also cooked on the embers.

YIELD: Serves 2 and can be multiplied as desired

METHOD: Caveman grilling (directly on the embers)

PREP TIME: 15 minutes

GRILLING TIME: 6 to 12 minutes

GRILL/GEAR: Sorry, gas grillers: You'll need a charcoal grill for this one. (But see an interesting plancha variation at the end of the recipe.) You'll want to use natural lump charcoal, not briquettes. You also need a grill hoe or garden hoe; newspaper for fanning the coals; long-handled tongs; heavy-duty grill gloves; and a 10-inch cast-iron skillet.

INGREDIENTS

FOR THE STEAK

1 porterhouse steak (20 to 24 ounces), cut 2 inches thick

Coarse salt (sea or kosher) and freshly ground black pepper

2 cloves garlic, peeled and minced (optional)

2 tablespoons extra virgin olive oil (optional)

FOR THE PEPPER HASH

½ cup extra virgin olive oil

1 poblano chile or green bell pepper, stemmed, seeded, and cut into matchstick strips

1 yellow bell pepper, stemmed, seeded, and cut into matchstick strips

1 red bell pepper, stemmed, seeded, and cut into matchstick strips

3 cloves garlic, peeled and thinly sliced crosswise

½ cup coarsely chopped fresh flat-leaf parsley

1. Build a charcoal fire following the instructions on page 27, and using a grill hoe, rake the coals into an even layer. (Leave the front third of your grill coal-free.) When the coals glow orange, fan them with a newspaper to disperse any loose ash.

2. Make the steak: Generously— and I mean generously—season the porterhouse on both sides with salt and pepper. If you want to go the Eisenhower route, sprinkle the steak with garlic (pat it into the meat) and drizzle with oil.

3. Lay the steak directly on the embers. Grill until cooked to taste, 3 to 5 minutes per side or as needed for rare (120° to 125°F); 4 to 6 minutes per side or as needed for medium-rare (130° to 135°F), turning with tongs. (Wear heavy-duty gloves to protect your hands.) Tip: Keep the steak moving every minute or so to make the cooking process more even.

4. Using tongs, lift the steak out of the fire, shaking it to dislodge any clinging embers. Using a stiff-bristled basting brush, knock off any loose ash and arrange the steak on a wire rack set over a sheet pan. Let rest, loosely tented with aluminum foil, for a minute or so, then transfer to a cutting board. Carve the filet mignon and strip steak sections off the bone, then cut each into ¼-inch-thick slices, running your knife slightly on the diagonal from top to bottom. Arrange the sliced porterhouse on a platter with the bone in the center.

5. Now, make the pepper hash: Pour the oil in a cast-iron skillet (it helps to use a long-handled skillet) and heat it directly on the embers. Add a strip of either pepper. When bubbles dance around it, the oil is ready. Add the poblano, bell peppers, garlic, and parsley. Cook until the peppers begin to brown, 2 minutes. Pour the sizzling peppers and oil over the sliced porterhouse and dig in!

SHOP: Porterhouse is another of the "noble" steaks (i.e., strip, rib-eye, and filet mignon). It is comprised of both a piece of filet mignon and a strip steak, separated by a T-shaped bone.

INSIDER TIP: Grilling steak directly on the embers isn't new, and it certainly isn't limited to steak. But there's something about laying a slab of beef on a red-hot bed of embers that astonishes, horrifies, and ultimately thrills in a way that no other grilling method can rival. And there's more to the practice than mere theatrics: The strong but uneven heat, the micro-charring of the meat's surface, and even the tiny bits of cinder add a texture and taste to a steak you simply can't achieve by conventional grilling.

VARIATION: PLANCHA METHOD

You can't caveman a steak on a gas grill, but you can sear it on a fire-heated plancha or cast-iron skillet. You'll achieve a savory crust quite unlike what you'd get with conventional grilling. It's not the same as a caveman crust, but it's remarkable nonetheless.

Set up your grill for plancha grilling following the instructions on page 28. Heat the plancha well (a few drops of water splashed on it will evaporate in 2 seconds). Oil and season the steak well and grill it on the plancha following the cooking times in Step 3, page 129.

ROTISSERIE PRIME RIB
WITH HORSERADISH CREAM

YIELD: Serves 6 to 8

METHOD: Rotisserie/spit-roasting

PREP TIME: 15 minutes

COOKING TIME: 1 to 1½ hours

GRILL/GEAR: You'll need a grill with a rotisserie. If you're lucky enough to own a wood-burning rotisserie (like a Kalamazoo), you can smoke the prime rib while you grill it. Ditto for a charcoal-burning rotisserie, like a Weber kettle. You can even add a little smoke flavor on a gas grill (see page 22). You also need butcher's string; 2 hardwood chunks or 1½ cups wood chips (optional), the latter soaked in water to cover for 30 minutes, then drained; an instant-read thermometer; and heavy-duty grill gloves.

The English call it roast beef, and for untold generations, a rib roast rotating on a spit in front of a wood fire has represented not just gustatory bliss, but material and spiritual comfort. So essential is roast beef to the British sense of well-being, a special breed of dog was developed in the sixteenth century to turn a treadmill attached to the rotisserie spit. (Before that, the task fell to miserable scullery lads, and later, elaborate clockworks.) You've probably had prime rib cooked in the oven. Spit-roasted next to a wood or wood-enhanced fire, prime rib is nothing less than a revelation.

INGREDIENTS

1 prime rib roast
(3 bones, 7 to 8 pounds)

1 bunch fresh rosemary, torn or cut into 1-inch sprigs

3 cloves garlic, peeled and cut lengthwise into matchstick slivers

Coarse salt (sea or kosher) and cracked black peppercorns

Extra virgin olive oil for drizzling

Horseradish Cream (recipe follows)

1. Set up your grill for spit-roasting and heat to medium-high. Place a large drip pan below the center of the spit (to collect meat drippings for the Horseradish Cream).

2. Using the tip of a paring knife, make a series of slits in the roast on all sides. Each slit should be about ½ inch wide and deep and spaced 1½ inches apart. In half the slits, insert sprigs of rosemary, and in the remainder, insert garlic slivers, taking care to intermix the flavorings. Generously—and I mean generously—season the roast on all sides with salt and pepper, patting the seasonings into the meat. Drizzle oil over the meat, rubbing it in with your fingertips.

3. Using butcher's string, tie the roast between the bones. (This keeps the collar of the meat from separating from the eye of the roast.) Wrap the string around the roast end to end to give it a compact shape.

4. Slip the first pronged fork on the spit. Thread the roast from end to end on the rotisserie spit and secure it with the second fork. Tighten the lock screws between the tines of a table fork. Fit the end of the spit in the motor socket. If your rotisserie kit has one, adjust the counterbalance to ensure the meat spins smoothly (it shouldn't wobble or seize during the rotation). If using wood chunks or chips on a charcoal grill, add them to the coals. On a gas grill, place the chunks on the metal heat diffuser over the burners.

5. Spit-roast the prime rib until crusty and brown on the outside and cooked to the desired degree of doneness on the inside, about 1 hour for rare (120° to 125°F); 1¼ to 1½ hours for medium-rare (130° to 135°F). Pause the rotisserie and use an instant-read thermometer inserted into the very center of the prime rib (through the large end but not touching the rotisserie spit or bone) to test for doneness. Remember, the prime rib will continue to cook even after it leaves the rotisserie.

6. Turn off the rotisserie motor and remove the spit from the rotisserie socket. Supporting the spit with both hands (heavy-duty grill gloves, please), transfer the roast to a large cutting board (preferably with a deep well around the periphery to collect the juices). Carefully remove the roast from the spit. Remove the butcher's string and let the prime rib rest for 5 minutes or so, loosely tented with aluminum foil.

7. Meanwhile, make the Horseradish Cream (page 132).

8. To carve the prime rib, remove the bones in one piece with a sharp knife following the curve of the meat. Set aside the bones for yourself or divvy among other lucky diners. Carve the roast crosswise into ¾-inch-thick slices and serve with the Horseradish Cream.

NOTE: Some folks like their prime rib well-done. Serve them end cuts.

SHOP: Paradoxically, not all prime rib is Prime (the majority of it is graded Choice—read about the difference on page 120). But either grade delivers beef in one of its most magisterial forms. There are 7 bones to a full prime rib (which will easily feed 14 to 16). A 3-rib roast makes a good compromise between grandeur and affordability. Ask your butcher to "french" it, that is, carve away the fat from the last inch or two of each bone.

INSIDER TIP: You can cook prime rib by indirect grilling and smoking (in my previous books you'll find instructions for both). But if you really want to maximize its deliciousness—crusty bones, sizzling fat, and sanguine beef—spit-roast it on a rotisserie. This gives you the searing and browning of direct grilling with the constant gentle heat of indirect grilling, and the slow and steady rotation bastes the beef both externally and internally. Try this with some barbecue buddies sometime: Have one smoke a prime rib; another indirect grill it; and yet a third spit-roast it. Taste them side by side (preferably a blind tasting) and I bet you'll find the spit-roasted version wins every time.

HORSERADISH CREAM

YIELD: Makes 1½ cups

The secret to a great horseradish cream sauce is to grate the horseradish fresh. Look for horseradish in the produce section of most supermarkets or order it online from Melissas.com.

INGREDIENTS

1 piece (3 to 4 inches) fresh horseradish (½ cup diced) or ¼ cup prepared horseradish

½ cup mayonnaise, preferably Hellmann's or Best Foods

½ cup sour cream

3 tablespoons heavy (whipping) cream or buttermilk

1 tablespoon soy sauce

2 tablespoons of drippings from the prime rib (optional)

Coarse salt (sea or kosher) and freshly ground black pepper

1. If using fresh horseradish, peel it with a paring knife and cut it into ½-inch pieces. Finely chop in a food processor. (Take care not to inhale the potent fumes.)

2. Add the mayonnaise, sour cream, heavy cream, soy sauce, and meat drippings (if using) to the fresh or prepared horseradish and process or stir until smooth. Work in salt and pepper to taste.

Insert the rotisserie skewer through the prime rib.

Tighten the rotisserie prong screw using a table fork.

A spit-roasted prime rib ready for carving.

THE RAICHLEN "CHEESESTEAK"
WHOLE BEEF TENDERLOIN STUFFED WITH GRILLED POBLANOS, ONIONS, AND PROVOLONE CHEESE

YIELD: Serves 6 to 8

METHOD: Direct grilling

PREP TIME: 20 minutes

GRILLING TIME: 12 to 18 minutes for the vegetables; 15 to 20 minutes for the tenderloin

GRILL/GEAR: Can be grilled over charcoal, wood, or gas. You also need butcher's string; bamboo skewers; and 2 hardwood chunks or 1½ cups wood chips (optional), the latter soaked in water to cover for 30 minutes, then drained.

SHOP: A whole beef tenderloin weighs 5 to 6 pounds. You want a trimmed tenderloin (about 3 pounds), but ask your butcher to leave a little fat on it. At the same time, ask him or her to remove the tail (the thin tapered section at the end), so the roast has an even shape. If you need to buy a whole tenderloin, save the tail section for cubing for kebabs.

Think of this as the *ultimate* low-carb steak sandwich, with the beef tenderloin standing in for the hoagie roll. I created it for Barbecue University, and it's been a Raichlen favorite ever since. In a nutshell, you start with the traditional Philly cheesesteak toppings—grilled peppers, onions, and provolone cheese—but you stuff them into the beef tenderloin rather than piling them on top. Once you master the butterflying technique, the stuffings are limited only by your imagination.

INGREDIENTS

FOR THE CHIPOTLE SAUCE

1 cup mayonnaise, preferably Hellmann's or Best Foods

2 canned chipotle chiles in adobo, minced, with 1 tablespoon adobo sauce

FOR THE BEEF

Vegetable oil for oiling the grill grate

2 poblano peppers

1 large sweet onion, peeled and cut crosswise into ½-inch-thick slices

Extra virgin olive oil

Coarse salt (sea or kosher) and freshly ground black pepper

1 trimmed beef tenderloin (about 3 pounds), preferably center-cut

6 ounces sliced aged provolone cheese

1. Prepare the Chipotle Sauce: Combine the mayonnaise, chipotle chiles, and adobo sauce in a small bowl and stir to blend. Cover and refrigerate until serving.

2. Set up the grill for direct grilling and heat to high. Brush or scrape the grill grate clean and oil it well.

3. Grill the poblanos until darkly browned on all sides, 3 to 4 minutes

per side. Transfer to a cutting board and let cool. Scrape off any burnt skin, remove the stems, and cut the chiles in half. Scrape out and discard the seeds.

4. Skewer the onion slices crosswise on slender bamboo skewers. Brush both sides with olive oil and season with salt and pepper. Grill the onions until browned on both sides, 3 to 5 minutes per side. Transfer to the cutting board, let cool, and remove the skewers.

5. Make a lengthwise cut in one side of the tenderloin to the opposite side (do not cut all the way through) and open it like a book. Season the meat, inside and out, with salt and pepper. Lay the strips of poblano end-to-end on the bottom section. Top with grilled onions and sliced provolone. Close the meat around the cheese and vegetables and tie crosswise at 2-inch intervals with butcher's string. Brush the outside of the tenderloin with olive oil.

6. Grill the tenderloin until well browned on the outside and cooked to taste, 4 to 5 minutes per side, 15 to 20 minutes in all for medium-rare (130° to 135°F). The provolone should be melted.

7. Transfer the beef to a cutting board and let rest for a couple of minutes. Remove the strings, then cut the tenderloin crosswise into ½-inch-thick slices. Serve with the chipotle mayonnaise.

INSIDER TIP: A beef tenderloin roast is a surefire showstopper. What you might not realize is how easy it is to cook. You basically direct grill it for 3 to 4 minutes per side, which gives you a crusty exterior, while leaving the center medium-rare. Its long cylindrical shape makes it easy to stuff. Ideally, you'll be working on a wood-burning grill. If not, enhance the fire with hardwood chunks or chips as described on page 22.

COFFEE-CRUSTED BEEF SHORT RIBS
WITH RED-EYE BARBECUE SAUCE

In my book *Project Smoke*, I explain how to smoke the biggest, baddest ribs on Planet Barbecue: beef plate ribs. Many of you have made them (I love when you share your photos on my Steven Raichlen Facebook page). Others lament that beef plate ribs are hard to find—especially at your local supermarket. So here's the next best thing: barbecued beef short ribs. Also cut from the rib cage, the short rib delivers an equally luscious texture and rich beefy flavor, but in a more manageable size that's readily available at most supermarkets. The flavorings are built on the triple pillars of cowboy cuisine: coffee, bacon, and beef.

YIELD: Serves 4

METHOD: Indirect grilling/ smoking

PREP TIME: 15 minutes

GRILLING TIME: 4 to 6 hours

GRILL/GEAR: Try to cook these ribs on a charcoal grill. The reason is simple: It's easy to smoke with charcoal, and challenging to achieve a rich smoke flavor on a gas grill. Don't own a charcoal grill? Here's a good excuse to buy an inexpensive kettle grill. You also need a food-safe spray bottle and 6 hardwood chunks or 4½ cups wood chips, the latter soaked in water to cover for 30 minutes, then drained.

SHOP: Beef short ribs are widely available. You want large short ribs with a thick cap of beef.

INSIDER TIP: Like all great barbecue, these beef ribs use a flavor-layering technique: a coffee rub on the raw ribs; then a coffee and Worcestershire sauce spray while they're cooking; and a not-too-sweet espresso barbecue sauce for serving.

INGREDIENTS

FOR THE SPRAY

½ cup cold brewed coffee

½ cup Worcestershire sauce

FOR THE RUB AND SHORT RIBS

3 tablespoons coarse salt (sea or kosher)

3 tablespoons freshly ground black pepper

3 tablespoons pimentón (Spanish smoked paprika) or sweet paprika

3 tablespoons ground coffee

1 tablespoon onion powder

Vegetable oil for oiling the grill grate

6 pounds beef short ribs

Red-Eye Barbecue Sauce (recipe follows)

1. Set up your grill for indirect grilling and heat to medium-low. To do this on a charcoal grill, use two thirds of a chimney of charcoal. If you're using a gas grill, set the outside burners on medium-low.

2. Make the spray: Place the coffee and Worcestershire sauce in a spray bottle and shake to mix. Set aside.

3. Make the rub: Place the salt, pepper, pimentón, coffee, and onion powder in a small bowl and stir to mix.

4. Brush or scrape the grill grate clean and oil it well. Place the short ribs in a large bowl and sprinkle with rub on all sides, tossing with your hands so all sides are coated. Arrange the ribs meat side up on the grate, away from the heat. Add 2 wood chunks or 1½ cups wood chips to the coals. When you see smoke, close the grill lid.

5. Indirect grill the short ribs until darkly browned on the outside, very tender inside, and the meat has shrunk back from the ends of the bones by at least ½ inch. Depending on the size of the ribs, the heat of your grill, and even the weather, this could take as little as 4 hours or as many as 6. Start spraying the ribs with the coffee mixture after 1 hour and spray twice more at 1-hour intervals—3 times in all. You'll need to replenish the coals every 40 minutes or so (if using natural lump charcoal, add it right to the fire; if using briquettes, light them in a chimney starter). Add wood as needed to keep up a thin but steady stream of smoke for the first 3 hours. But open the lid as little as possible to avoid losing heat.

NOTE: I like to eat the ribs right out of the smoker with the sauce on the side. If you like your ribs glazed with barbecue sauce, start basting them with sauce the last 30 minutes of cooking and baste once or twice before serving. For extra crunch, direct grill the ribs for the last 3 minutes to sear the sauce into the meat.

RED-EYE BARBECUE SAUCE

YIELD: Makes 1¼ cups

H ere's a bacon and coffee barbecue sauce in the best cattle wrangler tradition. Bacon makes it smoky; vinegar and coffee keep it from being too sweet.

INGREDIENTS

1 tablespoon butter

1 strip bacon or 1 ounce Smithfield ham, cut crosswise into ¼-inch slivers

1 scallion, trimmed, white and green parts finely chopped

¼ cup Worcestershire sauce

½ cup ketchup

2 tablespoons soy sauce

2 tablespoons rice vinegar

2 tablespoons packed brown sugar, dark or light, or to taste

3 tablespoons brewed espresso

2 tablespoons water

Coarse salt (sea or kosher) and freshly ground black pepper

1. Melt the butter in a saucepan over medium heat. Add the bacon and scallion and cook until both are browned, 4 minutes, stirring often with a wooden spoon.

2. Stir in the Worcestershire sauce and bring to a boil, scraping the bottom of the pan with the spoon to deglaze it. Stir in the ketchup, soy sauce, vinegar, brown sugar, espresso, and water, and gradually bring to a boil over medium-high heat. Reduce the heat and simmer the sauce until thick and richly flavored, 10 minutes, whisking often. Correct the seasoning, adding salt and pepper to taste; the sauce should be highly seasoned. Let cool to room temperature for serving. Store any extra in a covered container in the refrigerator: It will keep for several days.

BOOL KOGI BEEF KEBABS

YIELD: Serves 4

METHOD: Direct grilling

PREP TIME: 15 minutes, plus 2 to 4 hours for marinating the beef

GRILLING TIME: 8 to 12 minutes

GRILL/GEAR: Can be grilled over charcoal, wood, or gas. You also need 8-inch bamboo skewers.

SHOP: The traditional beef for *bool kogi* is rib-eye, a cut exceptional for both its intrinsic tenderness and generous marbling. Another good option are tenderloin tips. Gochujang (Korean chili paste) is available online, at Asian markets, and at a growing number of supermarkets. You could substitute sriracha or other hot sauce. I give a range so you can make these kebabs as fiery or as mild as you want to. Think of kimchi (pickled napa cabbage) as Korean sauerkraut, and yes, you can find it in the produce section of most supermarkets.

Here's an American twist on a Korean barbecue classic. Traditional *bool kogi* starts with wafer-thin rib steaks marinated in a sweet-salty mixture of soy sauce, sugar, sake, and sesame oil. These flavorings caramelize during the cooking, giving the meat a candied sweetness. I've turned the dish into shish kebab, piling the traditional accompaniments—chiles and scallions—onto a skewer. Serve these kebabs as they are, or for a Los Angeles food truck twist, unskewer them on grill-warmed tortillas with kimchi, cucumbers, and Chinatown Barbecue Sauce (page 156).

INGREDIENTS

FOR THE KEBABS

2 bunches scallions, trimmed

6 jalapeño peppers, preferably red

1½ pounds rib-eye steak, cut into ¾-inch cubes

FOR THE MARINADE

½ cup soy sauce

¼ cup sake (or rice wine or sherry)

⅓ cup packed brown (dark or light) or granulated sugar

¼ cup Asian (dark) sesame oil

1 to 3 tablespoons gochujang or favorite hot sauce (optional)

2 cloves garlic or 1 shallot, peeled and roughly chopped

1 teaspoon freshly ground black pepper

2 tablespoons butter, chilled, cut into cubes

Vegetable oil for oiling the grill grate

3 tablespoons toasted sesame seeds (see box, page 69)

OPTIONAL INGREDIENTS FOR SERVING

Small flour tortillas, warmed before serving

Kimchi

Thinly sliced cucumbers

Chinatown Barbecue Sauce (page 156)

1. Finely chop enough scallion greens to obtain ¾ cup. Cut the remaining scallions crosswise into ¾-inch pieces.

2. Cut each jalapeño in half lengthwise and discard the seeds. Cut each half in half crosswise.

3. Thread the beef cubes onto bamboo skewers, alternating with the scallion pieces and jalapeños. Arrange the kebabs in a baking dish just large enough to hold them.

4. Make the marinade: Combine the soy sauce, sake, sugar, sesame oil, gochujang (if using), garlic, and pepper in a blender and puree until smooth. Add ½ cup of the chopped scallion greens and pulse the blender just to mix. (Reserve the remaining ¼ cup scallions for serving.) Pour this mixture over the beef kebabs and let marinate in the refrigerator for 2 to 4 hours, turning the kebabs several times so they marinate evenly.

5. Set up your grill for direct grilling and heat to high.

6. Drain the beef kebabs well and strain the marinade into a saucepan. Boil the marinade for 3 minutes to sterilize it, then whisk in the butter. You'll use this sauce for basting and serving.

7. Brush or scrape the grill grate clean and oil it well. Grill the *bool kogi* kebabs until cooked to taste, 2 to 3 minutes per side (8 to 12 minutes in all) for medium. (In Korean cooking, beef is often done medium to medium-well.) Start basting the kebabs with the boiled marinade after 4 minutes and baste twice more as they cook.

8. Transfer the kebabs to a platter or plates. Pour any reserved basting sauce over them. Sprinkle with scallion greens and sesame seeds. To serve the beef Korean taco-style, unskewer it into warm flour tortillas. Pile on kimchi, cucumbers, and the Chinatown Barbecue Sauce (if using).

INSIDER TIP: Kebabs are one of the easiest ways to grill beef, but you need to keep two things in mind. First, use a relatively fatty cut of beef or add fat in the form of sliced bacon or a butter- or oil-based basting mixture. This adds flavor and keeps the beef moist during grilling. The second is to build your kebab with ingredients that all cook at roughly the same rate.

ROSEMARY-SMOKED VEAL CHOPS

Veal is back after decades of near-pariah status (on account of the cruel conditions under which factory farms raised calves.) A new generation of ranchers and meat companies like Strauss Meats are supplying veal from healthy, humanely raised animals that graze free in pastures. It's about time, because mild, meaty, sweet-tasting veal is one of the most satisfying meats you can grill. I, for one, have missed it. These chops feature one of the coolest smoking techniques on Planet Barbecue: charring fresh rosemary atop the sizzling veal chops with a blowtorch at tableside. Need I say more?

YIELD: Serves 2 and can be multiplied as desired

METHOD: Direct grilling

PREP TIME: 10 minutes, plus 1 hour for marinating the chops

GRILLING TIME: 6 to 8 minutes

INGREDIENTS

2 veal rib chops (each 14 to 16 ounces and 1 to 1¼ inches thick)

Coarse salt (sea or kosher) and cracked or freshly ground black peppercorns

3 tablespoons finely chopped fresh rosemary needles

1 Meyer lemon or conventional lemon for squeezing, plus 1 lemon, halved and seeded for grilling (latter lemon optional)

½ cup best-quality extra virgin olive oil, plus extra for drizzling

Vegetable oil for oiling the grill grate

3 fresh rosemary branches, tied together with butcher's string

4 large sprigs fresh rosemary for flambéing

1. Arrange the veal chops in a baking dish. Generously season each side with salt, pepper, and chopped rosemary. Using a Microplane or other fine-toothed zester, grate the zest of 1 lemon over the veal chops on both sides. Drizzle ¼ cup of extra virgin olive oil over the chops on both sides. Let the chops marinate while you make the basting mixture and light the grill.

2. Place the remaining ¼ cup of olive oil in a bowl. Squeeze in the juice from the zested lemon and mix with a fork.

3. Set up your grill for direct grilling and heat to medium-high. Brush or scrape the grill grate clean and oil it well.

4. Arrange the chops on the grill running diagonal to the bars of the grate. Grill until sizzling and browned on the bottom, giving each chop a quarter turn after 1½ minutes to lay on a crosshatch of grill marks. Turn the chops after 3 to 4 minutes and grill the other side the same way. After 3 minutes of grilling, brush the veal chops with the olive oil and lemon juice mixture, using the tied rosemary branches as a basting brush. Baste often. While you're at it, grill the lemon halves, if using.

5. Continue grilling the veal until both sides are sizzling and browned and the internal temperature is around 140° to 145°F (for veal with a blush of pink in the center); go a little longer for medium (160°F). Alternatively, use the poke test (see page 40): The veal will feel gently yielding when pressed with your finger. Total cooking time will be 3 to 4 minutes per side for medium-rare; 4 to 5 minutes for medium.

6. Transfer the veal chops to a heatproof platter and drizzle with a little more olive oil. Lay a branch of fresh rosemary on each chop. Carefully light a kitchen blowtorch. Direct the flame toward the rosemary branches atop the veal. Burn until the leaves singe, releasing fragrant rosemary smoke. Serve the chops with the grilled lemon.

GRILL/GEAR: You can grill these chops over charcoal or gas, but you'll get the best flavor over a wood or wood-enhanced fire. (Learn how to do the latter on page 21.) You also need butcher's string; Microplane or zester; 2 hardwood chunks or 1½ cups unsoaked wood chips; an instant-read thermometer; and a kitchen blowtorch.

SHOP: Shop for veal chops at butcher shops and high-end supermarkets, or order them online from a company like Lobel's of New York. Look for the words *pastured*, *group raised*, or *free raised*, which usually means the calves roamed free in open pastures and weren't penned up in cages indoors. At the very least, buy veal that displays a sticker reading "Certified Humane Raised and Handled."

This recipe calls for three different rosemary preparations—needles, branches, and sprigs. Be sure to buy plenty.

INSIDER TIP: Veal is much leaner than beef, so you need to grill it at a slightly lower temperature: medium-high instead of high. And because it has such a mild flavor, it picks up smoke like a magnet when you grill it over wood. An oil- or fat-based marinade helps keep it moist; so does conscientious basting during grilling.

PORK

The hog was not the first animal domesticated by man. (That honor goes to the dog.) But for the last 8,000 years, this other four-footed friend has brought us immeasurable pleasure. Without pigs there would be no Boston butt, pork belly, or baby backs. Italians would lack *porchetta*; Chinese, *char siu*; Jamaicans, jerk pork. And nobody would have bacon. In this chapter you'll learn how to grill pork in all its smoky glory: from mustard pulled pork to teriyaki pork loin, from Shanghai pork belly to "swine-apple" kebabs. You'll learn how to smoke-roast baby back ribs; how to butterfly a pork loin to make a pork loin "Reuben"; and how to assemble a real boneless rib sandwich that puts the fast food restaurant version to shame. Read this and pig out. We've been doing it for a long time.

PORK

It used to be that pork was always served medium-well or beyond—a holdover from the now-distant days when undercooked pork bore the risk of giving you trichinosis. Today, even the USDA has cut its minimum safe doneness temperature to 145°F (a point at which it still has a marked blush of pink in the center).

CUT	BLUE	RARE	MEDIUM-RARE	MEDIUM	MEDIUM-WELL	WELL	VERY WELL
Boston butt (Shoulder)					155°–160°F hot gray center; suitable for slicing	175°–185°F hot gray center; suitable for slicing	195°–205°F hot gray center; suitable for pulling
Loin and tenderloin				145°F pink blush center	155°–160°F hot gray center		
Belly						175°–185°F hot gray center; suitable for slicing	
Chops				145°F hot pink center	155°–160°F hot gray center		
Baby back ribs					155°–160°F hot gray center; ribs will have some chew to them	175°–185°F hot gray center; will be very tender	195°–205°F hot gray center; will be fall-off-the-bone tender
Spareribs						175°–185°F hot gray center; will be very tender	195°–205°F hot gray center; will be fall-off-the-bone tender

FIRST-TIMER'S PORK SHOULDER
SERVED WITH MUSTARD SLAW AND MUSTARD BROWN SUGAR BARBECUE SAUCE

Brisket is tricky (whole treatises have been written on its preparation) and steak requires a lot of last-minute legerdemain. So I'll let you in on a little secret: If you're new to the fire and smoke game, grill a pork shoulder. Not only is pulled pork one of the icons of American barbecue—claimed with equal partisanship by Memphians, Carolinians, and Kansas Citians—it's also utterly forgiving. Thanks to its generous fat and natural tenderness, it can withstand severe overcooking or temperature spikes. Cook it low and slow or cook it hotter and faster. Just cook its interior to 200°F and it will always be crusty and tender. What follows is a South Carolina–inspired version—rubbed with mustard powder and sauced with a sweet, smoky, fiery mustard barbecue sauce.

YIELD: Serves 6 to 8

METHOD: Smoke-roasting (indirect grilling with wood smoke)

PREP TIME: 10 minutes for the pork; 15 minutes for the sauce; 10 minutes for the slaw

GRILLING TIME: About 3 hours, plus 1 to 2 minutes for the buns

GRILL/GEAR: For the best results, cook the pork shoulder on a charcoal grill. (It's easy to smoke with charcoal; difficult with gas.) You also need 6 hardwood chunks or 4½ cups wood chips (the latter soaked in water to cover for 30 minutes, then drained) and heavy-duty grill gloves or meat claws.

SHOP: With pork, as in so much in life, you get what you pay for. The best taste comes from a heritage pork breed, like Berkshire or Mangalitsa—hogs raised for their flavor, not just their meat yield. Be sure to buy the top section of the shoulder, the "Boston butt" (it's named for the barrels in which salted pork shoulders were traditionally shipped). The other section of pork shoulder—the picnic shoulder—has a lower ratio of meat to connective tissue and bone.

INGREDIENTS

- 1 tablespoon coarse salt (sea or kosher)
- 1 tablespoon freshly ground black pepper
- 1 tablespoon dry mustard
- 1 tablespoon onion powder
- 1 Boston butt (also known as bone-in pork shoulder roast, 5 to 6 pounds)
- Vegetable oil for oiling the grill grate

- Mustard Brown Sugar Barbecue Sauce (recipe follows)
- Mustard Slaw (recipe follows) or shredded cabbage
- 12 hamburger buns, split
- 4 tablespoons (½ stick) butter, melted
- Pickled Red Onions (optional; page 146)
- Sweet pickle slices (optional)

1. Make the rub: Combine the salt, pepper, dry mustard, and onion powder in a small bowl and stir to mix. Generously season the pork shoulder on all sides with the rub. Store any extra rub in a lidded jar away from heat and light.

2. Set up your grill for indirect grilling and heat to medium. Brush or scrape the grill grate clean and oil it well.

3. Place the pork shoulder, fat side up, on the grate over the drip pan. Add wood chunks or chips to the coals following the instructions on page 21. You need 2 chunks or 1½ cups chips every hour. Indirect grill the pork until it is fall-off-the-bone tender and the internal temperature reaches about 200°F, about 3 hours. (The cooking time will depend on the size of the Boston butt and the heat

Pulling (shredding) the pork with meat claws.

INSIDER TIP: You may be surprised to find pulled pork in this book. Doesn't it require a half-day cook in a smoker? And isn't this a book about grilling, not smoking? Unlike brisket or spareribs, pork shoulder is intrinsically tender, so it's well suited to indirect grilling. The result: You can cook it a *lot* faster than the low and slow method used on the barbecue circuit.

PICKLED RED ONIONS:
Thinly slice 1 large red onion. Separate the slices into rings and soak in red wine vinegar for 20 minutes just to lightly pickle.

of the grill.) Replenish the charcoal as needed, roughly a half chimney every hour.

4. Meanwhile, prepare the Mustard Brown Sugar Barbecue Sauce and the Mustard Slaw.

5. Transfer the cooked pork shoulder to a cutting board and let rest for 10 minutes. Wearing insulated food gloves, break the pork shoulder into meaty chunks. Discard any skin, bones, and large lumps of fat. Using meat claws or forks, tear the pork into meaty shreds. Or finely chop it with a cleaver. Or thinly slice it with a knife.

6. Set up your grill for direct grilling. Brush the cut sides of the buns with melted butter and toast them on the grill, 1 to 2 minutes.

7. Pile the pulled pork onto the buns. Top each with a mound of Mustard Slaw and a spoonful of Mustard Brown Sugar Barbecue Sauce. Add the Pickled Red Onions and pickle slices, if using, and dig in.

MUSTARD BROWN SUGAR BARBECUE SAUCE
YIELD: Makes 2 cups

Yes, I know that tradition calls for cheap yellow mustard. But I like the winey finesse of Dijon mustard.

INGREDIENTS

1 tablespoon butter

1 strip bacon, cut crosswise into thin slivers

1 small onion, peeled and finely chopped

⅔ cup cider vinegar

⅔ cup packed brown sugar, dark or light, or to taste

⅔ cup Dijon mustard

1 tablespoon of your favorite hot sauce, or to taste

Coarse salt (sea or kosher) and freshly ground black pepper, to taste

1. Place the butter in a saucepan and melt over medium heat. Add the bacon and onion and cook, stirring with a wooden spoon, until the onion is golden brown, 4 minutes.

2. Stir in the cider vinegar and bring to a boil. Whisk in the brown sugar, mustard, and hot sauce. Reduce the heat and gently simmer the sauce until mellow and richly flavored, 10 minutes. Correct the seasoning, adding salt, pepper, and additional sugar or hot sauce as needed—the sauce should be sweet, tart, piquant, and very flavorful. Let cool to room temperature for serving.

MUSTARD SLAW

YIELD: Makes 4 cups

Like much of barbecue, slaw is distinctly regional, with mustard slaw associated with South Carolina and Georgia, vinegar slaw found in North Carolina, and creamy coleslaw found just about everywhere else. This one mellows the tang of Dijon mustard with the molasses sweetness of brown sugar.

INGREDIENTS

1 small head green cabbage

⅔ cup Mustard Brown Sugar Barbecue Sauce (page 146), or to taste

½ teaspoon celery seed, or to taste

Coarse salt (sea or kosher) and freshly ground black pepper

1. Cut the cabbage in half and remove the core. Cut the cabbage into 2-inch chunks, transfer to a food processor and finely chop—you should have about 4 cups. Transfer the cabbage to a mixing bowl.

2. Stir in enough of the Mustard Brown Sugar Barbecue Sauce to make the slaw moist, but not so much that it becomes soupy. Add the celery seed. Correct the seasoning, adding additional sauce as needed and salt, pepper, and additional celery seed to taste. The slaw tastes best served within a few hours of making.

PORK LOIN "REUBEN"

The pork loin is one of those blank canvas meat cuts—mild tasting and a great foil for whatever big-flavored ingredients with which you choose to stuff it. Notice I said "stuff": Thanks to its clean cylindrical shape and lack of bones, a loin is easy to butterfly and stuff. It's also lean, so I like to wrap it in bacon to keep the outside moist. The following pork loin channels a Reuben sandwich, and I think you'll find the pastrami, Swiss cheese, and sauerkraut stuffing as delectable as it is unexpected.

INGREDIENTS

1 center-cut pork loin (about 3 pounds)

Coarse salt (sea or kosher) and freshly ground black pepper

3 tablespoons Dijon mustard

6 ounces lean pastrami, thinly sliced

1 cup sauerkraut (not canned), drained well and wrung dry

6 ounces Gruyère cheese, thinly sliced

3 tablespoons chopped fresh chives

4 strips artisanal bacon, like Nueske's

Vegetable oil for oiling the grill grate

Russian Dressing (recipe follows)

1. Butterfly the pork loin: Place the pork loin on a cutting board. Using a long, slender, sharp knife, cut the loin almost in half lengthwise through one side, but not all the way through. Leave both sides attached. Open up the loin as you would a book. Lay a sheet of plastic wrap on top and pound the meat with the side of a cleaver to flatten it slightly. Season the inside with salt and pepper and spread with mustard.

2. Arrange the pastrami over one side of the pork loin, followed by the sauerkraut and cheese slices. Sprinkle with chives. Fold the roast back together (like closing a book).

3. Position four 12-inch pieces of butcher's string on your work surface so that the strings are parallel and roughly 2 inches apart. Lay a bacon strip across the strings so that it runs perpendicular to and in the center of them. Set the pork loin on top of the bacon so that the bacon runs down the length of the pork. Place a second bacon strip on top of the loin. Press the remaining 2 strips against the long sides of the loin. Bring the end strings and then the middle strings over the roast and tie it back into a tight cylinder with the bacon strips in place. Breathe a sigh of relief: The hard part is over. The pork loin can be stuffed to this stage several hours ahead, covered, and refrigerated.

YIELD: Serves 6 to 8

METHOD: Indirect grilling

PREP TIME: 20 minutes

GRILLING TIME: 1 to 1½ hours

GRILL/GEAR: Can be grilled over charcoal or gas. You also need butcher's string and an instant-read thermometer.

SHOP: Here, too, an heirloom pork variety, like Berkshire, Duroc, or Red Wattle, will reward you with an uncommon depth of flavor. One good source for heirloom pork is Heritage Foods USA. There are some wonderful new artisanal sauerkrauts that are traditionally fermented in small batches. Check your local farmers' market.

INSIDER TIP: Unlike a pork shoulder, which you can cook half to death so it will shred, you want to cook a pork loin to temperature: 145°F if you like it with a blush of pink (don't worry: the USDA now says it's safe); 155°F if you like your pork cooked through. Use an instant-read thermometer to guide you.

4. Set up the grill for indirect grilling and heat to medium. Brush or scrape the grill grate clean and oil it well.

5. When ready to cook, place the pork roast on the hot grate, over the drip pan and away from the heat, and cover the grill. Cook the roast until cooked through, 1 to 1½ hours. To test for doneness, insert an instant-read thermometer into the center of the meat; the internal temperature should be about 150°F. Transfer the cooked roast to a cutting board and let it rest for a few minutes, then remove and discard the strings. Cut the pork loin crosswise into ½-inch-thick slices and serve with the Russian Dressing.

RUSSIAN DRESSING

YIELD: Makes 1½ cups

Sure, you could buy commercial Russian dressing, but it's easy to make your own. The advantage: less sugar and fewer chemical additives.

INGREDIENTS

1 cup mayonnaise, preferably Hellmann's or Best Foods

⅓ cup chili sauce or ketchup

¼ cup sweet pickle relish

Place the mayonnaise, chili sauce, and pickle relish in a bowl and whisk to mix. Cover and refrigerate until using; it will keep for at least 3 days in the refrigerator.

Spread the pork with pastrami, sauerkraut, and cheese, and sprinkle with chopped chives.

Tie the pork loin into a tight roll with butcher's string.

PORK TENDERLOIN TERIYAKI

YIELD: Serves 4

METHOD: Direct grilling

PREP TIME: 15 minutes plus 2 to 4 hours for marinating the pork

GRILLING TIME: 9 to 12 minutes

GRILL/GEAR: Can be grilled over charcoal, wood, or gas. Wood smoke isn't really part of the Japanese flavor profile, so this is a great dish to cook on a gas grill.

SHOP: As always, try to source heritage pork from a full-flavored breed, like Kurobuta (Berkshire) or Duroc.

INSIDER TIP: Pork tenderloin tapers to a flat, slender tip. Invariably, this part will become crustier and more well done than the wide end. It's supposed to. That's the beauty of grilling pork tenderloin: You get three different degrees of doneness on a single plate.

I f you like your pork lean, tender, and affordable, grill a tenderloin. It costs a fraction of its beef analogue. It's loaded with flavor, too. And many of us can polish off a whole tenderloin, making it a great serving for one. In this dish, the pork gets the Japanese teriyaki treatment, marinated and basted with a sweet soy, sake, and sesame oil marinade that, when boiled, becomes the sauce. One nontraditional twist: I like to sweeten the marinade with maple syrup. If you like your pork sweet, salty, and crusty, fire up your grill.

INGREDIENTS

½ cup soy sauce

½ cup sake or rice wine

½ cup pure maple syrup

⅓ cup Asian (dark) sesame oil, plus 1 tablespoon for basting

4 scallions, trimmed, white parts flattened with the side of a cleaver, green parts thinly sliced on the diagonal

3 slices (each ¼ inch thick) fresh ginger, flattened with the side of a cleaver

2 cloves garlic, peeled and smashed

1½ to 2 pounds pork tenderloin, trimmed of any silverskin

2 tablespoons butter

Vegetable oil for oiling the grill grate

2 tablespoons sesame seeds, toasted (see page 69), for serving

1. In a large shallow bowl, whisk together the soy sauce, sake, maple syrup, ⅓ cup sesame oil, the scallion whites, and all but 3 tablespoons of the scallion greens, all the ginger, and all the garlic. Add the pork tenderloin, turning with tongs to coat with marinade. Marinate the pork, covered, in the refrigerator for at least 2 hours or as long as 4—the longer, the richer the flavor—turning several times so it marinates evenly.

2. Transfer the pork tenderloin to a wire rack to drain. Strain the marinade into a saucepan and boil until syrupy and reduced to about 1¼ cups, 5 minutes, whisking often. Whisk in the butter to make the sauce glossy. Set aside.

3. Set up your grill for direct grilling and heat to medium-high. Brush or scrape the grill grate clean and oil it well.

4. Brush the pork tenderloin with the remaining tablespoon of sesame oil. Grill until browned on the outside and cooked to the desired internal temperature, 145°F for medium-rare with a blush of pink; 155°F for medium. This will take about 3 minutes per side, 9 to 12 minutes in all. Start basting the pork with some of the boiled marinade after 5 minutes.

5. Transfer the pork tenderloin to a cutting board and let rest for a few minutes, then cut on the diagonal into ¼-inch-thick slices. Fan the pork slices out on a platter or plates, with the remaining boiled marinade (rewarm if desired) spooned over them and the sesame seeds and remaining scallion greens sprinkled on top.

PORCHETTA PORK CHOPS

Porchetta is one of the high holies of Italian barbecue—a whole young pig painstakingly boned, seasoned with an aromatic herb paste of rosemary, sage, and garlic, reassembled, spit-roasted, then sliced crosswise into some of the most luscious, soulfully seasoned pork you'll ever sink your teeth into. Boning a whole pig is beyond the knife skills of most of us, but the herb paste goes well with all cuts of pork, including these monster double-thick pork chops.

INGREDIENTS

¼ cup packed fresh rosemary leaves

¼ cup packed fresh sage leaves

3 cloves garlic, peeled and coarsely chopped

3 tablespoons coarse salt (sea or kosher)

3 tablespoons cracked black peppercorns

1 tablespoon fennel seeds or chopped fresh fennel fronds

2 strips (½ by 2 inches each) orange zest

¼ cup extra virgin olive oil, preferably Italian, or as needed

4 pork porterhouse chops (each 14 to 16 ounces and 2 to 3 inches thick)

Vegetable oil for oiling the grill grate

Fennel Slaw (recipe follows; optional)

YIELD: Serves 4

METHOD: Direct grilling followed by indirect grilling

PREP TIME: 15 minutes plus 2 to 4 hours for marinating the chops

GRILLING TIME: 8 minutes for searing, plus 15 to 20 minutes for indirect grilling

GRILL/GEAR: Can be grilled over charcoal or gas. You also need an instant-read thermometer.

SHOP: You have two options for chops: rib chops or loin chops. The former are more widely available. Order them double thick—that is, two joined chops with one rib bone removed. (Ask your butcher to prepare them.) Pork loin chops (often called pork porterhouse chops) come with a section of tenderloin as well as loin, giving you more bang for the buck. Make friends with your butcher and order them 2 to 3 inches thick.

INSIDER TIP: These chops call for a two-step grilling process: First, you sear them over a hot fire, then you move them to the cooler section of the grill to finish by indirect grilling. This lets you grill a pork chop, no matter how thick, without drying it out. Smoke isn't really part of the Italian flavor profile, so this is a great dish to prepare on a gas grill.

1. Place the rosemary, sage, garlic, salt, pepper, fennel seeds, and orange zest in a food processor (ideally fitted with a small chopping bowl) and finely chop them. (Alternatively, pound the ingredients into a paste in a mortar with a pestle.) Work in enough olive oil to obtain a thick paste.

2. Arrange the pork chops in a nonreactive baking dish. Spoon a few teaspoons of herb paste on both sides of each pork chop, spreading it onto the meat with the back of the spoon. Cover with plastic wrap and marinate in the refrigerator for 2 to 4 hours. (Any extra paste can be stored in the refrigerator for later use; it will keep for at least 3 days.)

3. Set up the grill for a two-zone fire (one side medium-high and the other side fire-free). Brush and scrape the grill grate clean and oil it well. Arrange the chops on a diagonal to the bars of the grill grate. Grill for 2 minutes, then rotate 90 degrees to lay on a crosshatch of grill marks. Repeat on the other side.

4. Using tongs, transfer the chops to the cooler side of the grill, close the lid, and continue to cook until the internal temperature when read on an instant-read thermometer (insert the probe through the side of the chop) is 150°F, 15 to 20 minutes, or as needed. The meat will still be slightly pink inside. Transfer the chops to a platter or plates and let rest for a minute or so before serving with the Fennel Slaw.

FENNEL SLAW

YIELD: Serves 4

This crisp anise-y fennel slaw makes a refreshing accompaniment to *porchetta* pork chops.

INGREDIENTS

1 large fennel bulb (ideally with a few of the feathery green leaves attached)

3 tablespoons fresh lemon juice

Coarse salt (sea or kosher) and freshly ground black pepper

1 navel orange, peeled and pith cut off, thinly sliced, juices reserved

⅓ cup extra virgin olive oil, preferably Italian

1. Cut the fennel crosswise into paper-thin slices. This is easiest done on a mandoline, but you can also use a food processor fitted with a thin slicing disk. While you're at it, finely chop 2 tablespoons of fennel leaves.

2. Combine the lemon juice, 1 teaspoon salt, ½ teaspoon pepper, and any orange juices in a medium-size bowl. Whisk until the salt crystals dissolve. Whisk in the olive oil. Add the fennel and orange slices and stir to mix. Correct the seasoning, adding salt or lemon juice to taste; the slaw should be highly seasoned. Sprinkle on the chopped fennel leaves and serve.

PORK BELLY STEAMED BUNS
WITH CHINATOWN BARBECUE SAUCE

How did we live without pork belly? We didn't, of course (we ate bacon). But pork belly as a meat you'd cook in its own right is a recent arrival to most American grills. It turns out that pork belly is easy and forgiving to grill, satisfying to serve, and easy on the wallet. Here's my Pac-Rim version, seasoned with a Chinese five-spice powder rub, grilled smoky and tender, and served on steamed buns.

YIELD: Makes 12 steamed buns, enough to serve 3 to 6

METHOD: Smoke-roasting (indirect grilling), followed by direct grilling

PREP TIME: 20 minutes

GRILLING TIME: 3 to 3½ hours

GRILL/GEAR: Can be grilled over charcoal or gas. You also need an instant-read thermometer and 2 to 4 hardwood chunks or 3 cups of wood chips (optional), the latter soaked in water for 30 minutes, then drained.

INGREDIENTS

FOR THE PORK AND THE RUB

1 piece (3 pounds) pork belly, skin removed

1 tablespoon coarse salt (sea or kosher)

1 tablespoon turbinado sugar, such as Sugar in the Raw brand

1 tablespoon Chinese five-spice powder

1 tablespoon freshly ground black pepper

½ teaspoon ground cinnamon

Vegetable oil for oiling the grill grate

FOR SERVING

12 Chinese steamed buns or slider rolls

2 cucumbers, peeled, seeded, and cut into matchstick slivers

1 bunch scallions, trimmed, white and green parts sliced sharply on the diagonal

Chinatown Barbecue Sauce (recipe follows)

3 tablespoons sesame seeds, toasted (page 69), for serving

1. Using a sharp knife, score both sides of the pork belly in a crosshatch pattern. The cuts should be ⅛ inch deep and ½ inch apart.

2. Make the rub: Place the salt, sugar, five-spice powder, pepper, and cinnamon in a small bowl and mix with a fork. Sprinkle the rub over the top, bottom, and sides of the pork belly, rubbing it into the meat with your fingers.

3. Set up your grill for indirect grilling and heat to medium-low. Brush or scrape the grill grate clean and oil it well.

4. Arrange the pork belly, skin-removed side up, on the grill grate over the drip pan away from the heat. Add wood chunks or chips to the coals (if using). Cook the pork belly until it is sizzling and browned on top and its internal temperature is 165°F, 3 to 3½ hours. Transfer the pork belly to a cutting board and let it cool slightly.

5. Meanwhile, set up your grill for direct grilling and heat to high. Be sure to leave a fire-free safety zone.

6. Cut the pork belly crosswise into ½-inch-thick slices. Arrange these slices on the grate and grill until sizzling and browned on both sides, 1 to 2 minutes per side. Don't overcrowd the grill. The melting fat may cause flare-ups—you want to leave plenty of maneuvering room to dodge the flames.

7. To serve, cut the grilled pork belly slices crosswise into 3-inch pieces. Place on steamed buns (or slider buns) with cucumber, scallions, and Chinatown Barbecue Sauce. Sprinkle the pork with sesame seeds and serve.

CHINATOWN BARBECUE SAUCE

YIELD: Makes 1¼ cups

Sweet and nutty (sesame oil will do that), with the signature Asian flavors of scallion and ginger, this barbecue sauce goes exceedingly well with pork, beef, and poultry. Be sure to use an Asian-style (dark-roasted) sesame oil, like Japanese Kadoya.

INGREDIENTS

¾ cup hoisin sauce

2 tablespoons rice wine, sake, or dry sherry

2 tablespoons honey

1 tablespoon soy sauce

2 tablespoons Asian (dark) sesame oil

2 tablespoons chopped fresh cilantro

2 teaspoons minced fresh ginger

2 teaspoons minced scallion, white part only

Combine the hoisin sauce, rice wine, honey, soy sauce, sesame oil, cilantro, ginger, and scallion in a saucepan and gently simmer over medium-low heat until thickened and richly flavored, 5 minutes, stirring from time to time to prevent scorching. Let the sauce cool to room temperature before serving. The sauce can be made ahead, covered, and refrigerated. It will keep for at least a week.

BLACK PEPPER BABY BACKS
WITH WHISKEY VANILLA GLAZE

If (for most people) ribs epitomize barbecue, the baby back epitomizes ribs. Cut from high on the hog (next to the backbone), baby backs have tender meat (more so than spareribs), abundant fat, and a convenient shape and size that makes one rack perfect for feeding one or two people. But don't ribs require low and slow smoking for the better part of a day? Well, that's one way to prepare ribs (you'll find this technique in my book *Project Smoke*). But ribs can also be grilled using the indirect method—in particular, a technique I call smoke-roasting (see page 21). Slow-smoked ribs are all about tenderness; smoke-roasted ribs retain some of the meaty chew that makes pork chops or loin so satisfying to bite into. You'll still get plenty of smoke flavor thanks to adding hardwood chunks or chips to the fire. The following ribs keep the seasonings simple: pepper, paprika, salt, brown sugar, and celery seed. The emphasis is on the pork. And because we Americans like our ribs sweet, I've added a whiskey brown sugar glaze with an unexpected note: the perfumed scent of vanilla extract.

YIELD: Serves 4 to 8 and can be multiplied as desired

METHOD: Smoke-roasting (indirect grilling)

PREP TIME: 20 minutes

GRILLING TIME: 3 to 3½ hours

GRILL/GEAR: If you want a pronounced smoke flavor, cook these ribs on a charcoal grill. You also need: 4 hardwood chunks or 3 cups hickory or other hardwood chips (the latter soaked in water for 30 minutes, then drained) and a rib rack (for cooking the ribs upright, optional).

SHOP: The usual caveats apply here: heirloom pork when possible. A 2½-pound rack will feed 1 to 2 people as part of a meal. Alternatively, use St. Louis style ribs, which are spareribs with the rib tips removed, trimmed to a rectangular shape. Because they are meatier and better marbled than baby backs, they may take longer to cook.

INSIDER TIP: "Fall-off-the-bone tender." Never have five words done more harm to the notion of what constitutes good eating. Fall-off-the-bone tenderness usually results from steaming or boiling ribs—a practice frowned upon in Raichlendia, just as it is at the big barbecue competitions, like Memphis in May and the American Royal. No, a proper rib is supposed to have a little chew to it—that's why God gave us teeth.

Ribs have a papery membrane (the pleura) on the concave side. I like to remove it for aesthetic reasons, which is easily done with a butter knife. Slide the blade under the skin and pry it away from the bones, then grab one end with a dishcloth or paper towel and gently pull it off the ribs. If you can't find it, it may have been removed by the butcher beforehand. There's no great harm in leaving it on.

INGREDIENTS

FOR THE RIBS AND RUB

4 racks baby back ribs (each 2 to 2½ pounds—membranes removed—see Insider Tip)

3 tablespoons cracked black peppercorns

3 tablespoons smoked or sweet paprika

3 tablespoons coarse salt (sea or kosher)

3 tablespoons packed brown sugar, dark or light

1 teaspoon celery seed

FOR THE GLAZE

½ cup rye, bourbon, or other whiskey

½ cup packed brown sugar, dark or light

8 tablespoons (1 stick) unsalted butter

1 teaspoon pure vanilla extract

Vegetable oil for oiling the grill grate

1. Place the ribs on a sheet pan. Combine the peppercorns, paprika, salt, brown sugar, and celery seed in a small bowl and mix with your fingers, breaking up any lumps in the brown sugar. Sprinkle the rub on the ribs on both sides, rubbing it into the meat with your fingertips, about 3 tablespoons per rack. Store any leftover rub in a sealed jar away from heat and light.

2. Make the glaze: Combine the whiskey, brown sugar, butter, and vanilla in a saucepan and boil until syrupy, 4 to 6 minutes, whisking to mix. Set the glaze aside.

3. Set up your grill for indirect grilling and heat to medium-low. Brush or scrape the grill grate clean and oil it well. Add half the wood chunks or chips to the coals. Arrange the ribs on the grate, bone side down, away from the heat, and lower the lid.

4. Smoke-roast the ribs until sizzling, browned, and tender. When ready, the meat will have shrunk back from the ends of the bones by about ½ inch and the ribs will be tender enough to pull apart with your fingers. Replenish the wood and charcoal as needed. Total cooking time will be 3 to 3½ hours. The last 30 minutes of cooking, baste the ribs with the glaze. Baste twice more before serving. Pour any remaining glaze over the ribs and serve.

NOTES: For sizzling crusty ribs, brush the racks on both sides with glaze and move them directly over one of the fire zones for the last few minutes of cooking. Direct grill for a couple of minutes per side.

So how do you grill 4 racks of ribs for a party on the standard 22½-inch kettle grill most of us have in our backyards? The answer is a rib condominium, aka a rib rack. You stand the ribs upright in the rack (which also helps drain off the fat).

THE 3-2-1 RIB SANDWICH

YIELD: Makes 2 sandwiches, enough to serve 4 to 8

METHOD: Smoke-roasting (indirect grilling)

PREP TIME: 20 minutes

GRILLING TIME: 4 hours

GRILL/GEAR: For the best results, use a charcoal grill. You also need 4 hardwood chunks or 3 cups hardwood chips, the latter soaked in water to cover for 30 minutes, then drained; 2 sheets heavy-duty aluminum foil, each 24 by 18 inches; and small bamboo skewers or toothpicks (optional).

SHOP: The usual advice about heirloom pork (see page 145).

INSIDER TIP: The secret to this sandwich is to *overcook* the ribs. You do this by wrapping them in foil so they steam as well as roast. This allows you to pop out the bones.

The 3-2-1 rib is the most frequently searched recipe on my website. The reason is simple: People still want their ribs fall-off-the-bone tender (despite my admonition to the contrary—see Insider Tip on page 158). One of the best ways to achieve this is to smoke the ribs uncovered for 3 hours, then wrapped in foil for 2 hours, then uncovered and slathered with sauce for 1 more hour. Hence 3-2-1 ribs. The result is so tender, you can pop out the bones, echoing the soft texture of the extruded meat product sold as "ribs" at fast food restaurants, but this version actually tastes like ribs. Which brings me to this sandwich. I've shortened the cooking time so that these ribs are really 2-1-1. This sounds less alphanumerically satisfying, but you'll get a better rib. Thanks to Rob Baas for the idea.

INGREDIENTS

2 racks baby back ribs, each 2 to 2½ pounds, membranes removed (see Insider Tip, page 158)

6 tablespoons of your favorite barbecue rub, or to taste

Vegetable oil for oiling the grill grate

6 tablespoons packed brown sugar, dark or light

4 tablespoons unsalted butter, thinly sliced

¼ cup apple cider or juice

1 cup Chipotle Molasses Barbecue Sauce (recipe follows) or other favorite barbecue sauce

2 loaves Italian-style bread (softer crust than French bread), sliced in half lengthwise through the side

4 tablespoons (½ stick) unsalted butter, melted

Dill pickle slices, for serving (optional)

1 sweet onion or pickled onion, thinly sliced, for serving (optional)

1. Set up your grill for indirect grilling and heat to medium-low.

2. With the racks of ribs meat side down, use the tip of a sharp paring knife to make shallow lengthwise incisions on either side of the rib bones (close to the bones). This step makes it easier to remove the bones once the ribs are cooked.

3. Sprinkle the rub on both sides of each rack, using your fingertips to rub it into the meat.

4. Brush or scrape the grill grate clean and oil it well. Arrange the ribs on the grate, bone side down, away from the heat. Add half the wood to the fire. Smoke-roast the ribs until sizzling and browned, about 2 hours. Add the remaining wood after 1 hour; replenish the charcoal as needed.

5. Layer 2 large sheets of aluminum foil (approximately 18 by 24 inches) shiny side down on a counter or work surface. Lay 1 rack of ribs, meat side up, in the center of the foil. Sprinkle it with half the brown sugar and dot with half the butter. Lay the second rack of ribs on top of the first, meat side up. Sprinkle with the remaining sugar and dot with the remaining butter. Bring up the sides of the foil and pour the apple cider over the ribs. Tightly wrap the ribs in the foil, crimping the edges to form a tight seal.

6. Return the foil-wrapped ribs to the grill and continue to cook for 1½ hours: The ribs should be fall-off-the-bone tender.

7. Unwrap the ribs and discard the foil. (Take care not to burn yourself on the escaping steam.) Pull on a bone: It should come out cleanly and easily.

8. Remove the remaining bones from both racks of ribs. Generously brush the ribs on all sides with the barbecue sauce. Place the ribs on the grill side by side for another 30 to 60 minutes to set the sauce.

9. To serve, brush the cut sides of the Italian bread with melted butter and toast over one of the fire zones of the grill, 1 to 2 minutes per side. Arrange one rack of boneless ribs on each loaf of bread. Top with pickles and onions, if using, and slather more sauce on top. Assemble the other sandwich the same way. Slice crosswise into 3-inch sections to make individual sandwiches. To make them easier to eat, pin each with a small bamboo skewer or long toothpick. Serve any remaining barbecue sauce on the side.

CHIPOTLE MOLASSES BARBECUE SAUCE

YIELD: Makes about 3 cups

Think of this as your basic brown sugar-molasses sweet barbecue sauce turbocharged with chipotle chiles. The Sambuca adds an unexpected note of anise.

INGREDIENTS

2 cups ketchup

¼ cup bourbon

¼ cup Dijon mustard

¼ cup packed dark brown sugar

2 tablespoons molasses

2 tablespoons Worcestershire sauce

1 tablespoon of your favorite hot sauce

1 tablespoon Sambuca or other anise-flavored liqueur, or to taste

1 to 2 canned chipotle chiles, minced, with 1 to 2 teaspoons of the can juices

½ teaspoon granulated garlic

½ teaspoon liquid smoke

Combine all the ingredients in a deep, heavy saucepan and bring to a boil over medium heat. Reduce the heat slightly and simmer the sauce, uncovered, until thick and richly flavored, 10 to 15 minutes. Correct the seasoning, adding any flavoring you need. To store, transfer the sauce to clean glass jars and let cool to room temperature. Refrigerate until serving; the sauce will keep for at least a week.

"SWINE-APPLE" KEBABS
(PORK, PINEAPPLE, AND JALAPENO)

When the "swine-apple" lit up the blogosphere a few years ago, it seemed like a revolutionary idea. You'd smoke pork (in some versions, loin, in other versions, ribs) inside of a hollowed fresh pineapple. Great name and interesting exchange of flavors. There was just one problem—the pork wound up stewed, not roasted or smoked. Well, the idea haunted me until I finally figured out a way to prepare it with the results I was looking for. Yes, the brash sweet-sour of pineapple has an affinity for pork; but the secret is to expose both to the searing heat of the fire, not to attempt to cook one inside the other. Which brings me to these "swine-apple" kebabs: pork, pineapple, and jalapeño peppers—all fire, fruit, and spice.

YIELD: Serves 4

METHOD: Direct grilling

PREP TIME: 20 minutes

GRILLING TIME: 8 to 12 minutes

GRILL/GEAR: Can be grilled over charcoal, wood, or gas. You also need 8-inch bamboo skewers and a sheet of heavy-duty aluminum foil, folded in thirds like a business letter, for a grill shield.

SHOP: Make your life easier— buy a pineapple that's already peeled and cored. Choose it by color: Dark yellow fruit tends to be sweeter and more flavorful than paler fruit.

INSIDER TIP: Use a fatty cut of pork for these kebabs. Fat equals flavor, of course, and as it melts, it bastes the other ingredients. Good candidates include country-style ribs (which may or may not come with bones) or pork neck or pork shoulder. The latter requires a little knifesmanship to cut the meat away from the bone, but it's worth the effort.

INGREDIENTS

FOR THE GLAZE

4 tablespoons (½ stick) unsalted butter

2 cloves garlic, peeled and thinly sliced

¼ cup chopped fresh cilantro, plus 3 tablespoons for serving

¾ cup pineapple juice

¼ cup dark rum

1 tablespoon soy sauce

FOR THE PORK KEBABS

½ fresh pineapple, peeled and cored (see Note)

4 jalapeño peppers

1 medium-size onion, peeled

1½ pounds boneless country-style pork ribs, cut into 1-inch cubes (choose ribs with plenty of visible fat)

1 tablespoon extra virgin olive oil, or as needed

Coarse salt (sea or kosher) and freshly ground black pepper

Vegetable oil for oiling the grill grate

1. Make the glaze: Melt the butter in a small saucepan over medium heat. Add the garlic and ¼ cup cilantro and cook until the garlic is lightly browned, 2 minutes. Stir in the pineapple juice. Increase the heat to high and boil the mixture until reduced by one third, 3 minutes. Stir in the rum and soy sauce and boil the glaze until syrupy, 3 minutes.

2. Cut the pineapple into 1-inch cubes. Cut the jalapeños in half lengthwise; seed them and cut each half in half crosswise. Cut the onion in half crosswise and cut each half into 6 wedges. Break the wedges into layers. You'll use the larger outside layers for the kebabs. Save the inside pieces for another use.

3. Thread the pineapple, jalapeños, onions, and pork on bamboo skewers, alternating ingredients. Arrange on a sheet pan. Brush on all sides with olive oil and season with salt and pepper.

4. Set up the grill for direct grilling and heat to high. Brush or scrape the grill grate clean and oil it well.

5. Arrange the pork kebabs on the grill grate and grill until browned on all sides and cooked through, 2 to 3 minutes per side, 8 to 12 minutes in all. Start basting the kebabs with glaze after 4 minutes and brush several times during the grilling. If the exposed ends of the bamboo skewers start to burn, slide an aluminum foil grill shield under them to protect them. Transfer the kebabs to a platter or plates. Spoon any remaining glaze over them, sprinkle with the 3 tablespoons fresh cilantro, and dig in.

NOTE: Reserve the remaining pineapple half for another use, such as a salsa, or for just enjoying on its own.

LEMONGRASS PORK BITES

emongrass and pork are a classic Vietnamese flavor combination. They come together here in these sizzling bite-size kebabs. A section of lemongrass stands in for the traditional bamboo skewer; grilling releases its aromatic oils. You eat the meat right off the lemongrass stalk.

YIELD: Serves 4

METHOD: Direct grilling

PREP TIME: 15 minutes plus 1 to 2 hours for marinating the pork

GRILLING TIME: 2 to 4 minutes

GRILL/GEAR: Can be grilled over charcoal, wood, or gas.

INGREDIENTS

FOR THE MARINADE/SAUCE

3 cloves garlic, peeled and minced

¼ cup granulated sugar

1 teaspoon freshly and coarsely ground black pepper

½ cup fresh lime juice

½ cup Asian fish sauce

¼ cup chopped fresh cilantro

2 Thai chiles or other hot peppers, sliced crosswise paper-thin

¼ cup water

FOR THE KEBABS

1½ pounds pork tenderloin, trimmed of silverskin

6 to 8 stalks fresh lemongrass

3 tablespoons Asian (dark) sesame oil or vegetable oil

Vegetable oil for oiling the grill grate

¼ cup finely chopped toasted peanuts

1. Make the marinade/sauce: Place the garlic, 2 tablespoons of sugar, and the pepper in a mixing bowl. Pound to a paste with the back of a wooden spoon. Stir in the remaining sugar, lime juice, and fish sauce and whisk until the sugar crystals are dissolved. Stir in the cilantro, chiles, and water. Set the marinade aside.

2. Cut the pork crosswise sharply on the diagonal into ¼-inch-thick slices. Make three 1-inch slits in each slice, one an inch from the top, one in the middle, and one an inch from the bottom.

3. Trim the dark green leaves off the lemongrass stalks. Cut each stalk crosswise into 5-inch sections. Insert 1 piece of lemongrass in each pork slice, weaving it between the slits. Arrange the skewered pork in a baking dish in a single layer.

4. Spoon half the marinade over the pork, turning the pieces to coat both sides. Marinate in the refrigerator for 1 to 2 hours, the longer the better. Reserve the remaining half of the marinade for serving.

Make sure the slits in the pork are evenly spaced. Then weave the slices onto the lemongrass stalks.

5. Drain the pork slices well on a wire rack over a sheet pan. Lightly brush the pork on both sides with sesame oil.

6. Set up your grill for direct grilling and heat to high. Brush or scrape the grill grate clean and oil it well.

Arrange the pork slices on the grate. Grill until the pork is sizzling and browned on both sides and cooked through, 1 to 2 minutes per side. Sprinkle the pork with the chopped peanuts and serve at once with the remaining marinade in small bowls so you can spoon it on top.

SHOP: You'll need one special ingredient here: fresh lemongrass. You can find this quintessentially Southeast Asian herb (think herbal lemon flavor without the acidity) in the produce section of many supermarkets (look for it with the packaged fresh herbs). However, it's a lot more economical to buy it by the bunch at an Asian market.

INSIDER TIP: Usually we add flavor to a kebab by means of a rub or marinade. In this one, a big part of the flavor comes from the skewer itself: a section of lemongrass. Can't find lemongrass? Use another flavorful skewer, such as sugarcane (Melissas.com sells precut sugarcane swizzle sticks) or even cinnamon sticks.

LAMB

Quick: What's the world's most popular meat for grilling? If you come from Texas (not to mention Tuscany or Argentina), you'll probably say beef. If you come from the American barbecue belt (or Germany or Eastern Europe), you'll name pork. But on any given night on Planet Barbecue, more people are likely grilling lamb than any other meat. The lamb belt begins in the southern Mediterranean (think Italian *scottadito*—"finger burner" lamb chops stung with three-alarm doses of hot red pepper flakes and black pepper). From there it's on to North Africa (try the Tunisian lamb kebabs on page 178), the Middle and Near East (see the kofta on page 188), India with its tandoori (page 170), Indonesia with its saté, all the way down to New Zealand, where the sheep population outnumbers humans twenty to one. Want to grill something different this evening? Try lamb.

LEG OF LAMB
WITH TANDOORI SEASONINGS

YIELD: Serves 6 to 8

METHOD: Indirect grilling

PREP TIME: 20 minutes to make the marinade plus 12 to 24 hours for marinating the lamb

GRILLING TIME: About 1½ hours

GRILL/GEAR: Can be grilled over charcoal or gas. You also need a food processor.

SHOP: You've got two options for lamb: bone-in or boneless. Bone-in looks more impressive (and it's how you'd get your leg of lamb in India). But boneless is easier to slice. Naan is Indian flatbread. One widely available brand is Tandoor Chef.

Tandoori is one of the world's great barbecued lamb dishes—the meat marinated in a pungent paste of ginger, garlic, chiles, spices, and yogurt. The "pit" is remarkable, too: a large charcoal-burning clay cooker called a tandoor, that thanks to its unique urn-like shape, roasts the meat by both direct and indirect grilling. The result? Lamb that is at once crusty and tender, full-flavored, and intensely aromatic. Don't be intimidated by the long list of ingredients. It's really just a dump-and-mix marinade you can prepare in a food processor in 10 minutes.

INGREDIENTS

FOR THE TANDOORI MARINADE

6 cloves garlic, peeled and coarsely chopped

3 shallots, peeled and coarsely chopped

1 piece (2 inches) ginger, peeled and coarsely chopped

1 fresh turmeric root (about 2 inches long), peeled and coarsely chopped, or 1 tablespoon ground turmeric

4 jalapeño peppers, coarsely chopped (for milder tandoori, remove the seeds)

½ cup chopped fresh cilantro, plus ¼ cup for serving

1 tablespoon coarse salt (sea or kosher)

1 tablespoon freshly ground black pepper

2 teaspoons ground coriander

2 teaspoons ground cumin

1 teaspoon ground cardamom

1 teaspoon finely grated fresh lemon zest

½ teaspoon ground nutmeg

½ teaspoon ground cinnamon

⅓ cup vegetable oil

¼ cup fresh lemon juice

3 tablespoons Dijon mustard

½ teaspoon orange food coloring (optional)

3 cups plain Greek-style whole milk yogurt

FOR THE LAMB

1 leg of lamb (5 to 6 pounds if bone-in; 3½ to 4 pounds if boneless)

Vegetable oil for oiling the grill grate

5 tablespoons salted butter, melted, for basting

FOR SERVING

1 large sweet onion, peeled and thinly sliced crosswise

1 bunch of cilantro, torn into sprigs

3 lemons, 2 sliced lengthwise into wedges, 1 sliced in rounds, for serving

Flaky salt, such as Maldon, and cracked black peppercorns

Naan (optional)

1. Make the tandoori marinade: Place the garlic, shallots, ginger, turmeric, jalapeños, ½ cup chopped cilantro, salt, pepper, coriander, cumin, cardamom, lemon zest, nutmeg, and cinnamon in a food processor and finely chop. With the motor running, add the oil in a thin stream. Process to a coarse paste. Work in the lemon juice, mustard, and food coloring (if using). Work in the yogurt.

2. Prepare the leg of lamb: Using the tip of a paring knife, make a series of small slits in the lamb, ½ inch deep and wide and 1½ inches apart. Place the lamb in a baking dish. Slather with the tandoori marinade, forcing it into the slits with a spatula. Marinate in the refrigerator for at least 12 hours, ideally 24, turning several times so the lamb marinates evenly.

3. Set up your grill for indirect grilling and heat to medium-high. Brush or scrape the grill grate clean and oil it well. Place the leg of lamb, fat side up, in the center of the grate over the drip pan and away from the heat. Close the lid and cook the lamb until crusty and browned on the outside and cooked to taste, 1¼ to 1½ hours for medium, 15 to 30 minutes more for well-done. (In India, this recipe would generally be cooked to well-done.) Halfway through cooking, start basting the lamb with melted butter, and continue basting every 15 minutes. Transfer to a platter and baste one more time before serving.

4. Place the lamb on a bed of sliced onions and cilantro sprigs, and sprinkle with the reserved chopped cilantro, lemon rounds, flaky salt, and cracked black pepper. Serve with lemon wedges for squeezing and naan, if using, warmed on the grill.

ASIAN-FLAVORED LAMB SHOULDER

YIELD: Serves 4 to 6

METHOD: Indirect grilling

PREP TIME: 10 minutes, plus 10 minutes for the sauce

GRILLING TIME: 3 to 3½ hours

The shoulder is one of my favorite cuts of lamb—well-marbled and full-flavored, so it comes out rich, moist, and crusty. This one sounds an Asian note, with a Chinese five-spice powder rub and a hoisin barbecue sauce. It's as simple to prepare as it is impressive, and you can serve it whole as a roast or shredded on buns to make sliders.

INGREDIENTS

1 lamb shoulder (about 3½ pounds)

2 cloves garlic, peeled and cut lengthwise into matchstick slivers

2 pieces (1 inch each) fresh ginger, peeled and cut lengthwise (along the grain) into matchstick slivers

1 tablespoon coarse salt (sea or kosher)

1 tablespoon turbinado sugar, such as Sugar in the Raw brand

1 tablespoon Chinese five-spice powder

1 tablespoon freshly ground black pepper

Hoisin Barbecue Sauce (recipe follows)

1. Using the tip of a paring knife, make a series of small slits in the lamb, ½ inch deep and wide and 1½ inches apart. In half of the slits insert garlic slivers and in half insert ginger slivers, being sure to intermix the flavorings. Tie the shoulder into a compact oblong using butcher's string.

2. Combine the salt, sugar, five-spice powder, and pepper in a small bowl and mix them together with your fingers. Season the lamb on all sides with the rub. Let it marinate in the refrigerator while you light the grill.

3. Set up your grill for indirect grilling and heat to medium. Smoke isn't usually part of the flavor profile for this kind of dish, but if you like a smoke flavor, add the wood to the coals or your gas grill's smoker box (see page 22).

4. Indirect grill the lamb until darkly browned on the outside and cooked to taste: 195°F on an instant-read thermometer for well-done, 3 to 3½ hours (the meat won't shred properly unless it's cooked to this temperature). If you prefer your lamb rarer, go for 135°F for medium-rare, or 150°F for medium, but you'll need to slice the lamb, not shred it.

5. Transfer the lamb to a cutting board and let it rest, loosely draped with aluminum foil, for 5 minutes or so. Then pull it into meaty shreds with meat claws or forks for serving (or chop it or slice it). Serve with Hoisin Barbecue Sauce.

GRILL/GEAR: Can be grilled over charcoal or gas. You also need butcher's string (optional); meat claws (optional); 2 hardwood chunks or 1½ cups wood chips (optional; the latter soaked for 30 minutes, then drained); and an instant-read thermometer.

SHOP: You need to know about one special ingredient here—five-spice powder—a smoky, licorice-flavored Chinese seasoning composed of star anise, fennel, cinnamon, cloves, and pepper (the formula varies by manufacturer). Look for it at an Asian market, well-stocked supermarket, or online.

INSIDER TIP: There are several ways to serve this lamb shoulder: sliced with Hoisin Barbecue Sauce (recipe follows), for example, or chopped or pulled and piled on slider rolls or into steamed buns.

HOISIN BARBECUE SAUCE

YIELD: About 2 cups

You could think of hoisin sauce as the Chinese version of ketchup—a dark, thick, sweet-salty soybean-based condiment with distinctive anise-y overtones. Look for it in the Asian foods section of most supermarkets. Good brands include Pearl River Bridge, Ma Ling, Amoy, and Koon Chun.

INGREDIENTS

½ cup hoisin sauce

3 tablespoons Chinese rice wine, sake, or dry sherry

2 tablespoons soy sauce

2 tablespoons honey

2 tablespoons Asian (dark) sesame oil

1 to 2 tablespoons rice vinegar or distilled white vinegar, or to taste

1 teaspoon minced fresh ginger

½ teaspoon garlic powder or minced fresh garlic

Combine all the ingredients in a nonreactive saucepan and slowly bring to a boil over medium heat. Reduce the heat slightly and simmer the sauce, uncovered, until richly flavored, 5 minutes. The sauce should be thick but pourable—if too thick, add a few tablespoons of water. Use right away or transfer to a jar; cool to room temperature, cover, and refrigerate. The sauce will keep for at least 1 week.

ASIAN-FLAVORED LAMB SLIDERS

YIELD: Makes 12 to 16 sliders

Here's one of my favorite ways to serve lamb sliders—on sweet Hawaiian slider rolls or on Chinese steamed buns. Kimchi is available at most supermarkets, at Asian markets, or online. All of these accompaniments are available on Amazon.

INGREDIENTS

1 hothouse (English) cucumber, thinly sliced (see Notes, page 205)

12 King's Hawaiian slider rolls or 16 Asian steamed buns

3 tablespoons butter, melted (optional)

Asian-Flavored Lamb Shoulder, cooked to 195°F and shredded (page 172)

Hoisin Barbecue Sauce (page 173)

1½ cups kimchi (Korean pickled cabbage)

1. Place cucumber slices on the bottom section of each bun. (The cucumber keeps the bun from getting soggy.) For extra flavor, brush the cut sides of the slider rolls or buns with melted butter and toast on a hot grill before adding the cucumber.

2. Pile the lamb onto the buns atop the cucumbers and finish with more cucumber slices and a spoonful of Hoisin Barbecue Sauce. Add kimchi and dig in.

GRILLED LAMB STEAKS
WITH MINT CHIMICHURRI

YIELD: Serves 4

METHOD: Direct grilling

PREP TIME: 15 minutes

GRILLING TIME: 6 minutes

GRILL/GEAR: Can be grilled over charcoal, wood, or gas. You also need a food processor.

SHOP: You don't often find lamb steaks in the supermarket meat department. Order them from your butcher.

INSIDER TIP: Most of the lamb sold in the United States comes from New Zealand and Australia. American lamb may cost a bit more, but the flavor is well worth the price. Can't find lamb steaks? This preparation works great for lamb rib or loin chops.

The "steak" is one of my favorite cuts of lamb—a ¾-inch cross section of the thigh possessing the rich flavor of leg of lamb and much of the tenderness of a chop. It's also a bargain, costing substantially less than rib chops or loin chops. It even looks cool, thanks to the elegant circle of leg bone in the center. The following recipe takes advantage of lamb's natural affinity for mint—in particular, a mint chimichurri. Think of it as lamb channeled by Argentinean asado.

INGREDIENTS

FOR THE MINT CHIMICHURRI

2 cups fresh mint leaves, washed and stemmed

2 cloves garlic, peeled and coarsely chopped

Coarse salt (sea or kosher) and freshly ground black pepper

½ teaspoon finely grated fresh lemon zest

¼ cup fresh lemon juice

¼ cup cold water

⅓ cup vegetable oil, plus more to oil the grill grate

¼ cup extra virgin olive oil, or more vegetable oil

FOR THE LAMB

4 lamb steaks (cut from the leg), each about ¾ inch thick

Coarse salt (sea or kosher) and freshly ground black pepper

1. Make the mint chimichurri: Finely chop the mint and garlic in a food processor. Add the salt and pepper (about ½ teaspoon each), lemon zest, lemon juice, and water and process to blend. Slowly add the vegetable and olive oils through the feed tube with the machine running to make a thick sauce. Taste for seasoning, adding more salt or lemon juice as necessary; the sauce should be highly seasoned. Serve within 2 hours of making.

2. Set up the grill for direct grilling and heat to high. Brush or scrape the grill grate clean and oil it well.

3. Season the lamb steaks generously on both sides with salt and pepper. Grill until done to your liking, about 3 minutes per side for medium-rare. Let the steaks rest for a minute. Serve with the mint chimichurri.

LAMB CHOP HOT POPS

Italians call these spicy grilled lamb chops *scottadito*—"finger scorchers"—served so hot off the grill, they burn your fingers when you dig in. And with your fingers is precisely how you're supposed to eat them. As with most Italian grilling, the seasonings are pretty simple—rosemary, garlic, salt, and pepper—with hot red pepper flakes to notch up the heat.

INGREDIENTS

1 bunch rosemary

3 pounds lamb rib chops, bones frenched (scraped clean)

Coarse salt (sea or kosher) and cracked or freshly ground black peppercorns

3 cloves garlic, peeled and minced

1 to 3 tablespoons hot red pepper flakes

Extra virgin olive oil

3 lemons, cut in half crosswise and seeded

Vegetable oil for oiling the grill grate

Pickled cherry peppers, for serving (optional)

1. Strip enough rosemary leaves off the bunch to obtain 3 tablespoons of leaves, then finely chop. Tie the remaining rosemary sprigs together at the stem end with butcher's string. Trim off any straggly leaves at the opposite end.

2. Arrange the lamb chops in a single layer on a sheet pan. Generously season on both sides with the salt, pepper, garlic, chopped rosemary, and hot red pepper flakes. Drizzle olive oil and squeeze one of the lemons over the chops on both sides and pat the flavorings into the meat with the flat part of a fork. Marinate the chops in the refrigerator for 20 minutes while you build your fire. Brush the remaining lemon halves with olive oil and season with salt and pepper.

3. Set up your grill for direct grilling and heat to high. In the best of all worlds, you'd grill over a wood fire. Barring that, add wood chunks or chips to your charcoal fire (or place wood chunks on the heat diffuser of your gas grill—see page 22). Leave one third of the grill fire-free as a safety zone.

4. Fold a 12-by-18-inch piece of aluminum foil lengthwise in thirds like a business letter. This is your grill shield—it will keep the exposed ends of the bones from burning.

YIELD: Serves 4

METHOD: Direct grilling

PREP TIME: 10 minutes

GRILLING TIME: 6 minutes

GRILL/GEAR: Can be grilled over charcoal, wood, or gas. You also need butcher's string; 2 wood chunks or 1½ cups unsoaked hardwood chips (optional); and aluminum foil to make a grill shield.

SHOP: You want lamb rib chops for this dish (the smaller the better), so you can pick them up by the bone.

INSIDER TIP: The seasonings here go great with virtually any grilled meat, poultry, or seafood. For heightened drama, make a basting brush with a bunch of fresh rosemary and use it for basting the lamb.

Grill the lemons with the lamb chops so you have smoky grilled juice to squeeze over them.

5. Brush or scrape the grill grate clean and oil it well. Arrange the lamb chops on the grate in a neat row, rib bones facing the front. Arrange the lemon halves, cut sides down, on the grate. Grill until the lamb chops and lemons are sizzling and browned on both sides, about 3 minutes per side for medium-rare for the lamb; the same amount of time on 1 side for the lemon. At some point, the ends of the rib bones will start to burn: Slide the foil grill shield under them. At some point, the dripping lamb fat may cause flare-ups. Move the meaty part of the chops onto the foil or away from the fire into the safety zone.

6. Transfer the chops to a platter or plates and let rest for a minute or so. Squeeze juice from the grilled lemons over them and eat—how else?—with your burning fingers. Serve the pickled peppers alongside, if desired.

NORTH AFRICAN LAMB KEBABS
WITH HARISSA MAYONNAISE

YIELD: Serves 4

METHOD: Direct grilling

PREP TIME: 15 minutes

GRILLING TIME: 10 minutes

GRILL/GEAR: Can be grilled over charcoal, wood, or gas. You also need flat metal or bamboo skewers and a grill basket.

These simple, colorful kebabs take their inspiration from Tunisia, where caraway, cumin, coriander, and black peppercorns are roasted whole, then ground to make a fragrant seasoning called *tabil*. Roasting gives the spices a smoky flavor that goes perfectly with the fire-seared lamb.

When building kebabs, use flat metal or bamboo skewers, which hold the ingredients in place without slipping. Try to intersperse lean cubes of lamb with fatty pieces, so they melt and baste the meat as it grills.

SHOP: Two good brands of harissa are made by Mina and Teeny Tiny Spice Co.

INSIDER TIP: For two other compelling flavor combinations, try spicing the lamb with the rub used in the Coffee-Crusted Beef Short Ribs (page 135) or Pork Belly Steamed Buns (page 155).

INGREDIENTS

FOR THE SPICE MIX

1 teaspoon caraway seeds

1 teaspoon cumin seeds

1 teaspoon coriander seed

1 teaspoon black peppercorns

1 teaspoon coarse salt
   (sea or kosher)

1 teaspoon hot red pepper flakes

FOR THE KEBABS

1½ pounds boneless lamb shoulder
   (not too lean—you need some fat
   to keep the kebabs moist)

2 tablespoons extra virgin olive oil, plus
   more for basting

1 medium-size onion, peeled

1 jar (16 ounces) sweet cherry peppers,
   drained

Vegetable oil for oiling the grill grate

3 tablespoons chopped fresh flat-leaf
   parsley (optional)

Harissa Mayonnaise (recipe follows)

1. Make the spice mix: Place the caraway, cumin, coriander, peppercorns, and salt in a dry cast-iron skillet. Roast over medium heat until the spices are fragrant and just beginning to brown, 2 minutes, shaking the pan so they cook evenly. Transfer the spices to a bowl and let cool, then coarsely grind in a spice mill or a mortar with a pestle. Stir in the hot red pepper flakes. Set aside.

2. Cut the lamb into ¾-inch cubes and place in a large mixing bowl. Sprinkle the spice mix over the meat and stir the cubes with a wooden spoon to coat. Stir in the olive oil. Let marinate while you prepare the onion and light the grill.

3. Cut the onion in half crosswise. Cut each half into 6 wedges and break each wedge into individual segments. Stir any really small pieces into the bowl with the marinating lamb.

4. Thread the lamb cubes onto the skewers alternating with pieces of onion. Place the cherry peppers in the grill basket.

5. Set up your grill for direct grilling and heat to high. Brush or scrape the grill grate clean and oil it well.

6. Grill the lamb kebabs until cooked to taste, 1 to 2 minutes per side, 4 to 8 minutes in all for medium. (People in North Africa tend to eat their lamb medium or medium-well.) Grill the cherry peppers in the grill basket for 1 minute per side. Transfer the lamb to a platter and sprinkle with parsley, if using. Scatter on the cherry peppers. Serve the Harissa Mayonnaise on the side for spooning over the lamb.

HARISSA MAYONNAISE

YIELD: Makes 1 cup

Harissa is a North African hot pepper sauce. It's available at upscale supermarkets like Whole Foods, and of course, at North African and Middle Eastern grocery stores. Alternatively, you could substitute sriracha or sambal oelek or other hot pepper paste.

INGREDIENTS

¼ cup harissa (North African hot pepper sauce), or to taste

¾ cup mayonnaise, preferably Hellmann's or Best Foods

A few drops of fresh lemon juice

Combine the harissa and mayonnaise in an attractive serving bowl and whisk to mix. Whisk in lemon juice to taste. Refrigerate, covered, until ready to serve.

GROUND MEAT

May 28 is National Hamburger Day. The hot dog, too, has its own month: July (proclaimed by the National Hot Dog and Sausage Council—yes, there is such an organization). As for bratwurst, reluctant to wait for Labor Day, Johnsonville has proclaimed August 16 the start of the "Twelve Days of Bratsgiving." These red-letter days remind us that ground meats command our respect all year long and that it's never too early to fire up your grill to cook them. In this chapter, you'll learn how to grill the perfect hamburger (hint: Use three cuts of beef) and how to construct an Italian cheeseburger (hint: There's a slab of real Gorgonzola cheese in the center). You'll learn how to hedgehog a hot dog (for the crustiest wiener ever) and how to give Italian sausage a smoke ring (and a smoke flavor you never dreamed sausage could possess)—served in a "mile-long" sandwich. So mark your calendar and get ready to grill some righteous ground meat.

TRIPLE STEAK BURGERS

YIELD: Serves 4

METHOD: Direct grilling

PREP TIME: 30 minutes

GRILLING TIME: 6 to 10 minutes

GRILL/GEAR: Can be grilled over charcoal, wood, or gas. You also need an instant-read thermometer.

SHOP: When possible, grass-fed or organic beef with 15 to 20 percent fat content.

INSIDER TIP: How far would you go for a great burger? Would you source and grind your own beef? If so, you need a real meat grinder: Good brands include Magic Mill and STX. KitchenAid also makes an optional food grinder attachment for the power hub on its stand mixers. Sorry folks, you can't get a proper grind in a food processor. If you don't have a meat grinder, find a butcher who will grind the burger meat to your specs.

So what makes a great burger? Obviously, the flavorings, the grill master's skill, and even the shape of the roll. But the most important factor may be the one over which few of us take any control: the composition of the meat. What's actually in the ground beef you buy in your supermarket cold case? Well, here's an occasion to take charge and determine the meat blend. My dream burger contains equal parts brisket, sirloin, and short ribs: the first for its beefiness; the second for its steakiness; and the third for its richness and fat. Note: I like to put the potato chips *on* the burger, not next to it, for extra crunch.

INGREDIENTS

FOR THE BURGERS

10 ounces sirloin, cut into 1-inch chunks, chilled

10 ounces beef brisket (not too lean), cut into 1-inch chunks, chilled

10 ounces boneless beef short ribs, cut into 1-inch chunks, chilled

Vegetable oil for oiling the grill grate

Coarse salt (sea or kosher) and freshly ground black pepper

4 thin slices (3 by 3 inches) sharp cheddar cheese or aged provolone (4 to 6 ounces; optional)

2 tablespoons butter, melted

4 brioche hamburger buns or sesame buns, split

4 lettuce leaves

ANY OR ALL OF THE FOLLOWING TOPPINGS

4 slices bacon, grilled and cut in half crosswise (page 50)

1 luscious ripe red tomato, sliced crosswise

Sliced avocado

Sliced dill or sweet pickles

1 cup potato chips

1 small sweet onion, peeled and thinly sliced

Ketchup, mustard, mayonnaise, and/or pickle relish to taste

1. Coarsely grind the sirloin, brisket, and short ribs in a meat grinder (make sure the parts are well-chilled; I place them in the freezer for 30 minutes first). Mix well with a wooden spoon. Wet your hands with cold water. Form 4 equal patties, each ¾ inch thick. Dimple the center slightly with your thumb (burgers rise more in the center as they cook, so these will remain an even thickness). Place the burgers on a

plate lined with plastic wrap. Cover with plastic wrap and refrigerate while you light the grill.

2. Set up your grill for direct grilling and heat to high. Ideally, you'll be grilling over wood or a wood-enhanced fire (page 21). Brush or scrape the grill grate clean and oil it well.

3. Season the burgers generously on both sides with salt and pepper. Arrange on the grate and grill until the bottoms are sizzling and browned, 3 to 5 minutes. Give them each a quarter turn after 1½ minutes so they grill evenly. Turn the burgers over and lay the cheese slices on top, if using. Close the grill lid and continue grilling until the cheese is melted

and the burgers are cooked through, 3 to 5 minutes more. The USDA recommends an internal temperature of 160°F. Insert the probe of an instant-read thermometer through the *side* of the burger to check it.

4. Meanwhile, butter the cut sides of the buns. Toast the buns, cut sides down, on the grill. This will take about 1 minute.

5. To assemble the burgers, line the bottom of each toasted bun with a lettuce leaf (this keeps the burger juices from making it soggy). Add the burger and any of the toppings, including your favorite condiments. Add the top bun and enjoy.

GROUND BEEF SPEAK

Ground Beef: Did you know there's a difference between ground beef and hamburger? Ground beef is made from trimmings (meat and fat) or offal from one or multiple animals. The fat content cannot exceed 30 percent and must come exclusively from the trimmings themselves. Additional fat cannot be added.

Hamburger: Like ground beef, hamburger is made from meat trimmings or offal from one or multiple animals and cannot exceed 30 percent fat. Unlike ground beef, however, pure beef fat (suet) can be added to the mixture to supplement fat in the trimmings.

Lean and Extra Lean Ground Beef: According to the USDA, ground beef that is labeled "lean" contains 10 percent fat. If the mixture is labeled "extra lean," it contains 5 percent fat

ITALIAN CHEESEBURGERS
WITH CRISPY PROSCIUTTO, GRILLED RADICCHIO, AND GORGONZOLA

Imagine if the cheeseburger had been born in Italy, not the United States. The cheese might be Gorgonzola; the bacon, prosciutto; the lettuce, raddichio; and the bun, ciabatta. And the meat itself might be a mixture of ground beef and pork. Here's a cheeseburger that's simultaneously familiar and exotic. Note the technique for sandwiching the cheese in the beef.

YIELD: Makes 4 burgers

METHOD: Direct grilling

PREP TIME: 15 minutes

GRILLING TIME: 10 minutes

GRILL/GEAR: Can be grilled over charcoal or gas, but for the best flavor, grill over wood. You also need an instant-read thermometer.

SHOP: Most supermarkets sell imported Italian Gorgonzola cheese. (If you can't find it, substitute another mild blue cheese or other Italian cheese.) Ditto for radicchio, a bitter, cruciferous, red-and-white salad green that comes in small heads.

INSIDER TIP: Did you ever notice how some hamburgers seem luscious and light, others leaden? One factor is how you handle the meat. Moisten your hands with cold water and touch the meat as little as possible.

INGREDIENTS

FOR THE BURGERS

1 pound ground sirloin

¾ pound lean ground pork (or more beef)

8 ounces Gorgonzola cheese in 4 slices

Coarse salt (sea or kosher) and freshly ground black pepper

Vegetable oil for oiling the grill grate

FOR SERVING

1 small head of radicchio, cut crosswise into ½-inch-wide slices

¼ cup extra virgin olive oil, or as needed

Coarse salt (sea or kosher) and freshly ground black pepper

4 thin slices prosciutto

4 ciabatta rolls, each cut in half

8 oil-cured sun-dried tomato halves, drained

1. Line a plate with plastic wrap. Mix the ground sirloin and pork together with a wooden spoon. Moisten your hands with cold water. Divide the mixture into 8 balls and flatten each into a square patty. Sandwich a slice of Gorgonzola between 2 patties, crimping the edges to encase the cheese. Place on the prepared plate. Cover with additional plastic wrap and refrigerate while you light the grill. Just before grilling, season generously on both sides with salt and pepper.

2. Set up the grill for direct grilling. Heat one side to high and one side to medium-high. Brush or scrape the grill grate clean and oil it well.

3. Lightly brush the radicchio slices on both sides with olive oil and season with salt and pepper. Lightly brush the prosciutto on both sides with olive oil. Lightly brush the cut sides of the ciabatta rolls with olive oil.

4. Grill the radicchio over high heat until browned on both sides, but still raw in the center, 1 to 2 minutes per side. Grill the prosciutto over medium-high heat until browned, 1 to 2 minutes per side. It will crisp as it cools. Set these ingredients aside.

5. Grill the burgers over high heat until sizzling and browned on both sides, 3 to 5 minutes per side. To test for doneness, insert an instant-read thermometer through the side of a burger into the center: The internal temperature should be about 160°F for medium. While you're at it, grill the ciabatta rolls over medium-high heat, cut sides down, 1 to 2 minutes.

6. Assemble the burgers: Place a slice of grilled radicchio on the bottom half of the ciabatta bun, then the burger, prosciutto, and finally, the sun-dried tomatoes. Now *that's* a cheeseburger.

LAMB BURGERS
WITH YOGURT AND DILL

YIELD: Serves 4

METHOD: Direct grilling

PREP TIME: 15 minutes

GRILLING TIME: 6 to 8 minutes

GRILL/GEAR: Can be grilled over charcoal, wood, or gas. You also need an instant-read thermometer.

SHOP: You want fairly fatty lamb for these burgers: 15 to 20% fat content.

INSIDER TIP: Lamb burgers can sometimes be tough. You're going to make a *panada*, bread soaked in milk or cream, and add it to the meat to keep it soft and moist.

Kofta. *Kubideh. Lula* (sometimes spelled *lyulya*). Vast is the world of ground grilled lamb dishes, and your repertoire isn't complete without at least one. Here's a Greek version, flavored with garlic, scallions, and dill. For a Middle Eastern lamb burger, replace the dill with fresh mint and add a teaspoon or two of sumac (a tart red spice available in Middle Eastern markets).

INGREDIENTS

FOR THE LAMB

1 clove garlic, peeled and minced

1 teaspoon coarse salt (sea or kosher)

1 slice country-style white bread, crust removed, cut into ½-inch cubes

3 tablespoons heavy (whipping) cream

1¾ pounds ground lamb, well chilled

2 scallions, trimmed, white and green parts finely chopped

3 tablespoons chopped fresh dill, plus 8 sprigs for serving

1 teaspoon ground cumin

1 teaspoon freshly ground black pepper

Vegetable oil for oiling the grill grate

FOR SERVING

4 fresh pita breads (white or whole wheat)

4 romaine lettuce leaves, washed and dried

1 cucumber, peeled and thinly sliced

1 ripe tomato, diced

¾ cup plain Greek yogurt

1. Place the garlic and salt in the bottom of a mixing bowl and mash to a paste with the back of a spoon. Stir in the bread and heavy cream and let the mixture soak for 5 minutes.

2. Add the lamb, scallions, dill, cumin, and pepper and stir just to mix with a wooden spoon. Wet your hands and form the lamb mixture into 4 oval patties. Arrange on a plate lined with plastic wrap. Cover with additional plastic wrap and refrigerate for 1 hour.

3. Set up your grill for direct grilling and heat to high. Brush or scrape the grill grate clean and oil it well.

4. Arrange the lamb burgers on the grate and grill until sizzling and browned on both sides and cooked through, 3 to 4 minutes per side. To test for doneness, insert an instant-read thermometer through the side of a burger into the center. The internal temperature should be 160°F for medium. While you're at it, lightly toast the pita breads on the grill, 30 to 60 seconds per side.

5. To serve, slice one edge and open each pita bread. Line each one with a lettuce leaf, then pile in the burger, cucumber, tomato, and generous dollops of yogurt. You'll need both hands to eat this one.

MILE-LONG ITALIAN
ITALIAN SAUSAGE SANDWICH FOR A CROWD

This colorful Italian sausage sandwich was inspired by the Italian street festivals that take place each summer in Boston's North End. Traditionally, the sausage and peppers are griddled on a gas-heated flat-top. But grilling with hardwood scents the ingredients with an inimitable smoke flavor. Butt two Italian breads end to end to create a "mile-long" sandwich. The recipe can be multiplied as many times as you want to create edible bliss by the yard.

YIELD: Serves 4 to 8 and can be multiplied as desired

METHOD: Indirect grilling for the sausages; direct grilling for the veggies and bread

PREP TIME: 15 minutes

GRILLING TIME: 12 minutes for the veggies, plus 30 to 40 minutes for the sausages

INGREDIENTS

Vegetable oil for oiling the grill grate

1 red bell pepper

1 yellow bell pepper

1 green bell pepper

1 large onion, peeled and cut into 12 wedges

Extra virgin olive oil for basting and drizzling

Coarse salt (sea or kosher) and freshly ground black pepper

8 Italian sausages

2 long Italian breads or French baguettes

2 cups giardiniera (Italian pickled vegetables), with 3 to 4 tablespoons juices

1 bunch dried oregano (available at Italian grocery stores) or 1 tablespoon dried oregano

GRILL/GEAR: Can be grilled over charcoal or gas. You also need toothpicks; basting brush; and 2 hardwood chunks or 1½ cups wood chips (optional; if using the latter, soak in water to cover for 30 minutes, then drain).

SHOP: There are two options for Italian sausage: sweet or hot, or you could grill and serve both. Giardiniera is an Italian pickled vegetable mix. Look for it in Italian markets and most supermarkets. Two good brands are Marconi and Mezzetta.

INSIDER TIP: Some years ago, having a very large number of bratwurst to grill and a small number of helpers (make that none) to do it, I set up a large charcoal grill for indirect grilling. Not only did the sausages come out supernaturally plump and juicy, there was nary a split casing or flare-up. Best of all, by adding wood chips to the fire, I gave the sausages a smoke flavor, complete with crimson smoke ring. This is the only way I grill any sausage now—German, Italian, or otherwise. Try it: It might just become your go-to method, too.

1. Set up your grill for direct grilling and heat to high. Brush or scrape the grill grate clean and oil it well.

2. Arrange the peppers on the grate and grill until darkly browned on all sides, about 3 minutes per side, 12 minutes in all. Transfer to a large cutting board to cool.

3. Meanwhile, insert a toothpick in each onion wedge. Lightly brush the onion wedges with olive oil and season with salt and pepper. Grill until sizzling, browned, and soft, 3 to 5 minutes per side, turning with tongs. Transfer to the cutting board to cool.

4. Cut the peppers lengthwise into ½-inch strips, discarding the stems and seeds. Remove the toothpicks from the onion wedges and cut them crosswise into ½-inch-wide slices. The peppers and onions can be prepped several hours ahead or even at a previous grill session.

5. An hour before serving, set up your grill for indirect grilling and heat to medium-high. Brush or scrape the grill grate clean and oil it well. Arrange the sausages on the grate over the drip pan away from the heat. If you want a smoke flavor (nontraditional, but decidedly tasty), add the wood chunks or chips to the coals.

6. Close the grill lid and indirect grill the sausages until crusty and golden brown on the outside and cooked through, 30 to 40 minutes. Use an instant-read thermometer to check for doneness—insert it in one end toward the center of the sausage—it should read 160°F. There is no need to turn the sausages; remember, you're indirect grilling.

7. Meanwhile, cut one end off each loaf of bread so you can butt them together. Cut each loaf almost in half lengthwise through the top. Open up the bread and brush inside and out with olive oil. I like to toast the bread on the grill, but tradition calls for leaving it soft. Your choice.

8. To assemble the mile-long sandwiches, join the breads together end to end to make one long sandwich. Line up the sausages in the sandwich. Top with the grilled peppers and onions and giardiniera. Drizzle more olive oil and the giardiniera juices on top. Rub the oregano bunch between the palms of your hands to sprinkle fragrant dried oregano on top. Let everyone admire the sandwich whole, then slice crosswise with a serrated knife into individual sausage lengths for serving.

HEDGEHOG HOT DOGS

YIELD: Makes 8 and can be multiplied as desired

METHOD: Direct grilling

PREP TIME: 15 minutes

GRILLING TIME: 8 to 10 minutes

GRILL/GEAR: Can be grilled over charcoal, wood, or gas.

SHOP: Lots of options for hot dogs here. Wagyu beef dogs (available from Snake River Farms) if you're feeling extravagant. Applegate if you want a natural nitrite-free hot dog. Hebrew National if you like the salty tang of tradition.

I always feel awkward about including a hot dog recipe in a cookbook. After all, hot dogs are the first food most of us grilled, and you don't need a cookbook to show you how. What special technique could I possibly bring to a food that's essentially ready to eat when it comes out of the package? Hedgehogging dramatically increases the ratio of crisp smoky crust to center meat. Tip o' the hat to Russ Faulk of Kalamazoo Outdoor Gourmet for this singular scoring technique and the idea of grilling the hot dog buns with mayonnaise and remoulade sauce. He calls his version a "Po' Dog." Amen.

INGREDIENTS

8 best-quality all-beef hot dogs

8 bakery-fresh hot dog rolls, preferably brioche rolls

6 tablespoons mayonnaise, preferably Hellmann's or Best Foods

Vegetable oil for oiling the grill grate

Creole Mustard Sauce (recipe follows)

Baby arugula or other micro-greens

2 luscious red ripe tomatoes or 1 pint cherry tomatoes, thinly sliced

1. Using a paring knife, make a series of crosshatch cuts on the surface of each hot dog, about ⅛ inch deep and ¼ inch apart, on all sides. (This will expose more of the hot dog to the direct heat of the grill.)

2. Slather the cut insides of the rolls with mayonnaise.

3. Set up your grill for direct grilling and heat to high. Brush or scrape the grill grate clean and oil it well. Arrange the hot dogs on the grate.

Grill until the exterior is sizzling, crisp, and browned, about 2 minutes per side, 6 to 8 minutes in all. While you're at it, grill the mayonnaise-slathered rolls until toasted, 1 minute per side.

4. Slather the rolls with Creole Mustard Sauce. Add the hot dogs, baby arugula, and tomato slices, and any other condiment you may fancy. This may be the best hot dog you've ever tasted.

INSIDER TIP: These hot dogs use a technique called "hedgehogging," in which you score the surface of the hot dogs in a crosshatch pattern. The edges puff and char during grilling, giving you an exceptionally crusty exterior and adding more wood smoke flavor. They also look cool as all get-out.

CREOLE MUSTARD SAUCE

YIELD: Makes 1 cup

Horseradish, hot sauce, and mustard give this slather sauce plenty of fire power. One good brand of Creole mustard is Zatarain's, from Louisiana.

INGREDIENTS

¾ cup mayonnaise, preferably Hellmann's or Best Foods

¼ cup Creole mustard

¼ cup prepared horseradish

1 tablespoon Worcestershire sauce

1 teaspoon of Tabasco or your favorite hot sauce, or to taste

3 tablespoons minced celery

3 tablespoons minced green olives

1 tablespoon drained capers

Combine the ingredients in a mixing bowl and whisk to mix. Any leftover sauce will keep in the refrigerator for several days.

POULTRY

Steak makes a carnivore's heart pound faster, and pork grabs top honors at barbecue competitions. But where's the glory in poultry? When's the last time you heard a food lover wax rhapsodic about a grilled chicken breast? Or a competition pit master take top honors with turkey or duck? Well, I cry fowl, and I'm not alone. *Pollo al mattone* (chicken under a brick) is one of the glories of Italian grilling. (Learn how to grill it under a salt brick on page 204.) *Poulet rôti à la broche* (rotisserie chicken) holds a sacred spot at French Sunday supper. From Peruvian cumin- and chile-scented *pollo asado* to Chinese barbecued duck, poultry ranks high elsewhere in the world's grill cultures. Come to think of it, and closer to home, more and more of us now smoke-roast that centerpiece of the Thanksgiving dinner: turkey. In this chapter, you'll learn how to grill, spit-roast, and smoke-roast superlative poultry. Cry fowl. Do it often.

POULTRY

Note: The USDA recommends cooking chicken and turkey to at least 165°F.

CUT	BLUE	RARE	MEDIUM-RARE	MEDIUM	MEDIUM-WELL	WELL	VERY WELL
Chicken (whole)				165°F cooked through	170°–175°F cooked through and then some: This is how I like whole chicken.	185°–190°F cooked through and suitable for pulling	
Chicken legs, thighs, and drumsticks				165°F cooked through	170°–175°F cooked through and then some	185°–190°F cooked through and suitable for pulling	
Chicken breasts				165°F cooked through			
Turkey (whole)				165°F cooked through	170°–175°F cooked through and then some		
Turkey pieces, including breast				165°F cooked through	170°–175°F cooked through and then some		
Duck (whole)			130°–135°F warm red center	140°–145°F warm pink center	155°–160°F hot pink center	175°–180°F cooked through and then some	
Duck breasts		120°–125°F cool red center	130°–135°F warm red center	140°–145°F hot pink center	155°–160°F hot pink center	175°–180°F cooked through and then some; gray center	

ROTISSERIE CHICKEN
WITH DRIP PAN POTATOES

Whenever my wife and I visit France, we have a ritual on the day of our departure from Paris. We stop at a local street market to buy a rotisserie chicken to eat on the way home. The French make the world's best rotisserie chicken—often with little more by way of seasonings than sea salt and butter. The quality of the bird helps: The French put a high premium on flavorful farm-raised breeds. But above all, it's the internal and external basting that results from the slow gentle rotation of the chicken on the rotisserie. Then, there's the heat source: a wood fire in the countryside, gas in the cities, but always live flames. The following chicken owes its extraordinary flavor to a generous basting with tarragon-shallot-lemon butter. If you've always found roast chicken underwhelming, this one will make you a convert.

YIELD: Serves 2 to 4

METHOD: Rotisserie/spit-roasting

PREP TIME: 15 minutes

GRILLING TIME: 1¼ hours

GRILL/GEAR: A grill with a rotisserie. You also need butcher's string; 2 basting brushes; a large (9-by-13-inch) aluminum foil drip pan; and an instant-read thermometer. Note: Although it's not typically French, if you want a wood smoke flavor, add 2 hardwood chunks or 1½ cups wood chips (if using the latter, soak in water to cover for 30 minutes, then drain) to the fire.

SHOP: Your rotisserie chicken will be only as good as the bird you start out with. Organic to be sure. One good source is Smart Chicken (smartchicken.com). Even better if it's a local farm-raised heritage breed like a Rhode Island Red, Plymouth Rock, or Araucana.

INGREDIENTS

FOR THE CHICKEN

1 roasting chicken (3½ to 4 pounds), preferably organic

Coarse salt (sea or kosher) and freshly ground black pepper

3 large shallots, peeled and minced

2 sprigs tarragon or other herb

2 strips fresh lemon zest for the cavity of the bird

FOR THE HERB BUTTER

6 tablespoons (¾ stick) unsalted butter

2 tablespoons minced shallots (from above)

2 tablespoons chopped fresh tarragon, or other fresh herb

½ teaspoon finely grated fresh lemon zest

FOR THE POTATOES

1½ pounds fingerling potatoes, scrubbed and blotted dry (cut any large ones in half on the diagonal)

4 sprigs fresh tarragon or other herb

1 tablespoon herb butter (from above)

Coarse salt (sea or kosher) and freshly ground black pepper

1. Prepare the chicken: Remove any giblets and large lumps of fat from inside the chicken. Season the front and main cavities with salt and pepper. Set aside 2 tablespoons of the minced shallots and place the remainder, plus 2 tarragon sprigs and the 2 strips of lemon zest, in the

Note that the chicken is secured to the rotisserie through the sides. Brush it often with the melted herb butter.

cavity. Truss the chicken by tying the ends of the drumsticks together with butcher's string. Fold the wing tips under the body. This gives the bird a neat cylindrical form so it will roast evenly. Generously season the outside of the bird with salt and pepper. Place the bird on a wire rack in the refrigerator and let it air-dry for 2 hours. This is optional, but it helps crisp the skin.

2. Make the herb butter: Melt the butter in a saucepan over medium-low heat. Add the reserved 2 tablespoons minced shallots, 2 tablespoons chopped tarragon, and ½ teaspoon grated lemon zest and cook over medium-high heat until the shallots lose their rawness, 2 minutes. Do not let brown. Set aside.

3. Place the potatoes and 4 sprigs of tarragon in an aluminum foil drip pan. Stir in 1 tablespoon of the herb butter and salt and pepper.

4. Set up your grill for spit-roasting following the manufacturer's instructions and heat to medium-high.

5. Spit the chicken from side to side (not from front to back), securing it to the spit with the rotisserie prongs. I'm not sure I can explain the physics of spitting the chickens side to side instead of front to back, but most of the world's grill masters do it this way, and the bird does seem to come out

juicier. Pour 2 tablespoons of the herb butter into a ramekin and brush it on all sides of the chicken.

6. Affix the spit with the chicken onto the rotisserie motor. Place the drip pan with the potatoes under the chicken (the spuds will roast in the chicken drippings). If using wood chunks or chips, add them to the coals. Switch on the motor.

7. Spit-roast the chicken until the skin is browned and crisp and the meat in the thigh reaches at least 165°F on an instant-read thermometer. (Insert it into the deepest part of the thigh, without letting it touch the bone.) Don't worry if the temperature goes higher: Overcooking just makes the bird more tender. Start basting the chicken with the remaining herb butter after 20 minutes, and baste it every 20 minutes. Use a different basting brush from the one that touched the raw chicken. Give the potatoes a stir while you're at it. Depending on the size of the bird and the potatoes, the cooking time will be 1 to 1¼ hours. Baste the chicken one last time before you take it off the fire.

8. Transfer the chicken to a cutting board and let it rest for 5 minutes or so. Carefully remove the chicken from the spit. Re-season the potatoes. Carve the bird and serve it with the potatoes on the side.

PERUVIAN GRILLED CHICKEN
WITH CREAMY SALSA VERDE

Peruvian chicken is one of the world's poultry wonders—skin crisp, meat moist and tender, the bird strongly scented with garlic and cumin, with *aji amarillo* (yellow chile) to pump up the heat and *huacatay* (black mint) to dampen the fire. It is, in other words, some of the most flavorful chicken on Planet Barbecue. It even has its own day on the Peruvian calendar— July 21. Curiously, we have a Swiss farmer to thank for it. His name was Roger Schuler and his farm outside Lima was on the verge of bankruptcy. In desperation, he set up four tables at the farm and advertised "all you can eat" chicken for only 5 *soles* (about $1.95) to local workers. Today, Granja Azul (Blue Farm) seats 450; the chicken still comes "all-you-can-eat," but it now costs 55 *soles* ($16.25). It's worth it.

INGREDIENTS

FOR THE WET RUB

4 cloves garlic, peeled and coarsely chopped

2 teaspoons coarse salt (sea or kosher)

2 teaspoons pimentón (Spanish smoked paprika) or sweet paprika

1½ teaspoons ground cumin

1 teaspoon freshly ground black pepper

1 to 2 tablespoons aji amarillo paste (see Shop) or 1 tablespoon hot paprika

1 tablespoon huacatay paste or finely chopped fresh mint

3 tablespoons fresh lime juice

2 tablespoons extra virgin olive oil, plus 1 to 2 tablespoons for basting

FOR THE CHICKEN

1 whole chicken, preferably organic (3½ to 4 pounds)

Vegetable oil for oiling the grill grate

Creamy Salsa Verde (Green Sauce, recipe follows)

1. Make the wet rub: Pound the garlic and salt to a paste in a mortar with a pestle or place in a bowl and mash with a wooden spoon. Work in the paprika, cumin, pepper, aji amarillo paste, huacatay, lime juice, and olive oil. Alternatively, puree the ingredients in a blender or food processor fitted with a small bowl. Set aside.

2. Remove any giblets and large lumps of fat from inside the chicken. Place the bird, breast side down, on a cutting board.

YIELD: Serves 2 to 4, and can be multiplied as desired

METHOD: Indirect grilling

PREP TIME: 15 minutes to make the marinade and spatchcock the chicken, plus 3 to 5 hours to marinate the bird

GRILLING TIME: About 40 minutes

GRILL/GEAR: Can be grilled over charcoal or gas. You also need kitchen scissors or poultry shears and an instant-read thermometer.

SHOP: To be strictly authentic, you'll need two typical Peruvian flavorings: *aji amarillo* and *huacatay*. The first is a piquant yellow chile with a mildly fiery bite. The second is a Peruvian black mint with an herbaceous minty flavor. Before you panic, know that both can be ordered from Amazon (or found at a Peruvian market). And that hot paprika makes a reasonable substitute for *aji amarillo*, and fresh spearmint or peppermint works fine in place of black mint.

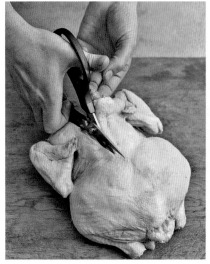

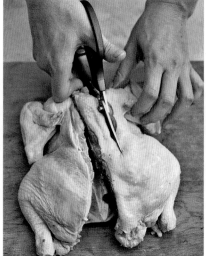

Using kitchen scissors, make a lengthwise cut in the chicken along the backbone from neck to tail.

Repeat along the other side and remove the backbone. Open up the chicken like a book and remove the breastbone as instructed in Step 4 (below).

Turn the chicken over and press down on the breast to flatten the bird.

INSIDER TIP: It's a challenge that faces most of the world's grillers: How do you grill a whole chicken on a grill that lacks a lid? (Most of the world's grills are open fire boxes without lids.) You could spit-roast it whole, as some Peruvians do. Or you could spatchcock it, that is, remove the backbone and open the bird up like a book. Spatchcocking has another advantage: It exposes more of the meat to the marinade and the searing heat of the fire. You'll find step-by-step photos above on how to do it.

3. Using kitchen scissors or poultry shears, cut through the flesh and bone along both sides of the backbone and completely remove the backbone. (Save it for chicken stock.)

4. Open out the bird (like opening a book) by gently pulling the halves apart. Using a sharp paring knife, lightly score the top of the breastbone. Run your thumbs along and under the sides of the breastbone and attached cartilage and pop them out.

5. Turn the bird over. Using a sharp knife, make a ½-inch slit in the skin between the lower end of the breastbone and the leg on each side. Stick the ends of the drumsticks through the slits. Spread the bird out flat, skin side down, in a baking dish

just large enough to hold it. Breathe a sigh of relief: The hard part is over.

6. Pour the wet rub over the chicken, spreading it over the meat on both sides. (The bird should end up skin side up.) If you're feeling ambitious, work some of the wet rub under the skin of the breasts and thighs. (Wear latex or other food-safe gloves.) Marinate the chicken, covered, in the refrigerator for 3 to 5 hours, or as long as overnight—the longer, the richer the flavor.

7. Set up your grill for indirect grilling (place a drip pan under the grate in the center), and heat the grill to medium-high. (Yeah, I know I said spatchcocking was developed to enable you to direct grill a whole chicken. But indirect grilling avoids the risk of flare-ups and produces an exceptionally moist bird.) When ready to cook, brush or scrape the grill grate clean and oil it well. Place the chicken, skin side up, in the center of the grate over the drip pan. Close the grill lid.

8. Indirect grill the chicken until the skin is golden brown and crisp and the meat is cooked through, 40 minutes, or as needed. Baste the chicken with olive oil halfway through. Use an instant-read thermometer to test for doneness; the internal temperature in the thickest part of the thigh should be at least 165°F. Transfer the chicken to a wire rack and let rest for a few minutes, then carve and serve with the Creamy Salsa Verde.

CREAMY SALSA VERDE (GREEN SAUCE)

YIELD: Makes 1 cup

Tip o' the hat to my assistant, Nancy Loseke, for this electrifying cilantro chile sauce, which is made creamy by the addition of mayonnaise.

INGREDIENTS

¾ cup chopped fresh cilantro leaves

1 jalapeño pepper, stemmed, seeded, and coarsely chopped

1 scallion, trimmed, white and green parts coarsely chopped

1 clove garlic, peeled and coarsely chopped

1 tablespoon aji amarillo paste (see Shop, page 201), or 1 teaspoon hot paprika

1 teaspoon huacatay paste (see Shop, page 201), or 6 fresh mint leaves

¾ cup mayonnaise, preferably Hellmann's or Best Foods

2 tablespoons fresh lime juice

Coarse salt (sea or kosher) and freshly ground black pepper

Place the cilantro, jalapeño, scallion, garlic, aji amarillo, and huacatay in a food processor (preferably fitted with a small bowl) and finely chop. Work in the mayonnaise, lime juice, and salt and pepper to taste; the sauce should be highly seasoned. Cover and refrigerate if not serving immediately, but try to serve it within 2 hours of making.

CHICKEN BREASTS GRILLED UNDER A SALT BRICK
WITH MEDITERRANEAN SALSA

YIELD: Serves 4

METHOD: Direct grilling under a salt brick

PREP TIME: 15 minutes, plus 30 minutes for marinating the chicken

GRILLING TIME: 8 minutes

GRILL/GEAR: Can be grilled over charcoal, wood, or gas. You also need 2 salt bricks or 1 salt slab (available at barbecue and cookware shops or online from Amazon); heavy-duty grill gloves; and an instant-read thermometer.

SHOP: As always, use organic chicken when possible. For a more interesting chicken breast, procure an "airline" cut (a boneless breast with the first joint of the wing attached).

INSIDER TIP: Warning: Do not make this recipe in cold weather. Hot salt bricks have been known to crack or explode when exposed to cold air.

Pollo al mattone (chicken under a brick) is one of the icons of Italian grilling; its origins are claimed with equal partisanship by Romans and Tuscans, and you find it across Italy. There's more to the dish than mere showmanship (although that plays a role, too). The brick seems to seal in moisture and helps lay on killer grill marks. Plus, it looks cool, and you should never underestimate the importance of looking cool on the grill. The traditional press is a brick wrapped in aluminum foil. You're going to up the ante—and the flavor—by using a brick or slab of Himalayan pink salt.

INGREDIENTS

4 skinless, boneless chicken breasts, preferably organic (each 6 to 8 ounces)

Coarse salt (sea or kosher) and freshly ground black pepper

Hot red pepper flakes (optional)

3 tablespoons chopped fresh rosemary and/or sage

2 cloves garlic, peeled and minced

1 Meyer or regular lemon

¼ cup extra virgin olive oil

Vegetable oil for oiling the grill grate

Mediterranean Salsa (recipe follows)

1. Trim any sinews or excess fat off the chicken breasts and arrange the meat in a baking dish. Generously season the breasts on both sides with salt, pepper, hot red pepper flakes (if using), rosemary, and garlic. Finely grate lemon zest over the breasts on both sides, then squeeze the lemon juice over them. Drizzle olive oil over the breasts, turning to coat both sides. Marinate the chicken breasts in the refrigerator while you make the Mediterranean Salsa and light the grill.

2. Set up your grill for direct grilling and heat to high. Brush or scrape the grill grate clean and oil it well.

3. Drain the chicken breasts, then arrange on the grate, all at a 45-degree angle to the bars of the grate. Place the salt bricks atop the chicken, one brick per 2 breasts. Grill the breasts until browned on the outside and cooked through, about 4 minutes per side, rotating each breast a quarter turn after 2 minutes to create an attractive crosshatch of grill marks. The internal temperature should be 165°F. Check it with an instant-read thermometer—insert the probe through the side. Wear grill gloves to move the hot salt bricks.

4. Transfer the chicken to a platter or plates and serve with the Mediterranean Salsa spooned on top or on the side.

INSIDER TIP: These quick, easy chicken breasts can be grilled over charcoal or gas. But for the ultimate flavor, grill them over wood. It's easier than you think: Simply fill your chimney with oak, hickory, or other hardwood chunks and light them as you would charcoal. Let the wood burn down to glowing embers and you're in business.

MEDITERRANEAN SALSA

YIELD: Makes about 2 cups

Think of this as *salsa fresca* from Mexico channeled by Provence, with olives and capers standing in for the jalapeños and fresh basil for cilantro.

INGREDIENTS

2 large ripe red tomatoes, peeled, seeded, and finely diced

2 scallions, trimmed, white and green parts thinly sliced crosswise

¾ cup finely diced cucumber (preferably English cucumber— see Notes)

6 kalamata olives, pitted and chopped

1 tablespoon drained small brined capers

4 fresh basil leaves, thinly slivered (see Notes)

3 tablespoons best-quality extra virgin olive oil

½ teaspoon finely grated fresh lemon zest

2 tablespoons fresh lemon juice (or more to taste)

Coarse salt (sea or kosher) and freshly ground black pepper

Place the tomatoes, scallions, cucumber, olives, capers, basil, olive oil, and lemon zest in a mixing bowl and gently stir with a rubber spatula to mix. Stir in lemon juice and salt and pepper to taste; the salsa should be highly seasoned.

NOTES: English cucumber is a seedless variety that comes shrink-wrapped in plastic. If using conventional salad cucumbers, peel and seed before dicing.

The easiest way to sliver basil is to stack 4 or 5 basil leaves on top of one another and roll them into a tight tube from one side. Using a chef's knife, cut the roll crosswise into the thinnest possible slices. Fluff the slices with your fingers to separate them into shreds.

GRILLED CHICKEN BREASTS
WITH SPANISH HAM, MANCHEGO CHEESE, AND SAFFRON BUTTER

YIELD: Serves 4

METHOD: Direct grilling

PREP TIME: 15 minutes

GRILLING TIME: 8 to 10 minutes

GRILL/GEAR: Can be grilled over charcoal, wood, or gas. You also need 4 toothpicks lightly oiled with vegetable oil and an instant-read thermometer.

SHOP: You'll need to know about a few special ingredients for this one. *Jamon serrano* is Spanish ham (think Iberian prosciutto—you could substitute prosciutto in a pinch). Regular serrano ham will work just fine; for a real treat buy *iberico* or *pata negra* (two super premium grades of Spanish ham). Manchego is a tangy sheep's milk cheese from the La Mancha region of Spain. If unavailable, use cheddar.

C hicken breast is the poultry cut serious grillers hate to love. It's milder (make that blander) than dark meat, and it has an annoying tendency to dry out when exposed to the high dry heat of the fire. The following recipe uses two time-honored techniques for keeping grilled chicken breasts juicy and flavorful. You stuff them with Spanish ham and Manchego cheese, which makes them moist from the inside out. And you baste the breasts with saffron butter as they grill. For even more flavor, use breasts with the skin on (admit it: the skin is the part we like best) and/or the first wing joint still attached (the latter is called an airline cut).

INGREDIENTS

FOR THE CHICKEN

4 skinless, boneless chicken breasts (each 8 ounces)

8 thin slices serrano ham

4 ounces thinly sliced Manchego cheese, cut into matchstick slivers

Extra virgin olive oil, for brushing

Coarse salt (sea or kosher) and freshly ground black pepper

FOR THE SAFFRON BUTTER

½ teaspoon saffron threads

2 teaspoons warm water

6 tablespoons (¾ stick) butter

1 shallot or garlic clove, peeled and minced

Vegetable oil for oiling the grill grate

2 tablespoons chopped fresh chives, for serving

1. Cut a deep pocket in the side of each chicken breast. Wrap a slice of ham around some cheese slivers to obtain a roll about ⅜ inch thick. Repeat to obtain 8 rolls.

2. Stuff 2 of these ham and cheese rolls into each chicken breast. (The rolls should run lengthwise.) Pin the

pocket shut with an oiled toothpick. Lightly brush the outsides of the chicken breasts with olive oil and season generously on both sides with salt and pepper.

3. Make the saffron butter: Soak the saffron threads in 2 teaspoons of warm water for 5 minutes. In a small

saucepan on the stovetop or the side burner of your grill, melt the butter over medium heat. Add the shallot or garlic and cook until just beginning to brown, 2 minutes. Do not let it burn. Stir in the saffron mixture.

4. Set up the grill for direct grilling and heat to high.

5. When ready to cook, brush or scrape the grill grate clean and oil it well. Arrange the chicken breasts on the grill running on a diagonal

to the bars of the grate. Grill until browned on both sides and cooked through (the internal temperature should be 165°F), 4 to 5 minutes per side, giving each breast a quarter turn after 2 minutes to lay on a crosshatch of grill marks. Start basting the chicken breasts with saffron butter after 2 minutes and continue basting.

6. Transfer the chicken breasts to a platter. Drizzle the remaining saffron butter over them and sprinkle with chopped chives.

Hold the chicken breast flat with one hand and cut a deep pocket in the side. Be careful not to cut completely through to the other side.

Insert 2 ham and cheese rolls in each pocket. Secure the pockets with oiled toothpicks.

SMOKE-ROASTED GAME HENS
WITH KENTUCKY FIRE DIP

These smoky game hens began as a mash-up between two of my favorite lesser-known Southern barbecue specialties: chicken with white barbecue sauce in the style of Big Bob Gibson's in Decatur, Alabama, and grilled pork steaks with vinegar dip from Monroe County, Kentucky. Both are dipped in a full-flavored vinegar sauce during and after cooking. Put them together and you get smoky, tender barbecued birds in a fiery dip that will send you lunging for a cold beer.

YIELD: Serves 4 as a main course

METHOD: Indirect grilling

PREP TIME: 15 minutes

GRILLING TIME: 40 minutes

GRILL/GEAR: Can be grilled over charcoal or gas. You also need an instant-read thermometer and 2 hardwood chunks or 1½ cups chips (if using the latter, soak in water to cover for 30 minutes, then drain).

SHOP: Organic game hens when possible. You could also use chicken quarters (the thigh and leg section), in which case, you'd need 8 for this amount of dip.

INSIDER TIP: A Cornish game hen is a small young chicken (originally a cross between a White Rock and Cornish chicken) typically weighing 1½ pounds. Despite the name, it's domesticated, not wild, and the bird can be female or male. Game hens taste pretty much like full-size chickens; their draw is that a whole bird serves one, so you get to savor both white and dark meat.

INGREDIENTS

FOR THE GAME HENS

4 Cornish game hens (each about 1½ pounds), thawed if frozen

Coarse salt (sea or kosher) and freshly ground black pepper

Vegetable oil for oiling the grill grate

FOR THE KENTUCKY FIRE DIP

8 tablespoons (1 stick) unsalted butter

2 cups distilled white vinegar

2 tablespoons hot sauce, such as Frank's RedHot

2 tablespoons freshly ground black pepper

2 tablespoons granulated sugar or packed brown sugar, dark or light, your choice

1 tablespoon cayenne pepper

1 tablespoon coarse salt (sea or kosher), or to taste

2 tablespoons finely chopped chives or scallion greens, for serving

1. Set up the grill for indirect grilling and heat to medium-high.

2. Spatchcock the game hens following the instructions on page 202. Very generously season each on both sides with salt and pepper.

3. Brush or scrape the grill grate clean and oil it well. Arrange the hens, skin side up, in a row in the center of the grate over the drip pan, away from the heat. Add wood chunks or chips to the coals. If working on a gas grill, use the gas grill smoking method on page 22. Close the grill lid.

4. Indirect grill the hens until the skin is browned and crisp and the meat is cooked through. Use an instant-read thermometer to test for doneness: The internal temperature in the thickest part of the thigh should be at least 165°F. The total grilling time will be 40 to 50 minutes.

5. Meanwhile, make the Kentucky Fire Dip: Melt the butter in a skillet or wide heavy saucepan over medium-high heat. Add the vinegar, hot sauce, pepper, sugar, cayenne, and salt. Reduce the heat and gently simmer for 3 minutes, whisking to dissolve the sugar and salt. Remove the dip from the heat and let cool slightly.

6. Ten minutes before the game hens are done, using tongs, dip each on both sides in the fire dip and return to the grill. Dip again the last 2 minutes and place game hens directly over the fire to sizzle the skin. Dip once more before serving. Sprinkle the hens with the chives and serve any remaining dip on the side.

CHINATOWN CHICKEN THIGHS

YIELD: Makes 8, enough to serve 4

METHOD: Indirect grilling

PREP TIME: 15 minutes

GRILLING TIME: 30 to 40 minutes

GRILL/GEAR: Can be grilled over charcoal or gas. You also need butcher's string and 2 hardwood chunks or 1½ cups wood chips (optional; if using the latter, soak in water to cover for 30 minutes, then drain); and an instant-read thermometer.

SHOP: Chinese sausage is a small, hard, sweet pork sausage—hence its nickname "meat candy." Look for it at Asian markets, or substitute your favorite hard sausage. Chinese ham is similarly sweet and salty: If unavailable, substitute Smithfield ham or Spanish serrano ham.

Quick and easy to assemble, these chicken thighs explode with Asian flavors—sweet-salty Chinese sausage and ham, musky shiitakes, sesame oil, and spicy Chinese mustard—with one non-Asian ingredient to hold them together: fontina cheese. Indirect grilling gives you crackling crisp skin and a moist interior, and you never need to worry about flare-ups. The Chinatown Barbecue Sauce on page 156 would make an excellent accompaniment (in addition to the mustard).

INGREDIENTS

8 large skin-on chicken thighs (8 ounces each with bone; 6 ounces each if boneless)

Coarse salt (sea or kosher) and freshly ground black pepper

3 tablespoons Chinese sweet-hot mustard, plus ½ cup for serving

4 ounces fontina cheese, cut into matchstick slivers

4 ounces Chinese sausage, cut into matchstick slivers

4 ounces sliced Chinese ham or other smoked ham, cut into matchstick slivers

8 shiitake mushrooms, stems removed, caps wiped clean with a damp paper towel, then thinly sliced

2 scallions, trimmed, white part thinly slivered lenthwise; green part thinly sliced on the diagonal, for serving

2 tablespoons Asian (dark) sesame oil, or more as needed

Vegetable oil for oiling the grill grate

1. If using bone-in chicken thighs, make a lengthwise cut through the flesh on either side of and underneath the bone. Pull out and discard the bone. Season the inside of the thigh with salt and pepper and spread it with mustard. Fill each thigh with an equal amount of cheese, Chinese sausage, ham, sliced shiitakes, and slivered scallion whites. Close the thighs to envelop the stuffing and tie shut with butcher's string. Brush the outsides of the thighs with sesame oil and season well with salt and pepper. Refrigerate until ready to grill.

2. Set up your grill for indirect grilling and heat to medium-high. Brush or scrape the grill grate clean and oil it well.

3. Arrange the chicken thighs skin side up on the grill grate. Add wood, if using, to the coals. If working on a gas grill, use one of the gas grill smoking methods on page 22. Close the lid.

4. Indirect grill the chicken thighs until the skin is sizzling, crisp, and golden brown, the cheese is melted, and the meat is cooked through, 30 to 40 minutes. The internal temperature should be at least 165°F on an instant-read thermometer.

5. Transfer the chicken thighs to a platter or plates and snip off and remove the strings. Sprinkle with scallion greens and serve with Chinese mustard.

INSIDER TIP: The chicken thigh is one of the best-kept secrets in poultry: moist, well-marbled, rich-tasting meat that costs a fraction of the more popular chicken breast. You can buy thighs boned already, but it's easy to bone them yourself (see instructions in Step 1). The stuffing is limited only by your imagination. A Cubano version, for example, might feature smoked ham, Swiss cheese, slivered sweet pickles, and mustard.

MAPLE-SRIRACHA CHICKEN DRUMSTICKS

I like to think of the drumstick as a chicken wing with a handle. Easy to eat (easier than wings) and easy on your wallet, it's an often overlooked cut that delivers a rich meaty flavor. My assistant, Nancy Loseke, came up with the sweet fiery maple-sriracha glaze. The Scotch whisky adds additional smoke flavor. It's simple (only four ingredients), but astonishingly tasty.

YIELD: Serves 4 to 6

METHOD: Smoke-roasting (indirect grilling)

PREP TIME: 10 minutes

GRILLING TIME: 40 to 50 minutes

GRILL/GEAR: Can be cooked over charcoal or gas. You also need 2 hardwood chunks or 1½ cups wood chips (if using the latter, soak in water for 30 minutes, then drain); an instant-read thermometer; and a basting brush.

INGREDIENTS

Vegetable oil for oiling the grill grate

FOR THE CHICKEN

12 large chicken drumsticks, preferably organic (3 to 4 pounds)

1 tablespoon coarse salt (sea or kosher)

1 tablespoon freshly ground black pepper

1 tablespoon hot red pepper flakes

2 tablespoons extra virgin olive oil

FOR THE GLAZE

6 tablespoons (¾ stick) unsalted butter

5 tablespoons pure maple syrup

¼ cup sriracha, or more to taste

3 tablespoons Scotch whisky (preferably single malt)

2 tablespoons finely chopped fresh cilantro, chives, or scallion greens, for serving

1. Set up your grill for indirect grilling and heat to medium-high. Just before cooking, brush or scrape the grill grate clean and oil it well.

2. Place the drumsticks in a large mixing bowl. Sprinkle with the salt, pepper, and hot red pepper flakes, stirring to coat well with the seasonings. Stir in the olive oil.

3. Arrange the drumsticks rounded side up in a single layer in the center of the grill. Add the wood to the coals. If working on a gas grill, use one of the gas grill smoking methods on page 22.

4. Close the grill lid. Indirect grill the drumsticks until the skin is crisp and well browned and the chicken is cooked through, 40 to 50 minutes. For maximum tenderness, cook the drumsticks to an internal temperature of 170°F.

5. Meanwhile, make the glaze: Melt the butter in a saucepan over high heat. Stir in the maple syrup, sriracha, and whisky and boil until the mixture is syrupy, 3 to 5 minutes. Set aside and keep warm.

6. About 5 minutes before the chicken is done, brush each drumstick on all sides with the glaze. Repeat just before removing the drumsticks from the grill. Arrange the drumsticks on a platter and pour the remaining glaze over them. Sprinkle with cilantro and serve.

YAKITORI
LIKE THEY MAKE IT IN TOKYO

YIELD: Serves 6 to 8 as an appetizer; 4 as a main course

METHOD: Direct grilling

PREP TIME: 20 minutes

GRILLING TIME: 6 to 8 minutes

GRILL/GEAR: Can be grilled over charcoal, wood, or gas. You also need small (6-inch) bamboo skewers and heavy-duty aluminum foil folded into thirds, like a business letter, to make a grill shield.

SHOP: In Japan, yakitori is usually made with dark meat (which is fattier and more flavorful than breast meat). But the teriyaki glaze keeps white meat moist, too. Extra points for skin on, which gives you extra richness. As always, organic chicken when possible. Mirin—sweetened rice wine— is available at Asian markets and most supermarkets. If unavailable, use sake or sherry and add a little more sugar.

Yakitori ("grilled chicken" literally) is Japan's national barbecue— enjoyed at innumerable grill parlors (many conveniently located in train stations), not to mention at family cookouts. In North America, we tend to marinate the meat before grilling, but in Japan it's dipped in a flavorful glaze during and just after the cooking. This sears the sauce into the meat, resulting in shiny, sweet-salty, delectably aromatic chicken kebabs—some of the most flavorful on Planet Barbecue.

INGREDIENTS

FOR THE SAUCE

1 cup chicken stock (preferably homemade)

1 cup soy sauce

½ cup sweet rice wine (mirin), sake, or white wine

½ cup granulated sugar (plus 2 tablespoons if using sake or white wine)

8 scallions, trimmed, the white part of 2 scallions gently crushed with the side of a cleaver, the green part thinly slivered on the diagonal for serving; the remaining 6 scallions cut crosswise into ½-inch pieces for skewering

2 slices fresh ginger (each ¼ inch thick), gently crushed with the side of a cleaver

1 clove garlic, peeled and gently crushed with the side of a cleaver

1 strip fresh lemon zest (½ by 2 inches)

FOR THE YAKITORI

1½ to 2 pounds chicken pieces (dark meat or white, skin on or off— your choice)

Vegetable oil for oiling the grill grate

2 tablespoons sesame seeds, toasted (see page 69), for serving (optional)

1. Make the sauce: Place the chicken stock, soy sauce, mirin, sugar, crushed scallion whites, ginger, garlic, and lemon zest in a nonreactive saucepan and bring to a boil over medium heat. Let the sauce simmer until syrupy, 6 to 10 minutes, stirring often to prevent scorching. Strain the sauce into a narrow deep saucepan you can place on the grill. (You want the sauce in the pot to be 3 to 4 inches deep.)

2. Make the yakitori (skewers): Cut the chicken into ½-inch cubes and thread onto skewers, alternating with pieces of scallion. Fill each skewer only halfway—leave the other half free as a handle. Intersperse lean pieces of chicken with fatty pieces or skin pieces. The chicken can be skewered several hours ahead; cover and refrigerate until ready to grill.

3. Set up your grill for direct grilling and heat to high. Brush or scrape the grill grate clean and oil it well. (A piece of chicken fat or skin held in tongs works great for greasing the grill grate.) Keep the sauce in the pot warm on one corner of the grill. If using a hibachi or other slender grill, arrange the chicken skewers on the grate so the handles hang over the edge. On a larger grill, place the aluminum foil grill shield on the grate and arrange the yakitori so that the meat is exposed directly to the fire and the bare skewers are protected by the grill shield.

4. Grill the yakitori until the chicken is mostly cooked (it will start to brown on the outside), about 2 minutes per side. Dip each skewer in sauce, then return it to the grate. Continue grilling until well browned on both sides and cooked through, another 1 to 2 minutes per side, 6 to 8 minutes in all. The sauce should cook to a shiny glaze and the meat should feel firm to the touch when done. Take care that it doesn't burn. Meanwhile, boil the extra sauce for 2 minutes.

5. Dip each yakitori in the reboiled sauce one more time and transfer to a platter or plate for serving. Sprinkle with the reserved scallion greens and sesame seeds, if using. Serve any remaining sauce in small bowls as a dipping sauce.

INSIDER TIP: Properly prepared yakitori comes lacquered with a sweet-salty glaze—the result of dipping the meat in the sauce twice—once during the cooking and again once the skewers are cooked. Japanese grill masters use the same pot of glaze (called *tare*) day after day, week after week, replenishing the ingredients as needed. Each successive dip of the chicken adds additional flavor to the glaze.

PLANCHA-GRILLED DUCK BREASTS
WITH FRESH CHERRY SALSA

I like to think of duck breast as the beefsteak of poultry—a dark, rich red meat you serve medium-rare (certainly unlike chicken breast)—with an added benefit: crisp, bacon-like rich skin. I like to serve it with a fresh cherry salsa (duck has a natural affinity for red fruit), and you can build on the cherry theme by smoking the duck with cherry wood. If you don't normally grill duck, this is a great way to try it, and it's a lot easier and neater than cooking a whole duck.

YIELD: Serves 4

METHOD: Plancha grilling

PREP TIME: 10 minutes for the duck; 10 minutes for the salsa

GRILLING TIME: 4 to 7 minutes

INGREDIENTS

4 skin-on boneless duck breasts (each 7 to 8 ounces)

1 tablespoon turbinado sugar, such as Sugar in the Raw, or granulated sugar

2 teaspoons coarse salt (sea or kosher)

2 teaspoons freshly ground black pepper

1 teaspoon Chinese five-spice powder

1 to 2 tablespoons Asian (dark) sesame oil

Vegetable oil for oiling the grill grate

Fresh Cherry Salsa, for serving (recipe follows)

1. Trim any tendons off the duck breasts with a sharp knife. Score the skin on each breast in a diamond pattern. The cuts should be about ⅛ inch deep and ¼ inch apart. (Cut the skin only, not the breast meat.)

2. Make the rub: Combine the sugar, salt, pepper, and five-spice powder in a small bowl and stir to mix. Generously sprinkle the rub on both sides of each duck breast. Drizzle with sesame oil, turning to coat both sides. Let marinate in the refrigerator while you make the salsa and light the grill.

3. Set up your grill for direct grilling and heat to medium-high. Brush or scrape the grill grate clean and oil it well. Place a cast-iron plancha on the grate and heat it as well. To test whether it's ready for grilling, sprinkle a drop or two of water on the plancha—if it evaporates in 1 to

GRILL/GEAR: Can be grilled over charcoal or gas. You also need a plancha (cast-iron griddle); 2 cherry wood chunks or 1 cup wood chips (optional; if using the latter, soak in water to cover for 30 minutes, then drain); and an instant-read thermometer.

SHOP: Duck breasts are available at many supermarkets, or you can special-order them from your butcher or online from mapleleaffarms.com. Five-spice powder is a Chinese spice mix with the smoky, licoricy flavor of star anise. Find it in the spice aisle of your supermarket or online.

INSIDER TIP: Imagine the perfect duck breast: dark, crisp skin; meat moist and rosy in the center. The best way to achieve this is to use a 2-step grilling process: First, brown the skin on a hot cast-iron plancha or skillet, then finish cooking the breast on the grill. For the full skinny on plancha grilling, see page 28.

Sear the duck breasts skin side down directly on the plancha.

To finish cooking, turn the duck breasts over and move them meat side down directly over the fire.

2 seconds, the plancha is hot. Lightly oil the plancha. Add wood chunks or chips to the coals (if using). If working on a gas grill, use one of the gas grill smoking methods on page 22. When you smell smoke, you're ready to go.

4. Arrange the duck breasts, skin side down, on the plancha. Sear until the skin is nicely browned and has begun to render its fat, 3 to 5 minutes. Close the grill to seal in the smoke.

5. Invert the breasts and move them from the plancha to directly over the fire. Cook until the meat side is seared and the duck is cooked to taste, 1 to 2 minutes for medium-rare. The internal temperature will be 130° to 135°F on an instant-read thermometer.

6. Serve the duck breasts whole or sliced crosswise and fanned out, with Fresh Cherry Salsa spooned over the meat on the side.

FRESH CHERRY SALSA

YIELD: Makes 3 cups

In the summer, I make this salsa with fresh cherries. (Make your life easy: Procure a cherry pitter at a cookware shop or online.) Other fruit salsas that go well with duck would be made the same way with diced mangoes, peaches, or pineapple.

INGREDIENTS

3 cups pitted fresh cherries (about 1½ pounds)

1 poblano pepper, seeded and cut into ¼-inch dice

1 to 2 jalapeño or serrano peppers, seeded (for spicier salsa leave the seeds in) and minced

1 tablespoon finely chopped candied ginger, or 2 teaspoons minced fresh ginger

2 scallions, trimmed, white and green parts thinly sliced crosswise

¼ cup chopped fresh mint or cilantro

3 tablespoons fresh lime juice, or to taste

1 tablespoon packed brown sugar, dark or light, or to taste

Combine the ingredients for the salsa in a mixing bowl and gently toss to mix. Correct the seasoning, adding lime juice or sugar to taste; the salsa should be sweet, sour, and very flavorful. This salsa tastes best served within 1 hour of mixing.

BOURBON-BRINED SMOKED TURKEY BREAST

Remember turkey breast—freshly roasted and carved off the bone? Unfortunately, the omnipresence of turkey roll (an awful product pumped full of water and preservatives, and often flavored with liquid smoke) has made real roasted turkey breast an endangered species—and with it a proper turkey or club sandwich. Here's how to brine and smoke-roast a real turkey breast from scratch.

INGREDIENTS

1 whole turkey breast (5 to 6 pounds), preferably bone-in

½ cup coarse salt (sea or kosher)

2 teaspoons Prague powder No. 1 (optional)

¼ cup pure maple syrup

1 quart hot water

1 quart ice water

¼ cup bourbon

Vegetable oil for oiling the grill grate

6 tablespoons (¾ stick) unsalted butter, melted, for basting

1. Thaw the turkey breast in the refrigerator, if frozen. Place it in a jumbo heavy-duty resealable plastic bag.

2. Place the salt, Prague powder (if using), maple syrup, and 1 quart of hot water in a large pot and bring to a boil, whisking to dissolve the salt crystals. Remove the pot from the heat and stir in the ice water and bourbon. Let the brine cool to room temperature, then pour it into the resealable plastic bag over the turkey breast. Place the sealed bag with the turkey in a large bowl (to contain potential leaks) in the refrigerator and brine for 8 hours, turning the bag several times so the breast brines evenly.

3. Drain the turkey breast, discarding the brine, and blot dry on all sides with paper towels.

4. Set up your grill for indirect grilling and heat to medium. Brush or scrape the grill grate clean and oil it well.

5. Place the breast in the center of the grill, skin side up. Add 2 wood chunks or 1½ cups chips to the coals, or use one of the gas grill smoking methods on page 22. Close the grill lid.

6. Smoke-roast the turkey until the skin is golden brown and the turkey is cooked through, 1½ to 2 hours, replenishing the wood chunks or charcoal as needed. Start basting the turkey with melted butter after 30

YIELD: Serves 6 to 8

METHOD: Smoke-roasting/ indirect grilling

PREP TIME: 15 minutes plus 8 hours for brining the turkey breast

GRILLING TIME: 1½ to 2 hours

GRILL/GEAR: Can be cooked over charcoal or gas. You also need 2 hardwood chunks or 1½ to 3 cups wood chips (if using the latter, soak in water to cover for 30 minutes, then drain); a jumbo resealable plastic bag; and an instant-read thermometer.

SHOP: You'll want a full breast—ideally with the breastbone intact but the ribs removed. Organic, of course, and fresh when possible. (Fresh—never frozen—turkey tends to be available around Thanksgiving and Christmas.) Prague powder No. 1, also known as pink salt or Insta-Cure No. 1, is a curing salt that contains 6.75 percent sodium nitrite. I've made it optional, but it will give your turkey breast a rich umami flavor reminiscent of ham. Procure it from your butcher or order it from Amazon.

minutes, and baste every 30 minutes thereafter. The turkey breast is done when the internal temperature reaches 165°F on an instant-read thermometer. Baste one final time after the breast comes off the grill. (If the skin starts to brown too much, *loosely* tent the breast with aluminum foil. Do not wrap it tightly or you'll make the skin soggy.)

7. Transfer the turkey breast to a cutting board or platter. Let rest for 5 minutes before carving. Delectable hot or cold.

THE RAICHLEN BUTTER BIRD
SMOKE-ROASTED TURKEY WITH COGNAC INJECTOR SAUCE AND HERB BUTTER OR TRUFFLES UNDER THE SKIN

YIELD: Serves 8 to 10

METHOD: Indirect grilling

PREP TIME: 20 minutes

GRILLING TIME: 3 to 3½ hours

GRILL/GEAR: Can be grilled over charcoal or gas. (For the most pronounced smoke flavor, use charcoal.) You also need a marinade injector; butcher's string for trussing; an instant-read thermometer; and 6 hardwood chunks or 4½ cups wood chips (optional; if using the latter, soak in water to cover for 30 minutes, then drain).

This turkey takes me back to my cooking school days in Paris. French birds were leaner than their American counterparts, so we learned to stuff butter (and sometimes thinly sliced truffles) under the skin. The butter melted into the breast meat as the turkey roasted, producing an astonishingly moist and flavorful bird every time. To this I add two distinctly American techniques: injecting the bird with a sauce and indirect grilling. Succulence guaranteed. I've made the hardwood optional; if you like your turkey smoked (and who doesn't?), add it. But if you use truffles, you may wish to omit smoking so you can focus on the truffles' unique flavor.

SHOP: In the best of all possible worlds, you'd use a fresh organic heritage turkey. Fresh birds tend to be available right before Thanksgiving. (If you use frozen, figure on one day of thawing in the refrigerator per 4 pounds of turkey.) Heritage turkeys are antique breeds raised for their flavor, not necessarily for their breast size. (One good source is marysturkeys.com.) Organic speaks for itself.

INSIDER TIP: Here's one holiday turkey you'll never complain about being dry. To keep it moist, I use two techniques: injecting it with melted butter and broth and stuffing herb butter under the skin. For a completely over-the-top bird, buy a fresh truffle (white or black, winter or summer—your choice) and insert paper-thin slices under the skin. (If using truffles, omit the herbs.) Yes, I know European truffles are hideously expensive; American truffles from the Pacific Northwest are a lot more affordable. One source is foodsinseason.com.

INGREDIENTS

FOR THE TURKEY AND COGNAC INJECTOR SAUCE

1 organic turkey (12 to 14 pounds)

Coarse salt (sea or kosher) and freshly ground black pepper

5 tablespoons unsalted butter

5 tablespoons unsalted or low-sodium chicken broth, preferably homemade

1 tablespoon Cognac

FOR STUFFING UNDER THE SKIN

10 tablespoons (1¼ sticks) cold unsalted butter, thinly sliced, plus 6 tablespoons (¾ stick), melted

1 bunch fresh sage leaves, stemmed, or tarragon sprigs, or 1 black or white truffle, thinly sliced

Vegetable oil for oiling the grill grate

1. Thaw the turkey in the refrigerator, if necessary. (Start 4 days early.) Remove the neck and giblets from both the front and main cavities (be sure to check both cavities). Remove and discard any lumps of fat from the main cavity. Blot the turkey dry inside and out with paper towels. Season the inside of the cavities with salt and pepper.

2. Make the injector sauce: Melt the butter in a saucepan over medium heat. Stir in the chicken broth and Cognac and let cool to room temperature.

3. Starting at the top of the neck cavity, tunnel your finger under the skin. Start with one finger, then two. Gently loosen the skin from the meat, taking care not to tear it. Gradually work your whole hand under the skin, loosening it from the breast meat, then the thighs. (Yes, I know this will feel weird the first time you do it; it gets easier with practice.)

4. Insert the butter slices between the skin and meat, positioning them over the thighs and especially over the breast. Insert sage leaves or tarragon sprigs (or truffle slices) under the skin, positioning them in an attractive pattern. Truss the turkey: Tie the ends of the drumsticks together with butcher's string to give it an attractive shape. Fold the wing tips under the body.

5. Using an injector, inject the broth-butter-cognac mixture deep into the turkey, especially into the thighs, drumsticks, and deep into the breast. (See Grilling Hack on page 19.) Brush the outside of the turkey with the 6 tablespoons of melted butter and season generously with salt and pepper. Breathe that sigh of relief—the hard part is over.

6. Set up your grill for indirect grilling and heat to medium. Brush or scrape the grill grate clean and oil it well. For a smoke flavor, add half the wood chunks or chips to the coals. If working on a gas grill, use the gas grill smoking method on page 22.

7. Smoke-roast the turkey for 1 hour. Baste the turkey with some of the melted butter. Add charcoal and wood to the fire as needed. Continue roasting for another hour and replenish the charcoal and wood as needed. Smoke-roast the bird until the skin is a dark golden brown and the meat is cooked through, 3 to 3½ hours. Start basting the turkey with melted butter after 1 hour and baste every 30 minutes. The internal temperature in the thickest part of the thigh, taken without the thermometer touching the bone, should be at least 165°F. If the skin starts to brown too much, *lay* a sheet of aluminum foil over the bird. (Note that I said "lay." Do not bunch the foil around the bird or you'll make the skin soggy.)

8. Transfer the turkey to a cutting board or platter and baste with melted butter one final time. Let it rest for 5 to 10 minutes before removing the butcher's string, carving, and serving.

Use an instant-read thermometer to check for doneness.

SEAFOOD

Fish on the grill. Four simple words that strike fear into the hearts of novice grillers. What if it sticks to the grill grate? (It will at first, then it will release—be patient and see the fish grilling tips throughout this chapter.) Or what if it breaks apart when you turn it? (That's why we grill on cedar planks, salt slabs, in grill baskets, and even on shovels.) Or what if the fish dries out? (It won't if you use the marinades, bastes, and sauces included here.) So, fear no more—I'm here to walk you through every step of the fish grilling process—from grilling fillets (try the Grill Basket Halibut with Maple Teriyaki on page 249) to steaks (how about the Albacore Tuna "Filets Mignons" with Peppercorn Cream Sauce on page 244) to whole fish (don't miss the Salt-Slab Grilled Rockfish with Mango Mint Relish on page 251). And while we're at it, I'll show you how to grill over-the-top shellfish, including oysters, mussels, lobster, and shrimp. Fresh fish. Hot fire. There's no better way to cook seafood.

GRILLED OYSTERS
WITH ASIAN AROMATICS

YIELD: Serves 4 to 6 as an appetizer

METHOD: Direct grilling or indirect grilling

PREP TIME: 20 minutes

GRILLING TIME: 4 to 6 minutes for direct grilling; 8 to 12 minutes for indirect grilling

GRILL/GEAR: Can be direct grilled over charcoal, wood, or gas; indirect grilled over charcoal or gas. You also need a shellfish grilling rack (optional— see the Variation, page 228); and 2 hardwood chunks or 1½ cups unsoaked wood chips (optional).

SHOP: You need fresh oysters in the shell. Shucking them takes time. I pay my fishmonger a little extra to do it for me. (He saves the oyster juices, which I pour back over the oysters just before grilling.) Mirin is sweetened Japanese rice wine. Look for it at Asian markets and most supermarkets, or use sake.

INSIDER TIP: There are two ways to cook the oysters: by direct grilling, in which case you sizzle them right in the shells. Or by indirect grilling, in which case you can add hardwood to the coals to smoke the oysters (also in their shells) as well as grill them. The first is a little faster. The second delivers a more complex flavor.

I f you've read my previous books or watched my shows, you know my enthusiasm for grilled oysters. Over the years, I've flavored them with tequila and chiles, bread crumbs and Parmigiano-Reggiano, smoked butter, and a wide range of barbecue sauces. The following oysters look to the Far East with a triad of Asian aromatics—ginger, scallion, and cilantro— and a trio of Asian condiments: soy sauce, mirin, and sesame oil. Do you have a favorite topping for grilled oysters? Post descriptions and photos on reddit.com/r/BarbecueBible/ or on my Steven Raichlen Facebook page.

INGREDIENTS

24 oysters in the shell

2 scallions, trimmed, white and green parts thinly sliced

2 tablespoons finely minced peeled fresh ginger

¼ cup chopped fresh cilantro

Soy sauce (about 2 tablespoons)

Sweet rice wine (mirin) or sake (about 2 tablespoons)

Asian (dark) sesame oil (about 2 tablespoons)

DIRECT METHOD

1. Shuck the oysters, sliding the knife under each bivalve to loosen it from the bottom shell. Discard the top shell. Arrange the oysters in a shellfish grilling rack, if using.

2. Place a small spoonful (about ¼ teaspoon) each of scallion, ginger, and cilantro on each oyster. Save some cilantro for sprinkling on at the end. Add ¼ teaspoon each of soy sauce, mirin, and sesame oil.

3. Meanwhile, set up your grill for direct grilling and heat to high. Brush or scrape the grill grate clean; there's no need to oil it.

4. Place the oysters on their rack on the grate. If you don't have a shellfish rack, balance the shells between the bars of the grate so they lie flat. Close the lid and grill the oysters until the juices bubble and the oysters are just cooked, 4 to 6 minutes. Do not overcook: The oysters should stay rare in the center. Add a pinch of fresh cilantro to each oyster and dig in.

Variation: Indirect grilling method with wood smoke

Prepare the oysters as described in Steps 1 and 2 on page 226. Place the oysters on their rack on the grate. Alternatively, arrange the oysters on a sheet pan or baking dish spread with a ½-inch-thick layer of coarse salt to hold them flat. Set up your grill for indirect grilling and heat to medium-high. Add wood chunks or chips to the coals. (You want a quick smoke, so you don't need to soak the wood.) Smoke-roast the oysters until cooked as described previously, 8 to 12 minutes.

Place the oysters on a shellfish rack, if you own one, before adding the soy sauce, mirin, and sesame oil.

A shellfish grilling rack keeps the oysters steady, with less chance of spilling any of the tasty juices when transferring the oysters to the grill.

GRILLED CLAMS
WITH LINGUIÇA AND PEPPERS

YIELD: Serves 4 as an appetizer; 2 as a light main course

METHOD: Direct grilling

PREP TIME: 15 minutes

GRILLING TIME: 6 to 10 minutes

Every summer, we have a little ritual—a beach barbecue on Chappaquiddick with our friends Mitch, Stephanie, and Jared Reiter (who, incidentally, own a terrific summer camp called Towanda). Clams are dug that morning; grills are piled into the backs of SUVs; lobsters are procured alive and wriggling from Edgartown Seafood. As the sun sets over Cape Pogue Bay, we dig into a sort of deconstructed clambake made all the more remarkable by the fact that the ingredients are grilled, not steamed.

INGREDIENTS

24 littleneck clams in the shell

8 ounces cooked linguiça or chorizo sausage

8 ounces padrón or shishito peppers, or 1 green bell pepper, stemmed, seeded, and cut into 1-inch dice, or 3 jalapeño peppers, cut crosswise into ¼-inch-thick slices (for milder clams, seed the jalapeños)

4 scallions, trimmed, both green and white parts cut crosswise into 1-inch sections

4 tablespoons (½ stick) unsalted butter, melted

1. Scrub the clams with a stiff-bristled brush. Drain well and blot dry.

2. Set up your grill for direct grilling and heat to high. Brush or scrape the grill grate clean; there's no need to oil it. While you're at it, heat the grill wok or mesh grill basket.

3. Place the littlenecks, linguiça, peppers, and scallions in the grill wok and stir to mix. Grill over high heat, stirring with tongs, until the clam shells open (discard any that don't), the sausage sizzles, and the peppers are lightly browned, 6 to 10 minutes, or as needed.

4. Transfer the mixture to a large serving bowl and stir in the melted butter. The best way to eat? With your fingers, of course.

GRILL/GEAR: Can be grilled over charcoal, wood, or gas. You also need a grill wok or deep wire mesh grill basket (see Insider Tip).

SHOP: You want small tender clams for this dish—littlenecks if you live on the East Coast, Manila clams if you live out West. As with all bivalves, choose clams with tightly closed shells. They should smell like the ocean, not fishy. You could also grill razor clams in this manner, and for that matter, mussels or cockles. Linguiça is a spicy, garlicky smoked Portuguese pork sausage. It was originally brought to New England by Portuguese seafarers who came to work the fishing boats and whaling ships. Look for it at Iberian markets and many supermarkets. Alternatively, substitute cooked chorizo or kielbasa. As for peppers, you have lots of choices: jalapeños if you like heat, diced green pepper if you like sweetness, padrón or shishito peppers if you like a little of both.

INSIDER TIP: This dish calls for a grilling accessory that may not yet be part of your arsenal: a grill wok. Picture a wok-shaped bowl, but with holes in it to allow the smoke and fire flavors to come through. You could also use a deep wire mesh grill basket or a grilling grid. Another interesting variation is to grill the clams on a plancha (see page 16), adding hardwood to the fire to infuse them with wood smoke.

HAY-GRILLED MUSSELS
WITH CHARCOAL BUTTER

When most Americans think of smoked food, we imagine cooking it with hickory, apple, or other hardwoods. Not so in Italy, where mozzarella is often smoked with hay or straw, or on the Atlantic coast of France, where mussels are smoke-grilled with pine needles. This dish merges the two, and if you like wood-smoked seafood, you'll love the delicate herbaceous smoke produced by hay. You'll certainly appreciate the theatrics of grilling the mussels on a smoking, burning bed of hay. And talk about simple: This recipe calls for only two ingredients, but the flavors—and high drama—will leave you gobsmacked.

INGREDIENTS

1½ pounds mussels

3 large handfuls of hay or straw

Charcoal Butter (recipe follows)

1. Pick through the mussels, discarding any with cracked shells or gapped shells that fail to close when the bivalve is tapped. Right before grilling, pull out and discard the tuft of threads (called the beard) at the hinge of each mussel, using needle-nose pliers. Alternatively, pinch the threads between your thumb and the back of a paring knife (see page 232). Twist the knife away from the mussel to pull them out.

2. Set up your grill for direct grilling and heat to high. Brush or scrape the grill grate clean; there's no need to oil it.

3. Fill the bottom 2 inches of the grill wok or basket with hay. Arrange the mussels on top in one or two layers.

4. Place the grill wok with the mussels on the hottest part of the grate. After a minute or two, the hay should start smoking, then burst into flames. You may need to touch a match to it to help it along.

5. Continue grilling until the mussel shells open, 3 to 6 minutes, or as needed.

6. Transfer the grill wok with the mussels to a heatproof tray and serve the mussels right out of the wok with the Charcoal Butter on the side. Eat with your fingers (use an empty mussel shell as tweezers to remove the mussels from their shells), dipping each mussel in melted butter before popping it into your mouth.

YIELD: Serves 2

METHOD: Direct grilling/hay grilling

PREP TIME: 10 minutes

GRILLING TIME: 3 to 6 minutes

GRILL/GEAR: Can be grilled over charcoal, wood, or gas. (It helps to use charcoal, so you have an ember for the butter.) You also need a grill wok or mesh grill basket (about 12 inches across); needle-nose pliers; and safety matches or a butane match.

SHOP: When possible, buy mussels from a fish store with a high turnover rather than at the supermarket. (Chances are they'll be fresher.) There's a simple test for freshness: The shells should be tightly closed (or should close promptly when tapped). Avoid any mussels that smell fishy or ammoniated. As for hay, if you live in horse or farm country, you'll be able to find it at a tack or garden shop. Otherwise, order timothy hay from Amazon. Straw will work, too. You'll need about 2 quarts.

The best tool
for hay grilling is a grill wok
or mesh grill basket—sturdy
enough to hold the mussels,
but perforated to let the flames
reach the hay. In a pinch you
could use a large cast-iron
skillet.

CHARCOAL BUTTER

This smoky butter joins the new boom in charcoal-flavored foods (my neighborhood bakery serves a jet black charcoal croissant). It tastes like you're sitting around a campfire.

INGREDIENTS

6 tablespoons (¾ stick) unsalted butter

1 lit piece of natural charcoal or charcoal briquette (do not use instant light charcoal)

Melt the butter in a small saucepan over medium heat. Add the glowing charcoal. The butter will hiss and sputter. Let the flavors infuse for a minute or so, then return the briquette to your grill.

Pinch the "beard" at the hinge between the knife blade and your thumb, then twist to pull it out.

Plunge a piece of lit charcoal into the melted butter to flavor it with smoke.

SHRIMP TIMES TWO

SHRIMP PINTXOS WITH PIMENTON BUTTER

*P*intxos (pronounced "pin-chos") are small Spanish kebabs traditionally served at tapas bars. (*Pintxo* literally means "spike," and while the food is often held together with a skewer or toothpick, not all *pintxos* are kebabs.) These shrimp skewers buzz with Iberian seasonings, such as cumin, oregano, and *pimentón* (smoked paprika). For an extra layer of flavor and to keep the shrimp moist, you baste them with a *pimentón*-scallion butter. It's remarkable how changing the usual grilled shrimp flavorings (bacon and barbecue sauce) gives you a whole new perspective on this popular crustacean.

INGREDIENTS

FOR THE SHRIMP

1½ pounds jumbo shrimp, cleaned and deveined

1½ teaspoons coarse salt (sea or kosher)

1½ teaspoons coarsely ground black pepper

1½ teaspoons pimentón (smoked Spanish paprika)

1½ teaspoons ground cumin

1½ teaspoons dried oregano

TO FINISH THE PINTXOS

1 medium-size Spanish onion, peeled

1 red bell pepper, stemmed, seeded, and cut into 1-inch squares

Extra virgin olive oil, preferably Spanish

Vegetable oil for oiling the grill grate

Pimentón Butter (recipe follows)

1. Dry the shrimp as described in the Insider Tip on page 234.

2. Make the rub: Combine the salt, pepper, *pimentón*, cumin, and oregano in a small bowl and mix with your fingers. Set aside.

3. Cut the onion in half widthwise (through its equator), then cut each half into sixths. Discard the furry stem end. Separate the onion into pieces, each about 1 inch. Trim to fit, if necessary. Save the small center pieces of onion for the Pimentón Butter.

YIELD: Serves 3 or 4

METHOD: Direct grilling

PREP TIME: 15 minutes

GRILLING TIME: 4 to 6 minutes

GRILL/GEAR: Can be grilled over charcoal, wood, or gas. You also need bamboo skewers, preferably flat skewers; and a grill shield or a 12-by-18-inch piece of aluminum foil folded into thirds, like a business letter.

SHOP: Use fresh local shrimp when possible: Maine shrimp in New England; Key West pinks if you live in Florida; spot prawns on the West Coast. The Carolinas and Gulf Coast states also have excellent local shrimp.

INSIDER TIP: Much as we all love grilled shrimp, it's surprisingly hard to grill well. One challenge is shrimp's small size (it's easy to go from undercooked to overcooked in a few seconds). Another is that so much of our shrimp come frozen, which gives it a tendency to stew rather than grill. (If this is the case with yours, thaw the shrimp in the refrigerator, then drain well, blot dry with paper towels, and air-dry uncovered on a wire rack in the refrigerator for 1 hour before cooking. Of course, your best leg up is to start with fresh wild shrimp.)

Seriouseats.com recommends dry-brining the shrimp with salt and baking soda (1 teaspoon of the former, ¼ teaspoon of the latter per pound) for 30 to 60 minutes, which helps improve the texture and flavor.

4. Thread the shrimp, onion pieces, and peppers alternately onto the skewers. (The *pintxo* can be made up to several hours ahead if covered and refrigerated.)

5. Brush each *pintxo* on all exposed sides with olive oil and season with the reserved rub.

6. Set up your grill for direct grilling and heat to high. Brush or scrape the grill grate clean and oil it well.

7. Lay the grill shield down on the grill grate. Arrange the *pintxos* on the grate, making sure the exposed handles of the skewers are positioned over the grill shield. (This keeps them from burning.)

8. Grill the *pintxos* until browned and cooked through, 2 to 3 minutes per side, 4 to 6 minutes in all. Start basting the shrimp with the Pimentón Butter after 2 minutes and baste on both sides. Arrange the *pintxos* on a platter or plates and drizzle the remaining Pimentón Butter over them.

PIMENTON BUTTER

YIELD: Makes ½ cup

Pimentón is smoked paprika from Spain; you'll love the smoky sweetness it adds to the butter. Look for it in your supermarket spice rack or online. Two good brands are La Vera and La Dalia.

INGREDIENTS

6 tablespoons (¾ stick) salted butter

Reserved onion pieces from the Shrimp Pintxos, finely chopped

1 teaspoon pimentón (smoked Spanish paprika)

1 teaspoon hot red pepper flakes

1 tablespoon Spanish sherry (optional)

Melt the butter in a small saucepan over medium heat. Add the onion, *pimentón*, and hot red pepper flakes, increase the heat to medium-high and cook until the onions are golden and the butter is slightly browned. Add the sherry, if using, and bring to a boil, then remove from the heat.

GRILLED SHRIMP WITH SALMORIGLIO

YIELD: Serves 4

This vibrant shrimp features a condiment that may be new to you—a Sicilian olive, caper, parsley, basil, mint sauce called *salmoriglio*. (Think of it as Sicilian chimichurri.) You use half the sauce as a marinade and serve the remainder as the sauce on the side.

INGREDIENTS

⅓ cup fresh flat-leaf parsley leaves, washed and shaken dry

⅓ cup fresh basil leaves, washed and shaken dry

⅓ cup fresh mint leaves (or more basil), washed and shaken dry

2 tablespoons capers

8 pitted green or black olives

½ teaspoon hot red pepper flakes, or to taste

⅔ cup extra virgin olive oil

½ teaspoon finely grated fresh lemon zest

Juice of 1 lemon (about 3 tablespoons)

⅓ cup water, or as needed

Coarse salt (sea or kosher) and freshly ground black pepper

1½ pounds jumbo shrimp, cleaned and deveined

Bamboo skewers (preferably flat skewers)

1. Make the salmoriglio: Place the parsley, basil, mint, capers, olives, and red pepper flakes in a food processor and finely chop. With the blade running, gradually add the olive oil. Work in the lemon zest, lemon juice, water, and salt and pepper to taste; the salmoriglio should be highly seasoned and thin enough to pour.

2. Thread the shrimp onto skewers and arrange in a baking dish just large enough to hold them. Pour half of the salmoriglio over the shrimp, turning the kebabs to coat both sides. Marinate in the refrigerator for 1 hour.

3. Set up your grill for direct grilling and heat to high. Brush or scrape the grill grate clean and oil it well. Grill the shrimp as described in Step 8 on page 234. Serve with the remaining salmoriglio on the side.

CAVEMAN LOBSTER
WITH ABSINTHE BUTTER

I'm lucky to live in two places where lobster is our local seafood. In the summer, I grill Maine lobster (*Homarus americanus*), while in the winter, our crustacean of choice is spiny lobster, aka Florida lobster (of the *Palinuridae* family). The Maine shellfish is a little sweeter, but trickier to grill. (Tradition calls for cutting it in half while it's still alive.) Florida lobster consists mostly of tail, which is often sold split already. Either lobster is delectable grilled—the high dry heat brings out its natural sweetness. Especially when basted with a simple garlic butter made sweet and anise-flavored with a shot of a spirit that was outlawed for a hundred years. I'm referring, of course, to absinthe—the drink alleged to drive poets and painters to madness on account of one of its primary flavorings: wormwood. Happily, absinthe has been exonerated and its anise-y tang makes a perfect foil for the sweet smoky meat of Caveman Lobster.

YIELD: Serves 4

METHOD: Grilling in the embers (caveman grilling)

PREP TIME: 15 minutes

GRILLING TIME: 4 to 6 minutes

GRILL/GEAR: As with all caveman grilling, you need newspaper for fanning the coals; a charcoal grill; long-handled tongs; and heavy-duty grill gloves.

SHOP: Maine lobsters should be purchased live and wriggling—preferably from a fish store with a saltwater lobster tank. Spiny lobsters are generally sold as tails, which makes them easier to split for grilling. Absinthe can be purchased at a high-end liquor store or online: Exemplary brands include St. George, Duplais, and Nouvelle-Orleans. If unavailable, use an anise-flavored spirit like Pernod or Ricard from France.

INGREDIENTS

FOR THE ABSINTHE BUTTER

12 tablespoons (1½ sticks) unsalted butter

2 cloves garlic, peeled and minced

3 tablespoons finely chopped flat-leaf parsley and/or chives

2 tablespoons absinthe or pastis

FOR THE LOBSTER

4 spiny lobster tails (each 8 to 10 ounces), split in half lengthwise (remove the vein running the length of the tail)

Coarse salt (sea or kosher) and cracked black pepper

1. Make the absinthe butter: Melt the butter in a heavy saucepan over medium-high heat. Add the garlic and parsley and/or chives and cook until just beginning to brown, 2 minutes. Stir in the absinthe and cook for 1 minute. Remove the butter from the heat and let it cool slightly.

2. Build a charcoal fire and rake the coals into an even layer. (Leave the front third of your grill coal-free.) When the coals glow orange, fan them with a newspaper to blow off any loose ash.

3. Generously, and I mean generously, season the lobster tails with salt and cracked pepper. Place the lobsters

INSIDER TIP: I call for caveman grilling here (directly in the embers—see page 27), which delivers a charred smoky flavor you just won't get on a conventional grill. (The process is pretty eye-popping to watch, too.) That's not to say that you can't grill great lobster on a conventional charcoal, wood, or gas grill—see instructions in the Variation.

directly on the embers cut sides down, 2 inches apart. Grill until the bottoms are browned, 2 minutes. Invert the lobsters and cook shell sides down until the shell juices bubble and the lobster meat is firm, white, and cooked, 2 to 4 minutes more.

4. Using tongs, lift the lobsters out of the coals, shaking each to dislodge any clinging embers. Using a basting brush, brush off any loose ash and arrange the lobster tails on a platter or plates. Pour some of the absinthe butter over the lobster, and serve the rest on the side for dipping.

Variation

Conventional grill method: Don't have a charcoal grill or aren't up for caveman grilling? Set up your grill (charcoal, wood, or gas) for direct grilling and heat to high. Brush or scrape the grill grate clean and oil it well. Brush the cut sides of the lobsters with some of the absinthe butter. Arrange the lobster tails, cut sides down, on the grate and grill until browned, 3 to 4 minutes, giving each a quarter turn after 1½ minutes to lay on a crosshatch of grill marks. Invert the lobsters and continue grilling, cut sides up, until the lobster meat is firm, white, and cooked.

SEAFOOD
The FDA recommends cooking fish to 145°F.

CUT	BLUE	RARE	MEDIUM-RARE	MEDIUM	MEDIUM-WELL	WELL	VERY WELL
Whole fish			130°F (for people who like their salmon pink in the center)	140°-145°F (fully cooked)			
Fish steaks	100°-110°F cold red center; suitable for tuna	120°-125°F warm red center; suitable for tuna	130°F hot pink center; good for tuna and salmon (for people who like salmon that's pink in the center)	140°-145°F (fully cooked—would be too much for tuna)			
Lobster and other shellfish				140°-145°F (flesh will be milky white)			

SALMON STEAKS ON A SHOVEL

I first chronicled this singular method of grilling lamb from Australia's Outback in *Planet Barbecue* and on my *Primal Grill* TV show. It was love at first sight and first bite: We loved the vision of lamb chops sizzling away on a shovel blade over a smoky wood fire. Theatrics aside, shovel grilling delivers two big flavor dividends—first in the crust that comes from searing meat (or fish, in this case) on a hot slab of metal over a fire, and second in the wood smoke that subtly flavors the food. This recipe features the common salmon flavorings of scallion, dill, and lemon, but I think you'll find they're utterly transformed by shovel grilling.

INGREDIENTS

4 thick salmon steaks (preferably center cut), each 6 to 8 ounces and 1¼ to 1½ inches thick

Extra virgin olive oil for brushing and drizzling

Coarse salt (sea or kosher) and cracked or freshly ground black pepper

2 scallions, trimmed, white parts finely minced, green parts thinly sliced on the diagonal and set aside for the sauce

¼ cup chopped fresh dill

2 teaspoons finely grated fresh lemon zest (save ½ teaspoon lemon zest and 1 tablespoon lemon juice for the sauce)

Lemon Dill Coriander Sauce (optional—recipe follows), or lemon wedges

1. Build a wood campfire with a good base of glowing embers. Feed fresh logs to the fire from time to time to pump out plenty of wood smoke.

2. Working on a sheet pan, brush the salmon steaks on both sides with olive oil. Season very generously on both sides with salt and pepper, then sprinkle with the minced scallion, dill, and lemon zest, patting these flavorings into the fish with the flat of a fork. Just before grilling, drizzle a little more olive oil over the salmon.

3. Heat the shovel blade in the fire. This serves two purposes. It helps clean and sterilize the cooking surface and preheats the metal so it will sear the meat.

4. Arrange the salmon steaks on the shovel blade, leaving an inch between them. Don't overcrowd the shovel—it's okay to work in batches. Remember, in the Outback, grilling

YIELD: Serves 4

METHOD: Direct grilling (on a shovel)

PREP TIME: 10 minutes, plus time for building a campfire

GRILLING TIME: 6 to 10 minutes

GRILL/GEAR: To be strictly authentic, you'd grill the salmon over a campfire. You could also work over a charcoal or gas fire. You also need a *clean* flat-bladed shovel. If using a new shovel, be sure to scrub off any factory grease or remove any plastic coating. If your shovel has been used for gardening, scrub it clean with soap and water, then sterilize it by heating it in the fire.

SHOP: For the best results, grill fresh wild king or coho salmon. That limits your grilling to May through October, when wild salmon is in season, but believe me, the flavor is worth it. Some of the best salmon comes from the Copper River in Alaska.

INSIDER TIP: As the name implies, shovel grilling requires a shovel. But you can get similar results by grilling the fish on a plancha (see page 241) ideally over a wood fire or on a charcoal or gas fire enhanced with wood chunks.

isn't just about cooking a meal—it's an evening's entertainment. Thrust the shovel over the fire or lay it directly on the embers. Grill until the salmon steaks are sizzling and browned on the outside and cooked to taste, 3 to 4 minutes per side for salmon with a blush of pink in the center; a minute longer per side for fully cooked (see Note).

5. Serve the salmon steaks right off the shovel with the Lemon Dill Coriander Sauce (if using) on the side.

NOTE: When it's time to turn the salmon steaks over, ask a helper to hold the shovel while you flip the fish with a long-handled spatula.

Variation

Plancha method: Set up your grill for direct grilling and heat to high. Place a plancha or large cast-iron skillet on the grill and heat it as well. If using logs, wood chunks, or chips, toss them on the coals (of a charcoal grill) or use one of the gas grill smoking methods on page 22. Arrange the salmon steaks on the plancha or skillet and cook and serve as described above.

Heat the shovel over a wood fire to sterilize it.

Grill the salmon steaks directly on the shovel.

When done, lift the shovel carefully—you don't want the salmon sliding into the fire.

LEMON DILL CORIANDER SAUCE

YIELD: Makes 1¼ cups

Mustard dill sauce often accompanies smoked salmon in Scandinavia. This one explodes with coriander and lemon flavors, plus mayonnaise and sour cream for richness.

INGREDIENTS

½ cup mayonnaise, preferably Hellmann's or Best Foods

½ cup sour cream, or more mayonnaise

2 tablespoons Dijon mustard

2 tablespoons finely chopped fresh dill

2 tablespoons thinly sliced scallion greens (reserved from main recipe)

½ teaspoon finely grated fresh lemon zest (reserved from main recipe)

½ teaspoon ground coriander seed

1 tablespoon fresh lemon juice (reserved from main recipe)

Coarse salt (sea or kosher) and freshly ground black pepper, to taste

Combine the ingredients for the sauce in a mixing bowl and whisk to mix. Cover and refrigerate if not using immediately. Eat within a few hours of making.

WOOD-GRILLED SWORDFISH
WITH BUTTER-FRIED OLIVES

YIELD: Serves 4

METHOD: Direct grilling

PREP TIME: 10 minutes

GRILLING TIME: 8 minutes

GRILL/GEAR: Can be grilled on charcoal, wood, or gas. You also need an instant-read thermometer and oak or other hardwood logs, chunks, or unsoaked chips (optional).

People often ask me what I grill at home. This simple swordfish comes as close to a weekly meal as any dish I cook on the grill. In the summer, we get superlative Atlantic swordfish and season it with salt, pepper, olive oil, and lemon juice—nothing more. I grill it over a wood fire and top it with a simple sauce of olives or capers fried in butter. Sometimes less really is more.

INGREDIENTS

FOR THE SWORDFISH

4 swordfish steaks, preferably harpooned, each 6 to 8 ounces and at least 1 inch thick

Coarse salt (sea or kosher) and freshly ground or cracked black peppercorns

3 Meyer or conventional lemons, cut in half widthwise and seeded

Extra virgin olive oil

FOR THE BUTTER-FRIED OLIVES

8 tablespoons (1 stick) unsalted butter

¼ cup diced pitted green olives or drained capers or both

Vegetable oil for oiling the grill grate

---

1. Arrange the swordfish steaks in a nonreactive baking dish. Generously season the swordfish on both sides with salt and pepper. Squeeze the juice of 1 lemon over the fish on both sides. (Squeeze it through your fingers to catch the seeds.) Drizzle olive oil on both sides, patting it and the seasonings into the meat with the back of a fork. Marinate the fish in the refrigerator for 20 minutes while you light the fire and make the sauce.

2. Make the Butter-Fried Olives: Melt the butter in a skillet over medium-high heat. Add the olives or capers and fry until crisp, 2 to 4 minutes. Set aside and keep warm.

3. Set up your grill for direct grilling and heat to high. Ideally, you'll grill over wood, or at least add wood chunks or chips to the coals (or place on the heat diffuser or in the smoker box of your gas grill). Brush or scrape the grill grate clean and oil it well.

4. Drain the swordfish, reserving the marinade. Arrange the steaks on the grate (all should run in the same direction—slightly on the diagonal to the bars of the grate). Grill until cooked through, about 4 minutes per side, giving each steak a quarter turn after 2 minutes to lay on a crosshatch of grill marks. When you invert the fish, pour the reserved marinade over the steaks. While you're at it, grill the remaining 4 lemon halves.

5. There are two ways to test for doneness. The first is the "poke" test: Press the fish with your index finger. If it feels firm and starts to break into clean flakes, it's cooked. Alternatively, insert an instant-read thermometer through the side of one of the steaks. The internal temperature should be about 140°F.

6. Transfer the swordfish to a platter or plates. Rewarm the olive butter and pour it over the fish. Serve the grilled lemon halves for squeezing on the side.

SHOP: Swordfish is widely available, but the fish is not the same everywhere. In Martha's Vineyard, we seek "harpooned" swordfish, which means that the fish was speared from a small boat and brought to market within 24 hours. In Florida, we look for "pink swordfish," which owes its alluring coral color to a diet of pink shrimp. Can't find swordfish in your area? Any steak fish can be grilled in this fashion, from tuna to salmon to wahoo. Meyer lemons (a cross between a lemon and a mandarin orange) have a distinctive floral fragrance.

INSIDER TIP: With a preparation this simple, the dish thrives or flops by the quality of the ingredients and the fuel. That fuel is wood—a pure wood fire if your grill allows, otherwise, wood-enhanced charcoal or gas (see page 21). Here's a great trick if you have a charcoal grill: Fill your chimney starter with oak or other hardwood chunks and light as you would charcoal. Once the coals glow red, spread them over the lower grate. Bingo: You're grilling over wood just like an Argentinean *asador* or Italian grill master. You can even grill on wood on a gas grill: Place hardwood chunks between the Flavorizer Bars (found in Weber gas grills) or on the heat diffuser plates. Note: Do not soak the wood. You want a light wood flavor, not the heavy smoke of barbecue.

ALBACORE TUNA "FILETS MIGNONS"
WITH PEPPERCORN CREAM SAUCE

YIELD: Serves 4 to 6

METHOD: Plancha grilling/ direct grilling

PREP TIME: 20 minutes

GRILLING TIME: About 6 minutes, depending on desired doneness

GRILL/GEAR: Can be grilled over charcoal, wood, or gas. You also need butcher's string; a plancha or cast-iron skillet; and 2 hardwood chunks or 1½ cups unsoaked wood chips.

SHOP: You'll want an albacore tuna loin—a long cylindrical cut—for this dish. Tuna often comes portioned this way on the West Coast; otherwise, ask your fishmonger to cut it for you. Of the seven species of tuna commonly eaten, "albie" (as we call albacore on Martha's Vineyard) has the lightest color and mildest flavor. (It's one species of tuna that goes into canned tuna fish.) If unavailable, use yellowfin, bluefin, or whatever variety looks freshest in your area.

Most of the dishes you see on my TV shows are carefully planned in advance. This one I created on the spot to showcase some gorgeous, astonishingly fresh albacore fillets a local fisherman brought to the set of *Project Smoke*. Plancha searing gives you a crisp smoky bacon crust on the outside, but you keep the grilling sufficiently brief to leave the fish sushi-rare in the center. Cut crosswise, the albacore looks like bacon-wrapped filet mignon. To continue the beef metaphor, you serve it with a Peppercorn Cream Sauce.

INGREDIENTS

FOR THE PEPPERCORN CREAM SAUCE

2 tablespoons (¼ stick) unsalted butter

1 large shallot, peeled and minced

1 tablespoon cracked black peppercorns

¾ cup dry white wine

1 cup heavy (whipping) cream

1 tablespoon Dijon mustard

2 tablespoons chopped fresh tarragon, plus extra sprigs for garnish

A few drops of fresh lemon juice or tarragon vinegar

Coarse salt (sea or kosher)

FOR THE ALBACORE

2 trimmed sushi-quality albacore tuna loins, each ¾ to 1 pound

Coarse salt (sea or kosher) and freshly ground black pepper

6 to 8 strips artisanal bacon

Vegetable oil for oiling the plancha or grill grate

1. Make the Peppercorn Cream Sauce: Melt the butter in a heavy saucepan over medium heat. Stir in the shallot and pepper and sauté until lightly browned. Increase the heat to high and add the white wine. Boil until reduced by half. Stir in the cream and mustard and boil until the sauce is reduced to about 1 cup—it should be thick enough to coat the back of a

spoon. Stir in the chopped tarragon, lemon juice, and salt to taste; the sauce should be highly seasoned. The sauce can be made several hours ahead.

2. Prepare the tuna: Season the tuna loins well on all sides with salt and pepper. For each loin, cut 4 lengths of butcher's string, each about 10 inches

long, and line them up parallel to one another, 1½ to 2 inches apart. Place a strip of bacon in the center, perpendicular to the strings. Lay a tuna loin on the bacon. Lay 2 more strips of bacon on top of the tuna (3 if the loins are large). Bring the ends of the strings over the loin, and tie so that the bacon is held firmly in place. Repeat with the other loin.

3. Set up your grill for direct grilling and heat to high. Place a cast-iron plancha on the grate and heat it as well. To test whether it is ready for grilling, sprinkle a drop or two of water on the plancha—if it evaporates in 1 to 2 seconds, the plancha is hot. Lightly oil the plancha.

4. Arrange the tuna loins on the plancha (or directly on the grill grate if not using a plancha) and grill until the bacon is browned and crisp, about 2 minutes per side, 6 minutes in all (less if the loins are really small), turning with tongs. Do not overcook; the fish should stay rare or raw in the center.

5. Transfer the tuna loins to a cutting board. Reheat the cream sauce as needed. Remove the strings from the tuna, then slice the loins into 1-inch-thick medallions and serve with the sauce spooned under or over them and tarragon sprigs on top.

INSIDER TIP: This recipe calls for a technique I call plancha grilling: You cook the fish on heated cast iron, adding hardwood to the fire to generate wood smoke. Alternatively, you can direct grill the tuna, but the bacon won't be quite as crisp.

CEDAR-PLANKED STRIPED BASS
WITH MISO GLAZE

For many years, I adhered to conventional wisdom: You soak a cedar plank in water before putting it on the grill. The water kept it from burning, the logic went, releasing a cedar-scented steam to flavor your food. One day on the set of *Project Smoke*, we left some cedar-planked trout in a Big Green Egg too long. When we opened the lid, the plank was aflame and the fish . . . was absolutely delicious. Since that time, I've skipped the soaking and I char the plank to generate cedar smoke. Believe me, smoke is a lot more flavorful than steam. Boosting that flavor is a sweet-salty umami-rich glaze made with miso and maple syrup that goes great with the luscious rich flesh of the bass. Serve the bass with the Fennel Orange Salad that also accompanies the trout on page 256.

YIELD: Serves 4

METHOD: Direct grilling/ indirect grilling/plank grilling

PREP TIME: 10 minutes

GRILLING TIME: 15 to 20 minutes

GRILL/GEAR: Can be grilled over charcoal or gas. You also need a cedar grilling plank (6 to 8 by 12 to 14 inches).

SHOP: This recipe calls for striped bass (preferably wild), but it's also excellent with wild salmon. Pick a section cut from the head end or center of the fillet. As for miso, it's a traditional Japanese cultured soybean and/or grain paste with rich sweet-salty umami flavors. (And it's probably available in the produce section of your local supermarket.) I call for white miso—the most common (made with soybeans and rice), but feel free to experiment with yellow or red miso.

INSIDER TIP: This bass uses a two-step grilling process: direct grilling to char the plank and indirect grilling to cook the fish. However, if you're feeling adventurous (or simply pyromaniacal), you can do the entire process by direct grilling. Use the thickest plank you can find and be ready with a water pistol to extinguish any serious flames (little flames are fine).

INGREDIENTS

FOR THE MISO GLAZE

3 tablespoons sweet rice wine (mirin) or sake

2 tablespoons pure maple syrup

½ cup white miso

⅓ cup mayonnaise, preferably Hellmann's or Best Foods or the Japanese Kewpie brand

½ teaspoon finely grated fresh lemon zest

FOR THE BASS

1 striped bass fillet (1½ to 2 pounds), center-cut, skin and bones removed

Coarse salt (sea or kosher) and freshly ground black pepper

2 tablespoons black or white sesame seeds

Fennel Orange Salad (page 256; optional)

1. Set up your grill for indirect grilling and heat to medium-high. Brush or scrape the grill grate clean; there's no need to oil it.

2. Meanwhile, make the glaze: Place the mirin and maple syrup in a saucepan and bring to a boil over high heat. Remove the pan from the heat and whisk in the miso. Let cool to room temperature. Add the mayonnaise and lemon zest and whisk until smooth. Set aside.

3. Place the plank directly over one of the fires and grill until lightly charred on the bottom, 1 to 2 minutes. Place on a heatproof surface and let cool.

4. Generously season the fish with salt and pepper. Lay it on the charred side of the plank. Spread the glaze over the fish. Dot the top with sesame seeds.

5. Return the plank to the grill away from the heat. Close the lid and indirect grill until the glaze is browned and bubbling and the fish is cooked through (to 140°F on an instant-read thermometer), 15 to 20 minutes. Serve the bass on the plank with the salad on the side, if using.

GRILL BASKET HALIBUT
WITH MAPLE TERIYAKI

Here's a New England riff on a Japanese favorite: teriyaki sweetened with maple syrup. You might think that the fish will stick to the grill grate. It won't. You might think that the sugar in the maple syrup will burn. It will—but just enough to impart a sweet-smoky caramel crust to the fish. Teriyaki comes from the Japanese words *teri*, meaning "luster" or "shine," and *yaki*, meaning "grilled." Rarely do four simple ingredients deliver such a big dividend of flavor.

INGREDIENTS

FOR THE MARINADE

½ cup soy sauce or tamari (a high-quality soy sauce brewed exclusively from soy beans)

½ cup sweet rice wine (mirin), sake, or white wine

½ cup pure maple syrup

½ cup Asian (dark) sesame oil

1 scallion, trimmed, white part smashed (reserve the green part, thinly sliced on the diagonal, for serving)

FOR THE FISH

1½ to 2 pounds fresh halibut, cut into 4 even pieces

Cooking oil spray for the grill basket

Vegetable oil for oiling the grill grate

1. Make the marinade/sauce: Combine the soy sauce, mirin, maple syrup, sesame oil, and scallion white in a saucepan and whisk to mix.

2. Arrange the halibut in a baking dish just large enough to hold it. Pour the marinade over the halibut, turning it a few times to coat well. Marinate the fish, covered, in the refrigerator for 1 to 2 hours, turning two or three times.

3. Drain the halibut well, pouring the marinade back into the saucepan.

Place the fish pieces in a grill basket that you've oiled well with oil spray.

4. Boil the marinade over high heat until syrupy and reduced by about one third, whisking often. You should have about 1¼ cups. Set this glaze aside for serving.

5. Set up your grill for direct grilling and heat to high. Brush or scrape the grill grate clean and oil it well. Lay the grill basket with the fish in it on the grate and grill the halibut until sizzling and browned on the outside

YIELD: Serves 4

METHOD: Direct grilling

PREP TIME: 10 minutes, plus 1 to 2 hours for marinating

GRILLING TIME: 6 to 10 minutes

GRILL/GEAR: Can be grilled over charcoal, wood, or gas. You also need a hinged grill basket and oil spray.

SHOP: Halibut is a semi-firm white fish with a mild sweet flavor. And it's one of the rare wild fish you find on both the East and West Coasts. Can't find halibut in your area? Teriyaki goes equally well with salmon, bluefish, and bass. You'll need to know about a couple of special ingredients for this dish. Asian sesame oil—pressed from roasted sesame seeds—has an alluring nutty flavor. One good brand is Kadoya from Japan. Mirin is Japanese sweet rice wine—you can substitute sake or white wine plus a little extra maple syrup.

Grill Basket Halibut with Maple Teriyaki

and cooked through, 3 to 5 minutes per side. After 3 minutes, start basting the fish with some of the teriyaki glaze. Baste several times.

6. Carefully open the grill basket and transfer the fish to a platter or plates. Reboil the remaining glaze, whisk well, then strain it over the fish. Sprinkle with the scallion greens and serve. FYI, our food stylist, Nora Singley, likes to serve the halibut with grilled scallions.

INSIDER TIP: So how do you grill a delicate stick-prone fish, like halibut, without leaving half of it stuck to the grill grate? One solution—used by grill masters in Europe and Central Asia—is to cook it in a grill basket. The beauty of this method? You turn the basket, not the fish.

SALT SLAB-GRILLED ROCKFISH
WITH MANGO MINT SALSA

Salt slab grilling may be new, but the pink salt mountain in the Pakistani Himalayas from which the slabs are mined has been around for hundreds of millions of years. (Alexander the Great stopped there to give his horses salt on his march to conquer India.) So is salt slab solely about the theatrics or does it actually improve the taste? The answer is a little of both. Yes, a whole fish roasting on a salt slab looks dramatic (especially when you serve it on the slab). But a salt slab also delivers on cooking performance and flavor—the former by providing a steady even heat (think of it as turbo-charged indirect grilling); the latter by mixing with the fish juices and infusing a salt flavor back into the fish. In short, it will make you look better and make your fish taste better, too. The following dish counterpoints salt with the fresh sweet-tart tang of Mango Mint Salsa.

YIELD: Serves 2 to 3

METHOD: Salt slab grilling/ indirect grilling

PREP TIME: 20 minutes

GRILLING TIME: 30 to 40 minutes

GRILL/GEAR: Can be grilled over charcoal or gas. You also need a pink salt slab large enough to hold the fish and an instant-read thermometer.

INSIDER TIP: Warning: Do not make this recipe in cold weather. Hot salt slabs have been known to crack or explode when exposed to cold air.

INGREDIENTS

FOR THE FISH

1 whole rockfish, snapper, or other fish (2 to 2½ pounds), cleaned

Coarse salt (sea or kosher) and freshly ground black pepper

3 fresh mint sprigs

Extra virgin olive oil

FOR THE MINT BUTTER BASTE

5 tablespoons unsalted butter

1 clove garlic, peeled and minced

3 tablespoons finely slivered fresh mint

Coarse salt (sea or kosher) and freshly ground black pepper, to taste

Mango Mint Salsa (recipe follows)

1. Set up your grill for indirect grilling and heat slowly to medium-high. Gradually heat the salt slab at the same time.

2. Prepare the fish: Make 3 slashes to the bone in each side of the fish. (This helps the fish cook more evenly.) Generously season the inside and outside of the fish with salt and pepper. Stuff mint sprigs inside the cavity. Drizzle the outside of the fish with olive oil.

3. Make the mint butter baste: Melt the butter in a small saucepan. Add the garlic and mint and cook over medium-high heat until lightly browned, 2 minutes. Stir in salt and pepper to taste.

4. Arrange the fish directly on the hot salt slab. Grill until sizzling and browned on the outside and cooked through, 30 to 40 minutes. Start basting the fish with the mint butter baste after 15 minutes and baste once or twice more as the rockfish cooks.

5. To check for doneness, look in one of the slits: The fish at the bone should be white and should separate into flakes when pressed with a fork. The internal temperature will be about 140°F.

6. Transfer the fish on its salt slab to a heatproof platter. Serve with the Mango Mint Salsa.

MANGO MINT SALSA
YIELD: Makes about 2 cups

You could serve the salt slab fish solely with the Mint Butter Baste (above), but the tropical freshness of Mango Mint Salsa takes it over the top.

INGREDIENTS

1 large or 2 medium ripe mangoes, pitted and cut into ¼-inch dice (enough to make 1½ cups)

1 small cucumber, peeled, seeded, and cut into ¼-inch dice (enough to make ½ cup)

¼ cup finely diced red onion

1 to 2 jalapeño peppers, seeded and finely diced (for a spicier relish, leave the seeds in)

2 tablespoons finely chopped candied ginger

¼ cup chopped fresh mint leaves

3 tablespoons fresh lime juice, or to taste

2 tablespoons packed light brown sugar, or to taste

Place all the ingredients in a mixing bowl and toss to mix. Correct the seasoning, adding lime juice or brown sugar to taste; the relish should be a little sweet and a little sour.

SARDINES GRILLED IN GRAPE LEAVES
WITH TOMATO OLIVE SALSA/LEMON SESAME SAUCE

Grilled sardines turn up across the Mediterranean region—from Portugal, where they sizzle on innumerable street corner grills during sardine season, to Italy, where the silvery fish gave its name to the island of Sardinia. Here's a Greek version featuring sardines grilled in grape leaves. The acidity of the pickled grape leaves balances the oily richness of the fish, and the visuals are off the charts. I offer two options for sauces: a Tomato Olive Salsa or a nutty Lemon Sesame Sauce. Better yet, serve both.

YIELD: Serves 4

METHOD: Direct grilling/leaf grilling

PREP TIME: 15 minutes

GRILLING TIME: 6 to 8 minutes

GRILL/GEAR: Can be grilled over charcoal, wood, or gas. You also need toothpicks and an instant-read thermometer.

INGREDIENTS

FOR THE SARDINES

12 fresh sardines (about 2 pounds)

Coarse salt (sea or kosher) and freshly ground black pepper

Dried oregano, preferably Greek for seasoning

1 lemon

12 large pickled grape leaves (more if the leaves are small)

FOR THE TOMATO OLIVE SALSA

1 lemon (use the one from the sardines)

1 pint cherry tomatoes (red, yellow, or a mix), cut in half

½ cup pitted kalamata olives, diced

1 scallion, trimmed, white and green parts thinly sliced crosswise

3 tablespoons fresh lemon juice

3 tablespoons extra virgin olive oil

½ teaspoon dried oregano, preferably Greek

Coarse salt (sea or kosher) and freshly ground black pepper

Lemon Sesame Sauce (recipe follows)

1. Rinse and dry the sardines. Season each inside and out with salt and pepper. Season the cavity with dried oregano. Using a vegetable peeler, remove strips of zest from the lemon and place 1 in the cavity of each fish. Wrap each sardine in a grape leaf (use 2 if the sardines are large or the grape leaves are small), leaving the head and tail uncovered. Refrigerate until ready to grill.

2. Make the salsa: Peel off the rind and white pith of the lemon and discard. Cut the flesh into ¼-inch dice, discarding the seeds. Place in a mixing bowl. Stir in the tomatoes, olives, scallion, lemon juice, and

Fresh silvery sardines ready for grilling.

olive oil. Add dried oregano (about ½ teaspoon) and salt and pepper to taste; the salsa should be highly seasoned.

3. Set up your grill for direct grilling and heat to high. Brush or scrape the grill grate clean and oil it well.

4. Arrange the sardines on the grate and grill until the grape leaves are charred and the fish is cooked through, 3 to 4 minutes per side. (Insert an instant-read thermometer in the cavity to check for doneness: The internal temperature should be 140°F.)

5. Transfer the sardines to a platter or plates. Spoon the salsa over them and dig in. The easiest way to bone a sardine is to eat the top fillet, then lift the tail to pull out the backbone and head. The grape leaves are edible.

SHOP: Sardines are available fresh at select fish markets (especially Iberian markets) and frozen at fish markets and many supermarkets. Pickled (brined) grape leaves can be found canned or jarred at most supermarkets or online. One popular brand is Krinos.

INSIDER'S TIP: Ask your fishmonger to scale and clean the sardines. I personally think sardines look naked without the heads, but you can remove them if desired. Can't find sardines? Cut salmon or tuna fillets into 1½-by-4-inch strips. Wrap and grill as described on page 253.

LEMON SESAME SAUCE

YIELD: Makes 1 cup

This creamy, nutty, lemony sauce takes its inspiration from Middle Eastern *taratoor*. You'll need one special ingredient—tahini (sesame paste)—which is available in the ethnic foods section of most supermarkets or online.

INGREDIENTS

1 clove garlic, peeled and minced

½ teaspoon coarse salt (sea or kosher)

½ teaspoon freshly ground black pepper

½ cup tahini

⅓ cup fresh lemon juice, or to taste

¼ cup hot water, or as needed

Place the garlic, salt, and pepper in the bottom of a mixing bowl and mash to a paste with the back of a spoon. Whisk in the tahini, lemon juice, and enough hot water to obtain a pourable sauce. Add lemon juice and salt to taste; the sauce should strike a balance between sesame, lemon, and salt. Let cool to room temperature for serving. Refrigerated, the sauce will keep for at least 3 days.

BACON-GRILLED TROUT
WITH FENNEL ORANGE SALAD

YIELD: Serves 4

METHOD: Direct grilling

PREP TIME: 15 minutes

GRILLING TIME: 8 to 12 minutes

GRILL/GEAR: Can be grilled over charcoal, wood, or gas. You also need a mandoline for slicing the fennel (optional) or food processor and butcher's string.

SHOP: If you're a fisherman (especially a good one with a fly rod), you won't need to shop at all. The rest of us will have to buy trout—two good online sources are Anderson Seafoods and Hy-On-A-Hill Trout Farm.

INSIDER TIP: Grill masters in the south of France often grill fish over fennel stalks. So when you buy fennel, try to find bulbs with the stems and feathery leaves. You can add them to the fire fresh or dried.

If you're grilling a whole fish for the first time, trout is a great way to start. Trout cooks evenly thanks to its long slender shape. And one fish serves one person, so you don't need to worry about filleting or portioning. You don't even have to worry about the fish sticking to the grill grate, because you grill the trout wrapped in bacon. Tip o' the hat to *Project Smoke* TV field chef, Chris Lynch, who serves the smoky trout with a refreshing salad of fennel, orange, and mint.

INGREDIENTS

4 trout, cleaned and trimmed (each 12 to 16 ounces)

Coarse salt (sea or kosher) and freshly ground black pepper

1 large fresh fennel bulb (ideally with stalks and feathery leaves attached)

2 large navel or Cara Cara oranges

1 bunch fresh mint, stemmed

2 scallions, trimmed, white part cut lengthwise in quarters, green part thinly sliced on the diagonal

2 tablespoons (¼ stick) cold butter, cut into 8 thin slices

8 strips artisanal bacon

2 tablespoons fresh lemon juice (or to taste)

2 tablespoons extra virgin olive oil

Vegetable oil for oiling the grill grate

1. Season the trout inside and out with salt and pepper.

2. Trim the stalks and leaves off the fennel and set aside. Cut the bulb crosswise into paper-thin slices (this is most easily done on a mandoline or in a food processor fitted with a slicing blade). Cut 2 of the slices in half and set aside. Place the remaining fennel slices in a mixing bowl for the salad. Chop the feathery leaves and add them to the mixing bowl.

3. Remove 4 strips of orange zest with a vegetable peeler and stuff one into each trout. Peel off the orange rind, and white pith, and make V-shaped cuts in each section to remove the individual segments from the membranes. (The French call these *supremes*.) Work over the fennel bowl to catch any juices. Drop each supreme into the bowl as it is removed from its membranes. Set aside.

4. Stuff each trout with a half slice of the reserved fennel and a mint sprig. Thinly sliver the rest of the mint and add it to the mixing bowl with the fennel and orange supremes.

5. Stuff half the white part of the scallion into each trout. Add the scallion greens to the mixing bowl.

6. Stuff 2 of the butter slices into each trout.

7. Lay 3 ten-inch lengths of butcher's string on your work surface, each parallel to the next, about 2 inches apart. Lay a strip of bacon perpendicular to the strings down the center. Lay a trout on top. Top the trout with a second strip of bacon. Loop the ends of the strings over the bacon and tie tightly. Snip off the ends of the strings and discard. Wrap and tie the remaining trout the same way. All this sounds a lot more complicated than it really is. And the trout can be stuffed and wrapped several hours ahead, covered and refrigerated.

8. Set up your grill for direct grilling and heat to medium-high. Lay the fennel stalks under the grate on the coals or on the heat diffusers of your gas grill.

9. While the grill is heating, finish the salad. Add the lemon juice, olive oil, and salt and pepper and toss to mix. Correct the seasoning, adding salt or lemon juice to taste; the salad should be highly seasoned.

10. Brush or scrape the grill grate clean and oil it well. Arrange the trout on the grill over the fennel stalks, running on the diagonal to the bars of the grate. Grill until the bacon is browned and crisp and the fish is cooked through, 4 to 6 minutes per side, giving each a quarter turn after 2 minutes to lay on a crosshatch of grill marks. To check the trout for doneness, cut a small slit in the back behind the head: The flesh at the backbone should be white and should come away from the bones easily.

11. Transfer the grilled trout to a platter or plates. Snip and remove the strings. Serve the hot trout with the Fennel Orange Salad on the side.

VEGGIES AND TOFU

I recently dined at an edgy new restaurant in Chicago, and no, it wasn't a meat palace or grill joint. Bad Hunter proposes a "vegetable forward" menu with the likes of grilled radish salad and ember-charred snap peas served hot off a wood-burning J & R Oyler pit. A gentle reminder how much progress grilled vegetables have made in a country that, when I was growing up, scarcely acknowledged their existence. Today, we grill not just the obvious peppers, corn, and mushrooms, but artichokes, kale, and chiles rellenos. And we're using grilling techniques that were unheard of for vegetables a decade ago. Beer-Brined Rotisserie Cauliflower, for example (see page 268). Or Caveman Cabbage roasted on the embers (see page 263). Or salt slab-grilled acorn squash (see page 283). There has never been a more interesting time to grill or eat your vegetables. Here's how.

CHIVE-GRILLED ARTICHOKES
WITH CHARRED LEMON AIOLI

YIELD: Serves 4

METHOD: Direct grilling

PREP TIME: 30 minutes for trimming and boiling the artichokes

GRILLING TIME: 8 minutes

GRILL/GEAR: Can be grilled over charcoal, wood, or gas. But for the most flavor, use wood or a wood-enhanced fire (see page 21). You also need 2 hardwood chunks or 1½ cups unsoaked wood chips (optional); a melon baller or grapefruit spoon; a metal skewer; a wire rack; and a basting brush.

SHOP: When buying artichokes, look for flowers (for that's what an artichoke is) that feel heavy and compact. When in season, baby artichokes are great for grilling. You'll need three to four baby artichokes to equal one large globe artichoke. A Meyer lemon is a cross between a lemon and a mandarin orange. It has a wonderful perfumed flavor, but a conventional lemon will do just fine.

At first glance, the dense, fibrous artichoke would seem like a poor choice of vegetable for grilling. Just don't tell any Sicilians, who cook them on massive charcoal-burning grills set up in market streets in Catania and Palermo. Or the Spaniards or Californians, for whom wood-grilled artichokes are not only a popular vegetable, but an article of barbecue faith. The following makes a great starter as well as an uncommon vegetable side dish, and the smoky Charred Lemon Aioli takes it over the top.

INGREDIENTS

Coarse salt (sea or kosher)

4 artichokes, preferably large globe artichokes

2 lemons, preferably Meyer lemons

8 tablespoons (1 stick) melted unsalted butter, extra virgin olive oil, or a mix

3 tablespoons finely chopped fresh chives

Vegetable oil for oiling the grill grate

Freshly ground black pepper

Charred Lemon Aioli (recipe follows), for serving

1. Bring 1 gallon of water with 4 teaspoons of salt to a boil in a large stockpot.

2. Cut the thorny tips off the ends of the artichoke leaves with kitchen scissors. This is optional, but makes the artichokes easier to eat. Trim ⅛ inch off the stem end. (The rest of the stem is edible.) Using a chef's knife, cut each artichoke in half lengthwise (even if the artichokes are small). Using a melon baller, grapefruit spoon, or your fingers, scrape out and discard the "choke" (the clump of fuzzy fibers just above the heart).

3. Finely grate the zest of 1 lemon and set aside for the aioli (page 263; you should have about ½ teaspoon). Cut both lemons in half and remove the seeds with a fork. Rub the cut parts of the artichoke with one of the lemon halves to keep them from discoloring.

4. Place the artichokes in the boiling water and cook until just tender, about 20 minutes. Use a metal skewer to test for doneness; it should pierce the artichoke with just a little resistance. Do not overcook; the artichokes should remain firm. Drain the artichokes in a colander, running cold water over them until they are cold. Position the artichokes cut sides down and drain them well on a wire rack covered

with a dish towel or paper towels. The artichokes can be cooked ahead to this stage and refrigerated in a large resealable plastic bag for up to 24 hours.

5. Pour the melted butter or olive oil into a small bowl and stir in 2 tablespoons of the chives. Reserve the remainder.

6. Set up your grill for direct grilling and heat to high. If using a charcoal grill, place hardwood chunks or chips on the coals. If using a gas grill, lay a few wood chunks between the heat diffuser bars or on the ceramic heating elements. If using a wood grill, do nothing more than light it; don't let the flames die down completely—it's good to have some smoke and fire. Brush or scrape the grill grate clean and oil it well.

7. Brush the cut sides of the artichokes with chive butter and

dab more butter between and over the leaves. Season with salt and pepper. Arrange the artichoke halves, cut sides down, on the grill running diagonal to the bars of the grate. Grill for 2 minutes, then give each artichoke a quarter turn to lay on a crosshatch of grill marks. Baste the tops of the artichokes with the chive butter, dabbing it under the leaves. While you're at it, grill the remaining 2 lemon halves for the aioli.

8. When the bottoms are nicely browned and grill-marked, turn the artichokes over and grill the leaf side, again basting with chive butter. The artichokes are ready when sizzling hot and browned on both sides. Transfer the artichokes to a platter or plates. Drizzle with any remaining chive butter and sprinkle with the reserved chives. Serve the Charred Lemon Aioli for dipping.

Cut the barbed ends off the artichoke leaves using kitchen scissors.

Remove the fibrous choke from each artichoke half.

CHARRED LEMON AIOLI

YIELD: Makes 1 cup

Aioli (garlic mayonnaise) is a common condiment for artichokes in southern France, and it's about to get more interesting with the sweet smoky juice of fire-charred lemons.

INGREDIENTS

1 clove garlic, peeled and minced

½ teaspoon coarse salt (sea or kosher)

½ teaspoon finely grated lemon zest (see Step 3, page 260)

1 cup mayonnaise, preferably Hellmann's or Best Foods

Juice from the grilled lemon halves (see Step 7, facing page)

½ teaspoon freshly ground black pepper

Place the garlic, salt, and lemon zest in the bottom of a mixing bowl and mash to a paste with the back of a wooden spoon. Whisk in the mayonnaise, lemon juice, and pepper. Add salt to taste as needed. If not serving right away, cover and refrigerate until using. The aioli will keep for at least 3 days.

CAVEMAN CABBAGE
WITH SWEET AND SOUR FIRE SAUCE

Cabbage has long been a barbecue staple, but most of us consume it in the form of slaw. Here's a cabbage that's actually barbecued—make that smoke-roasted on the embers. Jamaicans use a similar technique with whole breadfruit.

YIELD: Serves 3 to 4

METHOD: Caveman grilling (on the embers)

PREP TIME: 5 minutes

GRILLING TIME: 15 to 30 minutes

INGREDIENTS

1 head savoy cabbage or green cabbage (about 2 pounds), cut in half from top to bottom

Coarse salt (kosher or sea) and freshly ground black pepper

Sweet and Sour Fire Sauce (recipe follows)

1. Set up your grill for caveman grilling and when ready to cook, rake the coals into an even layer, using a grill hoe or garden hoe. Fan with a folded newspaper to disperse any loose ash.

2. Lay the cabbage halves on the coals. Grill until charred black on all sides and very tender inside, turning often with tongs. This could take as little as 15 minutes or as long as 30, depending on the size and density of the cabbage. Use a slender metal skewer to test for doneness. It should pierce the cabbage easily.

3. Transfer the cabbage to a sheet pan and let it rest until cool enough to handle. Trim off the burnt outside leaves. Cut the cabbage into wedges and season with salt and pepper. Serve with the Sweet and Sour Fire Sauce.

Variation

Direct grilling method on a gas grill: Okay, so you don't have a charcoal grill. You can still approximate the smoky char of caveman cabbage on a gas grill.

1. Set up your grill for direct grilling and heat to high. Brush or scrape the grill grate clean and oil it well.

2. Cut the cabbage as described in Step 3 and place on the grate, cut side down. Direct grill until the cut side is very darkly browned, 10 minutes. Turn it over and direct grill the rounded side until charred black, 15 to 20 minutes. Serve as described above.

GRILL/GEAR: Cavemanning must be done over charcoal or wood. You also need a grill hoe or garden hoe and a newspaper for fanning the coals.

SHOP: I like savoy cabbage, with its crinkly leaves and sweet flavor, for cavemanning. You can certainly use regular green cabbage.

INSIDER TIP: This cabbage calls for a technique I call ember-smoking. In effect, you burn the outside of the cabbage on the embers. This drives smoke flavor to the center of the cabbage. You can approach the flavor of caveman cabbage on a gas grill by direct grilling it until the exterior is charred (see Variation). You can also grill the cabbage whole, in which case you'll need 40 to 50 minutes.

SWEET AND SOUR FIRE SAUCE

YIELD: About 1 cup

This sweet and sour fire sauce gives you plenty of balsamic sweetness and chile fire.

INGREDIENTS

6 tablespoons (¾ stick) unsalted butter

6 tablespoons balsamic vinegar

6 tablespoons of your favorite hot sauce

Coarse salt (kosher or sea) and freshly ground black pepper

Place the butter, vinegar, and hot sauce in a heavy nonreactive saucepan over high heat. Melt the butter, then boil the ingredients until syrupy, 3 to 5 minutes, whisking steadily. Remove the pan from the heat and let cool to room temperature. Add salt and pepper to taste.

SMOKE-ROASTED CARROTS
WITH SPICE-SCENTED YOGURT

YIELD: Serves 4 to 6

METHOD: Smoke-roasting/ indirect grilling followed by direct grilling

PREP TIME: 10 minutes

GRILLING TIME: 35 to 50 minutes

GRILL/GEAR: Can be grilled over charcoal or gas. You'll also need a disposable aluminum foil pan (9 by 13 inches) and 2 hardwood chunks or 1½ cups wood chips (if using the latter, soak in water to cover for 30 minutes, then drain).

SHOP: Buy organic rainbow carrots (which come in red, purple, and white in addition to the usual orange). They tend to taste more, well, carroty than cheap commodity carrots, and there won't be any residual pesticides. One sign of freshness is bright springy green tops (which you can use to make pesto).

INSIDER TIP: These carrots call for a two-step grilling process (indirect grilling followed by direct grilling), so although they're cooked in a foil pan and never directly on the grate, I feel comfortable including them in a book on grilling. The indirect grilling softens and smokes them, while direct grilling caramelizes and crisps the exterior.

Call it the carrot moment. This slender root vegetable is turning up on fashionable menus everywhere. (I recently had terrific roasted carrots with spiced yogurt at Jean-Georges Vongerichten's plant-based abcV restaurant in New York.) Sometimes roasted, sometimes smoked or grilled, carrots are now served as starters, desserts, and even in cocktails. Sometimes they precede the steak; sometimes they *are* the steak. Of course, they also make a killer side dish. Think of these sweet, smoky, crusty, meaty, tender carrots as vegetable brisket.

INGREDIENTS

2 pounds medium-size whole carrots, trimmed and peeled

2 tablespoons extra virgin olive oil, or more as needed

Coarse salt (sea or kosher) and freshly ground black pepper

Spice-Scented Yogurt (optional; recipe follows)

1 to 2 teaspoons fresh thyme for serving

1. Set up your grill for indirect grilling and heat to medium-high.

2. Arrange the carrots in a single layer in a large disposable aluminum foil pan. Drizzle with olive oil and season generously with salt and pepper.

3. Place the carrots in the foil pan on the grill grate away from direct heat. Add wood chunks or chips to the coals. Close the grill lid.

4. Smoke-roast the carrots until almost tender, 30 to 40 minutes. Move the carrots (still in the pan) directly over the fire and grill until the exteriors are darkly browned and crusty, 5 to 10 minutes, turning with tongs to ensure even browning.

5. Arrange the carrots on a platter or plates. Spoon the Spice-Scented Yogurt over them and sprinkle with thyme, if using.

NOTE: One easy way to sprinkle fresh thyme is to rub an upright bunch between the palms of your hands. The leaves will fall over the carrots.

SPICE-SCENTED YOGURT

YIELD: Makes 1 cup

Roasted carrots with spiced yogurt has become a new American culinary classic, playing the tart tang of the yogurt off the earthy sweetness of the carrots. Cumin, coriander, and hot red pepper flakes add a North African accent.

INGREDIENTS

1 teaspoon cumin seeds

1 teaspoon coriander seeds

1 cup plain Greek-style yogurt

½ to 1 teaspoon hot red pepper flakes

½ teaspoon finely grated fresh lemon or lime zest

1 tablespoon extra virgin olive oil

Coarse salt (sea or kosher) and freshly ground black pepper

1. Heat a dry cast-iron skillet over medium-high heat. Add the cumin and coriander seeds and roast until fragrant and lightly browned, 1 minute, stirring with a wooden spoon. Lightly crush the roasted spices with a pestle or the back of a smaller frying pan to crack the coriander seeds.

2. Place the yogurt in a bowl and stir in the toasted spices, hot red pepper flakes, lemon zest, olive oil, and salt and pepper to taste. The yogurt should be highly seasoned.

ROTISSERIE CAULIFLOWER

YIELD: Serves 2 as a meatless entrée; 4 as a side dish

METHOD: Rotisserie/spit-roasting

PREP TIME: 10 minutes plus 6 to 8 hours for brining

I like to think of cauliflower as the rib roast of the vegetable kingdom—large, dense, meaty, and well suited to methods traditionally associated with meat, such as grilling, roasting, and cavemanning. Like meat, you can brine it (in this case, in a soulful mixture of dark beer, orange zest, and fennel) and, like meat, you can spit-roast it or grill it. The result: cauliflower with a savory crust and rich umami flavors. You even get to carve it into steaks. Tip o' the hat to Rhubarb restaurant in Asheville, North Carolina, for the idea.

INGREDIENTS

FOR THE CAULIFLOWER AND BRINE

1 large head of cauliflower

1 bottle (12 ounces) dark beer

3 tablespoons coarse salt
(sea or kosher)

2 strips orange or lemon zest
(remove them with a vegetable
peeler)

1 teaspoon fennel seeds

1 teaspoon coriander seeds

1 teaspoon black peppercorns, plus
freshly ground black pepper for
seasoning

4 cups ice water

FOR THE CURRY BUTTER BASTE

4 tablespoons (½ stick) butter

3 tablespoons finely chopped shallot

2 teaspoons curry powder

1. Trim any green leaves off the cauliflower and prick it deeply all over with a carving fork.

2. Make the brine: Place the beer, salt, orange zest, fennel, coriander, and peppercorns in a large pot and bring to a boil. Boil for 2 minutes. Remove the pot from the heat and stir in 4 cups of ice water. When the brine is cool, add the cauliflower. Brine it, refrigerated, for 6 to 8 hours—the longer, the richer the flavor.

3. Set up your grill for spit-roasting and heat to medium-high. Drain the cauliflower and blot dry. Thread it onto the rotisserie spit (the spit should go from top to bottom). It helps to make a starter tunnel through the cauliflower with a slender metal skewer. Secure the cauliflower in place with the rotisserie prongs.

4. Make the baste: Melt the butter over medium heat in a small saucepan and stir in the shallots and curry powder. Cook until the shallots are fragrant and lightly browned, 2 minutes.

5. Spit-roast the cauliflower until the cauliflower is darkly browned and tender (it will be easy to pierce with a bamboo or metal skewer), 45 minutes, or as needed, basting often with the curry butter.

GRILLING TIME: 45 minutes

GRILL/GEAR: You need a grill with a rotisserie and a sharp-tined carving fork.

SHOP: These days, cauliflower comes in rainbow colors, but the traditional white works just fine, too.

INSIDER TIP: Spit-roasting combines the virtues of direct grilling and indirect grilling. As with direct grilling, you get the browning that occurs when food faces fire directly. As with indirect grilling, the food roasts slowly and evenly. If your grill lacks a rotisserie, indirect grill the cauliflower to cook it through, then quarter it and direct grill to brown it.

CHILES RELLENOS

YIELD: Serves 6

METHOD: Smoke-roasting/ indirect grilling

PREP TIME: 20 minutes

GRILLING TIME: 30 to 40 minutes

GRILL/GEAR: Can be grilled over charcoal or gas. You also need 2 hardwood chunks or 1½ cups wood chips (if using the latter, soak in water to cover for 30 minutes, then drain).

SHOP: Choose poblanos that are large, straight, and round; they're easier to stuff.

INSIDER TIP: Vegetarians generally get short shrift at a barbecue, but here's a dish that's loaded with protein, fiber, and flavor. It looks pretty impressive, too. You can vary the flavor profile by changing the spicing and beans. For a North African version, for example, use chickpeas flavored with coriander, turmeric, and paprika.

If ever there was a dish ready for a live-fire makeover, it's Mexico's chiles rellenos. The original—cheese-filled, batter-dipped, and deep-fried—weighs in at 600 calories per serving. But stuff the same chile with beans and smoke-roast it on a grill instead of deep-frying. You wind up with a Mexican classic that not only tastes cleaner and more vibrant, but at 380 calories, it's better for you, too. Call it barbecue health food, and yes, your vegetarian friends will love you.

INGREDIENTS

6 large poblano peppers

2 tablespoons extra virgin olive oil

1 medium-size onion, peeled and finely chopped

1 clove garlic, peeled and minced

2 jalapeño peppers, seeded and finely chopped (for a spicier filling, leave the seeds in)

¼ cup chopped fresh cilantro

1 teaspoon ground cumin

1 cup canned low-sodium black beans, drained, rinsed, and drained again

1 cup canned pinto beans, drained, rinsed, and drained again (or more black beans)

¾ cup grilled or plain cooked corn kernels (optional)

3 cups (about 12 ounces) coarsely grated pepper Jack, Monterey Jack, or white cheddar cheese

Coarse salt (sea or kosher) and freshly ground black pepper

Vegetable oil for oiling the grill grate

1. Cut the poblanos in half lengthwise and scrape out the seeds and ribs. Leave the stem intact. Arrange on a sheet pan.

2. Heat 2 tablespoons of olive oil in a large nonstick skillet over medium heat. Add the onion, garlic, jalapeños, cilantro, and cumin and cook until golden brown, about 4 minutes. Remove the skillet from the heat, stir in the black beans, pinto beans,

and corn and let the mixture cool to room temperature. Stir in 2 cups of the cheese and salt and pepper to taste; the mixture should be highly seasoned. Spoon the bean mixture into the poblano halves. Sprinkle the remaining cheese on top, dividing it evenly among the peppers.

3. Set up your grill for indirect grilling and heat to medium-high. Brush or scrape the grill grate clean and oil it well. Add wood chunks or chips to the coals or follow the gas grill smoking instructions on page 22.

4. Place the peppers in the center of the hot grill grate (arrange them so they run parallel to the bars of the grate), away from the heat, or in your smoker. Cover the grill and cook the peppers until they are tender and the cheese is browned and bubbling, 30 to 40 minutes. Transfer the peppers to a platter or plates and serve at once.

COCONUT-GRILLED CORN

I've been grilling corn since my earliest days in barbecue. Starting with the grilled corn with cilantro garlic butter in *The Barbecue! Bible*, I've profiled dozens of renditions—Mexican-style (slathered with mayonnaise and grated cheese), Indian (doused with lime juice and cayenne pepper), Japanese (brushed with sesame soy butter), and so on. My latest version features a sweet-salty baste of mayonnaise, soy sauce, and maple syrup. But where it really gets interesting is the coating—shredded coconut, which you toast right on the corn. Do *you* have an ingenious grilled corn recipe? Share photos on reddit.com/r/BarbecueBible/ or on my Facebook page.

YIELD: Serves 4

METHOD: Direct grilling

PREP TIME: 10 minutes

GRILLING TIME: 8 to 12 minutes

GRILL/GEAR: Can be grilled on charcoal, wood, or gas. You also need butcher's string (optional); wooden skewers or chopsticks; and aluminum foil to make a grill shield (optional).

SHOP: Select corn with the husk on—preferably a sweet local variety that's just come into season in your area.

INGREDIENTS

4 ears sweet corn in the husk

¼ cup mayonnaise, preferably Hellmann's or Best Foods

1 tablespoon soy sauce

1 tablespoon pure maple syrup

Vegetable oil for oiling the grill grate

1 cup unsweetened flaked coconut

1. Husk the corn, stripping the husks back as though you were peeling a banana, leaving the husks attached at the base. Remove the silk. Tie the husks back below the corn to make a handle, using a strip of husk or butcher's string. (Alternatively, strip off the husks altogether and impale the corn through the pith end on sturdy wooden skewers or chopsticks.)

2. Combine the mayonnaise, soy sauce, and maple syrup in a small mixing bowl and whisk to mix.

3. Set up your grill for direct grilling and heat to high. Brush or scrape the grill grate clean and oil it well.

4. Lightly brush the ears of corn with maple-soy mayonnaise. Grill the corn until well browned on all sides, 2 to 3 minutes per side, 8 to 12 minutes in all, rotating the ears so they grill evenly. Position the corn so that the tied husks hang over the edge of the grill or away from the hot coals, or slide a folded sheet of aluminum foil under them so they won't burn. Continue to baste the corn as it grills.

5. When the corn is browned, baste it one more time and transfer it to a sheet pan. Sprinkle it with most of the flaked coconut, gently patting it onto the corn with your fingertips. Return the corn to the grill and sprinkle it with the remaining coconut. When the coconut is lightly toasted, transfer the corn to a platter and dig in.

INSIDER TIP: The "grate" corn debate centers on grilling with the husk on or husk off. To me, there's no question: husk off. This enables you to caramelize the natural plant sugars in the corn. When you grill with the husk on, you steam the corn, rather than grill it. I don't remove the husk completely. Rather, I leave it attached at the bottom, but tie it back to form a handle for eating the corn. The aluminum foil grill shield keeps the husk from burning.

Grill the corn directly over the fire. Make sure the husks hang over the edge. Or slide an aluminum foil shield under the husks to keep them from burning.

If you wish, you can sprinkle the corn with shredded coconut while it's still on the grill. Or transfer the corn to a sheet pan, sprinkle it with coconut, and return it to the grill.

Grilling the corn over wood imparts a rich smoky flavor.

THAI GRILLED KALE

YIELD: Serves 3 to 4

METHOD: Direct grilling

PREP TIME: 10 minutes

GRILLING TIME: 6 to 10 minutes

GRILL/GEAR: Can be grilled over charcoal, wood, or gas. You also need a vegetable grid or grill basket (optional) if grilling small kale leaves.

SHOP: Kale comes in many varieties, including the common curly and red Russian varieties. All are good grilled, but my favorite is dinosaur kale (aka cavolo nero, lacinato kale, and black kale), recognizable by its long, slender, dark blue-green crinkly leaves and sweet earthy flavor. This is the easiest kind of kale to clean and grill. Note: Kale becomes sweeter after the first frost, so this is one vegetable that's great for grilling in autumn or winter.

INSIDER TIP: Kale stems are noticeably more fibrous and chewy than the leaves—especially in curly varieties. Remove them following the directions in Step 1. When grilling small kale leaves (like red kale), place them in a grill basket. Arrange larger leaves directly on the grate.

How did we live without kale? Once the province of Italian and Portuguese cooks (who boiled it in soups and stews), kale has become the "it" veggie of the millennials. We consume it by the ton in chips, salads, rice bowls, and even smoothies. So it was only a matter of time until kale hit the grill. At first glance, this broad leafy vegetable would seem like an odd candidate. You'd think the leaves would wilt or burn. They don't. Instead, the high dry heat of the grill delivers a smoky char and potato chip crispness. Think barbecue health food loaded with calcium, potassium, B vitamins, and fiber. And don't think of firing up your grill without trying it.

INGREDIENTS

2 bunches dinosaur kale (12 to 16 ounces in all)

2 tablespoons Asian (dark) sesame oil or vegetable oil

2 tablespoons soy sauce or Asian fish sauce

1 clove garlic or a small shallot, peeled and minced

3 tablespoons sesame seeds or chopped peanuts

Hot red pepper flakes, to taste

Vegetable oil for oiling the grill grate

1. Wash the kale and spin it dry in a salad spinner or shake it dry. Lay a leaf on a cutting board and, making an elongated V-shaped cut, remove the thick part of the stem. (You can leave the tender part of the stem near the top intact.) Repeat with the remaining leaves—you may not need to stem the tender inner leaves. Blot off any excess water with paper towels.

2. Combine the sesame oil, soy sauce, and garlic in a small bowl and mix with a fork. Lightly brush each kale leaf on both sides with this mixture using a pastry brush. Sprinkle the kale on both sides with sesame seeds and hot red pepper flakes.

3. Set up your grill for direct grilling and heat to medium-high. Brush or scrape the grill grate clean and oil it well.

Direct grill the kale until browned and crisp on both sides.

4. Arrange the kale leaves in a single layer on the grate, working in several batches as needed. If the kale leaves are small, you can grill them on a vegetable grid or in a grill basket (page 14). Grill the kale until browned and crisp, 3 to 5 minutes per side, turning with tongs. Transfer to a platter and serve. I like to eat grilled kale with my fingers. It's messy—it's supposed to be, so provide napkins. The kale should be sufficiently salty from the soy sauce, but don't hesitate to add salt if you want to.

MUSHROOM MIXED GRILL
WITH BACON, HERBS, AND PARMIGIANO-REGGIANO

YIELD: Serves 4

METHOD: Direct grill

PREP TIME: 20 minutes (including time for the onions)

GRILLING TIME: 5 to 8 minutes for the mushrooms

GRILL/GEAR: Can be grilled over charcoal, wood, or gas. But for the best flavor, use wood or a wood-enhanced fire (see page 21). You also need 2 hardwood chunks or 1½ cups unsoaked wood chips and a grill wok or open vegetable grilling basket.

SHOP: You want a selection of exotic mushrooms such as shiitakes, oyster mushrooms, and king mushrooms. You can find them at most supermarkets.

Travel the world's barbecue trail and you'll find mushrooms of all stripes on all manner of grills. The reasons are simple: Porous in texture, mushrooms absorb herb, spice, and smoke flavors like a sponge. And high in water content, they stay moist even when exposed to the withering heat of the fire. The mushrooms in this recipe get a triple blast of flavor: from smoky bacon, fresh herbs, and freshly grated Parmigiano-Reggiano cheese.

INGREDIENTS

1 pound mixed exotic mushrooms (choose a mix of shiitakes, porcini, oyster mushrooms, morels, hedgehog mushrooms, king, cremini, and/or others)

¼ cup chopped fresh flat-leaf parsley, cilantro, dill, and/or other fresh herbs

2 scallions, trimmed, white and green parts finely chopped

2 strips bacon, grilled (see page 50) and cut crosswise into ¼-inch slivers

Coarse salt (sea or kosher) and freshly ground black pepper

3 to 4 tablespoons extra virgin olive oil or melted butter

½ cup freshly grated Parmigiano-Reggiano cheese

1. Set up your grill for direct grilling and heat to high.

2. Trim the sandy ends off the mushroom stems. If using shiitakes, discard the whole stems. Wipe the mushrooms clean with a damp paper towel. Cut any large mushrooms in halves or quarters so all the mushrooms are about the same size. The pieces should be at least 1½ inches across.

3. Place the mushrooms in a large mixing bowl. Stir in the parsley or other herbs, scallions, and bacon. Add salt and pepper to taste. Right before grilling, stir in the olive oil.

4. Brush or scrape the grill grate clean; there's no need to oil it. Place the grill wok or basket on the grate and heat it as well. Add the mushroom mixture and grill until the mushrooms and bacon are sizzling, browned, and tender, 5 to 8 minutes, shaking the pan and stirring with a wooden spoon.

5. Transfer the mushrooms to a serving bowl (or serve right out of the grill wok). Sprinkle with the cheese and serve (see Note).

NOTE: These grilled mushrooms are awesome served on slices of grilled bread.

INSIDER TIP: There are two ways to grill large quantities of small vegetables: in a grill wok or wire grill basket or threaded onto bamboo skewers. The former are less labor intensive and their perforated or wire mesh construction allows plenty of smoke and fire flavors to reach the food. Just remember to preheat the wok empty so you start with a sharp blast of heat.

SWEET AND SOUR GRILLED ONIONS

These luscious fiery grilled onions were inspired by a Venetian classic: *cipolline in agrodolce* (sweet and sour onions). The *Project Fire* twist? Charring the onions first to caramelize their natural plant sugars.

INGREDIENTS

1 large sweet onion, peeled

Extra virgin olive oil

Coarse salt (sea or kosher) and freshly ground black pepper

Vegetable oil for oiling the grill grate

Sweet and Sour Fire Sauce (page 265)

YIELD: Serves 3 to 4

METHOD: Direct grilling

PREP TIME: 10 minutes

GRILLING TIME: 6 to 8 minutes

GRILL/GEAR: Can be grilled over charcoal, wood, or gas. For maximum flavor, grill over a wood or wood-enhanced fire (see page 21). You also need flat bamboo or metal skewers or toothpicks.

SHOP: You'll want a sweet onion for this one. Varieties that come to mind include Vidalia, Maui, Walla Walla, and Texas Sweet. Extra points for organic: Remember, root vegetables can easily absorb pesticides.

INSIDER TIP: Cutting the onions in wedges exposes the maximum flesh to the fire. But it also makes them prone to falling apart. Skewering them holds the wedges together. Insert the sharp point of the skewer through the narrow edge of the onion wedge first.

1. Set up your grill for direct grilling and heat to high.

2. Cut the onion into 12 wedges from the tip through the root end. Skewer the onion wedges onto bamboo skewers, or skewer each individual wedge with a toothpick. Brush the onions on all sides with extra virgin olive oil and season generously with salt and pepper.

3. Brush or scrape the grill grate clean and oil it well. Arrange the onion wedges on the grate and grill until sizzling, browned, and soft, 3 to 4 minutes per side, turning with tongs. Start basting the onions with the Sweet and Sour Fire Sauce after 3 minutes and baste several times.

4. Transfer the onion wedges to a platter or plates and unskewer. Spoon the remaining sauce over them and dig in.

SMOKE-ROASTED POTATOES
STUFFED WITH CARAMELIZED ONIONS AND CHEESE

YIELD: Makes 8 potato halves (enough to serve 4 to 8)

METHOD: Smoke-roasting

PREP TIME: 20 minutes

GRILLING TIME: About 1¼ hours

Smoke-roasted potatoes have long been a family staple. We love the crackling crisp skin and smoky flavor. I like to think of this version as a mash-up of baked potatoes and French onion soup. Like the latter, it's loaded with caramelized onions, and when you eat it (make that devour it), long gooey strings of melted cheese stretch from your fork.

INGREDIENTS

Vegetable oil for oiling the grill grate

4 large baking potatoes (12 to 14 ounces each), such as russets

8 tablespoons (1 stick) unsalted butter, at room temperature

Coarse salt (sea or kosher) and freshly ground black pepper

1 medium-size onion, peeled and diced (about 1½ cups)

6 ounces smoked ham, cut into matchstick slivers (optional)

½ cup crème fraîche or sour cream, or more as needed

2 cups (8 ounces) coarsely grated Gruyère or other full-flavored cheese

Pimentón (Spanish smoked paprika) for sprinkling

1. Set up your grill for indirect grilling and heat to medium-high. Brush or scrape the grill grate clean and oil it well.

2. Scrub the potatoes on all sides with a vegetable brush under running water. Rinse well and blot dry with paper towels. Prick each potato skin 5 to 6 times with a fork. If you wish to speed up the roasting time, insert a potato nail or ten-penny nail in each. (The metal conducts the heat to the center.) Brush each potato with the butter (you'll need about 2 tablespoons in all) and season generously with salt and pepper.

3. Place the potatoes on the grill grate away from the heat. Add the wood chunks or chips if using. Smoke-roast the potatoes until the skins are crisp and the flesh is soft, about 1 hour. (Insert a bamboo skewer to test for doneness; it should go in easily.)

4. Meanwhile, melt 2 tablespoons of butter in a skillet. Add the onions and ham (if using) and cook over medium heat until a deep golden brown, 5 to 8 minutes. Lower the heat as needed so the onions brown evenly. Transfer to a large mixing bowl.

5. When the potatoes are cooked, transfer them to a cutting board. Remove the nails, if using, and cut each potato in half lengthwise with a sharp knife. Using a spoon, remove most of the potato flesh, leaving a ¼-inch-thick layer next to the skin. (Note: For the best texture, scoop the potatoes while they are still hot.) Coarsely chop the scooped potato and place in the mixing bowl with the ham and onions.

6. Add the crème fraîche and 1 cup of grated cheese and gently stir to mix with a rubber spatula. Season to taste with salt and pepper. The mixture should be highly seasoned. Stir as little as possible so as to leave some texture to the potatoes.

7. Stuff the potato mixture back into the potato skins, mounding it in the center. Sprinkle each potato with the remaining cheese and dot the tops with butter. Sprinkle each stuffed potato with *pimentón*. The potatoes can be prepared up to 24 hours ahead to this stage, covered and refrigerated.

8. Just before serving, if the grill isn't still at the ready, set it up for indirect grilling and heat to medium-high. Place the potatoes on the grill grate away from the heat until the cheese is melted and browned and the filling is hot and sizzling, 15 minutes or as needed. (Potatoes that have been refrigerated will take a bit longer.)

GRILL/GEAR: Can be grilled over charcoal or gas. For a more pronounced smoke flavor, use charcoal. You also need potato grilling nails or 4 ten-penny nails (optional) and 2 hardwood chunks or 1½ cups wood chips (optional; if using the latter, soak in water to cover for 30 minutes, then drain).

SHOP: Organic baking potatoes and onions. Cave-aged Gruyère cheese. Excellence lies in provisioning.

INSIDER TIP: Of course, you can "bake" a potato on the grill, but if you're going to go to the trouble of firing it up, why not blast the potato with wood smoke? Smoke makes vegetables taste a lot more interesting, just as it does meats.

HASSELBACK POTATOES
WITH PARMIGIANO-REGGIANO

YIELD: Serves 4

METHOD: Smoke-roasting

PREP TIME: 20 minutes

GRILLING TIME: 1¼ hours

GRILL/GEAR: Can be grilled over charcoal or gas. If you want a smoke flavor, use charcoal. You also need a hasselback potato cutter (such as the one made by the Companion Group) or 2 wooden chopsticks or pencils and 2 wood chunks or 1½ cups hardwood chips (if using the latter, soak in water to cover for 30 minutes, then drain).

SHOP: Organic baking potatoes. Real Italian Parmigiano-Reggiano cheese.

INSIDER TIP: As a griller, I'm always trying to bring smoke and fire flavors from the outside of the food to the center. These potatoes call for an accordion cutting technique whereby you make a series of deep parallel cuts through the top of the potato almost to the bottom (the chopsticks on either side keep you from cutting all the way through). The resulting slices open the interior of the potato to the smoke flavor.

I think of these singular spuds as "potato chips on the bone." The slices fan out during roasting, giving the potatoes the vague appearance of an armadillo. This looks cool as all get-out and gives a baked potato some of the crispness of a potato chip. Incidentally, the name comes from the swanky Hasselbacken restaurant, which opened in Stockholm in 1853 and is still serving its eponymous potatoes.

INGREDIENTS

4 large baking potatoes, such as russets, scrubbed

8 tablespoons (1 stick) unsalted butter, melted

Coarse salt (sea or kosher) and freshly ground black pepper

Vegetable oil for oiling the grill grate

½ cup finely grated Parmigiano-Reggiano cheese

3 tablespoons finely minced chives

1. Set up your grill for indirect grilling and heat to medium-high.

2. Place each potato on a hasselback cutting guide or between 2 wooden chopsticks or pencils. Using a sharp knife, cut each potato crosswise into ⅛-inch-thick slices, but don't cut all the way through; you want the potato to stay intact. Do this right before cooking so the potato won't oxidize. (The guide or the chopsticks will prevent you from cutting too deeply.) Brush the potatoes with melted butter, forcing it between the slices. Season generously with salt and pepper. If you want to cut the potatoes ahead of time (up to 4 hours), drop them in a bowl of ice water once sliced. There's an added advantage here: This helps spread the slices apart.

3. Brush or scrape the grill grate clean and oil it well. Place the potatoes on the grill grate over the drip pan away from the heat. Add the wood chunks or chips to the coals. Close the grill lid. Smoke-roast the potatoes until the slices begin to fan, 30 minutes.

4. Brush the potatoes with melted butter, again dabbing it between the slices, and sprinkle with the grated cheese. Continue smoke-roasting until the cheese is melted and the potatoes are browned and tender, 30 to 45 minutes longer. Sprinkle with chives before serving.

EMBER-GRILLED SUGAR SNAP PEAS
WITH FRESH MINT

I first experienced fire-roasted sugar snap peas at Tar & Roses in Santa Monica. The next time was at The Dabney restaurant in Washington, D.C., where chef Jeremiah Langhorne placed the grill basket directly on the embers. On a recent trip to Chicago, I enjoyed them at the trendy Bad Hunter and El Che Bar, and they were so crusty and smoky-sweet, I vowed the next time would be on my own grill. You can char any small green vegetable, from snow peas to green beans to fiddlehead ferns, in a grill basket in the embers. The optional jalapeño pepper reinforces the heat.

INGREDIENTS

1 pound fresh sugar snap peas

½ cup thinly slivered fresh mint

1 jalapeño pepper, very thinly sliced crosswise (optional)

2 tablespoons extra virgin olive oil, or to taste

Coarse salt (sea or kosher) and freshly ground black pepper

1. Set up your grill for caveman grilling. Let the coals burn down to glowing embers.

2. String the peas by breaking the tip off the stem end and pulling the string away from the inside curve of the pea. Place in a large mixing bowl. Stir in the mint, jalapeño (if using), olive oil, and salt and pepper to taste. Transfer to a grill basket.

3. When ready to cook, rake the coals into an even layer, using a grill hoe or garden hoe. Fan with a folded newspaper to disperse any loose ash. Lay the grill basket with the peas directly on the embers. Grill the peas, stirring occasionally with tongs, until browned and charred in places, about 5 minutes. (A few burnt spots add flavor.) Transfer the peas to a platter and serve.

YIELD: Serves 4

METHOD: Caveman grilling (grilling on the embers; see page 27) in a grill basket

PREP TIME: 10 minutes

GRILLING TIME: 5 minutes

GRILL/GEAR: Grill over charcoal or wood. You also need a grill basket; a grill hoe or garden hoe; and a newspaper for fanning coals.

SHOP: Sugar snap peas (sometimes called snap peas) are a small pea variety you eat pod and all. Look for smaller sugar snaps—organic if possible.

INSIDER TIP: Sure, you can roast large vegetables, like beets and cabbage, in the embers (see pages 103 and 263). But what about small vegetables, like snap peas, snow peas, or green beans? The answer is simple: Grill them in a wire mesh grill basket positioned directly on the embers. You get a surface charring and resulting flavor that's different from conventional grilling. Shake the basket a few times (or stir with long-handled tongs) so all the peas roast evenly. If you own a gas grill, try charring them on a plancha (see page 28).

SALT SLAB SQUASH
STUFFED WITH WILD RICE, CRANBERRIES, AND PECANS

This rustic salt-grilled acorn squash makes a perfect Thanksgiving side dish. Wild rice, pecans, and cranberries speak to the season and the festivities and especially to the turkey, which of course, you'll grill or smoke (page 219 or 220).

INGREDIENTS

2 medium-size acorn squash

4 tablespoons (½ stick) butter

1 strip bacon, cut crosswise into ¼-inch-wide strips

1 shallot, peeled and minced

8 fresh sage leaves, thinly slivered

½ cup pecan pieces

½ cup dried cranberries

1½ cups fully cooked wild rice

Coarse salt (sea or kosher) and freshly ground black pepper

¼ cup pure maple syrup, or to taste

1. Set up your grill for indirect grilling and build a medium-hot fire. Brush or scrape the grill grate clean; there's no need to oil it. Place the salt slab in the center of the grate away from the heat and slowly preheat it as well. (Heating it quickly could cause the salt slab to crack.)

2. Cut each squash in half from top to bottom and scoop out the seeds. Place each squash half, cut side down, on the salt slab. Roast until just tender (squeeze the sides to check for doneness), 30 minutes, or as needed.

3. Meanwhile, make the stuffing: Melt 2 tablespoons of butter in a skillet over medium heat. Lightly brown the bacon, shallots, and sage leaves, 3 minutes. Stir in the pecans and cranberries and cook for 1 minute. Stir in the wild rice and salt and pepper to taste.

4. Invert the squash halves. Spoon the stuffing into the cavities. Pour 1 tablespoon of maple syrup over each squash half, covering the filling and the edges. Place ½ tablespoon of butter in the center of each half.

5. Return the stuffed squash to the salt slab (filling side up). Use grill rings or crumpled aluminum foil twisted into small doughnuts to hold them upright. Continue grilling until the butter melts and the filling is hot, 10 to 15 minutes.

NOTE: For a vegetarian version, omit the bacon and sauté the

YIELD: Serves 4

METHOD: Salt slab grilling/ indirect grilling

PREP TIME: 20 minutes

GRILLING TIME: About 45 minutes

GRILL/GEAR: Can be grilled over charcoal or gas. You also need a Himalayan salt slab (available at grill shops and gourmet shops) and grill rings or crumpled aluminum foil doughnuts (optional).

SHOP: Wild rice used to require a solid hour of boiling to make it edible. Save yourself some time and buy it par cooked or precooked. Two good brands are Fall River and Canoe.

INSIDER TIP: Salt slab grilling is a relative newcomer to the world of live-fire cooking, but it belongs in your repertory for at least three reasons. It subtly flavors the food. It provides a steady even heat source. And the process looks cool. **Warning:** Do not make this recipe in cold weather. Hot salt slabs have been known to crack or explode when exposed to cold air.

shallots, pecans, and cranberries in 2 tablespoons butter, or for vegans, olive oil.

Variation

For simple salt slab squash without the stuffing, grill the squash halves on the salt slab as described through Step 2. Invert and brush the edges and cavities with 2 tablespoons melted butter. Sprinkle each with 1 tablespoon cinnamon sugar and drizzle with 2 teaspoons maple syrup. Place 2 teaspoons butter in each squash cavity. Continue grilling on the salt slab until these flavorings cook into the squash, 10 to 15 minutes.

TOFU STEAKS
WITH KOREAN BARBECUE SAUCE

YIELD: Serves 2 as a main course, 4 as a starter

METHOD: Plancha grilling/direct grilling

PREP TIME: 15 minutes

GRILLING TIME: 8 minutes

GRILL/GEAR: Can be grilled over charcoal, wood, or gas. You also need a well-seasoned plancha or cast-iron skillet.

Grilled tofu is a barbecue staple in Korea, Japan, and elsewhere in Asia, and it turns up more and more at forward-thinking restaurants and barbecue joints in North America. If you eat tofu already, I don't need to sell you on its health benefits (high in protein and calcium and mercifully low in fat), or how its porous texture and mild taste soak up smoke and spice flavors like a sponge. Confession time (surprising for a grill guy like me): My wife and I grill tofu at least once a week. Skeptical? The following grilled tofu "steaks" with fiery Korean Barbecue Sauce will turn you into a believer.

INGREDIENTS

1 pound fresh extra-firm tofu, drained well

½ cup sake or rice wine

¼ cup water or as needed

2 tablespoons soy sauce

½ cup packed light brown sugar

1 cup (8 ounces) gochujang (see Shop, facing page)

1 scallion, trimmed, white part minced, green part thinly sliced

1 tablespoon Asian (dark) sesame oil, plus 2 tablespoons for brushing on the tofu

Vegetable oil for oiling the plancha and the grill grate

1. Press the tofu (optional): Cut the tofu in half widthwise, then cut each half in half through the narrow side to make 4 flat steaks. Place these on a cutting board with one end slightly raised. Place a second cutting board on top of the tofu and press it for 15 minutes. This extracts the excess liquid and makes the tofu firmer. Otherwise, simply cut the tofu into steaks as described above.

2. Meanwhile, make the Korean Barbecue Sauce: Place the sake, water, soy sauce, and brown sugar in a saucepan and boil, whisking occasionally, until the sugar dissolves. Add the gochujang, scallion white, and sesame oil. Gently simmer the ingredients for 3 to 5 minutes, whisking well, to obtain a smooth, pourable sauce. If too thick, whisk in more water. The tofu can be pressed and the sauce made up to 24 hours ahead to this stage, covered and refrigerated.

3. Set up your grill for direct grilling and heat to high. Place a plancha or cast-iron skillet over the fire and gradually heat it as well.

4. Brush the tofu slices with sesame oil on both sides. Oil the plancha and arrange the tofu slices on it. Cook until firm and browned on both sides, 3 to 5 minutes per side.

5. Brush or scrape the grill grate clean and oil it well.

6. Brush the browned tofu slices with some of the barbecue sauce. Arrange the tofu slices on the grate running on the diagonal to the bars of the grate. Grill until sizzling and browned on both sides, about 2 to 3 minutes per side, giving each slice a quarter turn after 1 minute to lay on a crosshatch of grill marks. Brush with more barbecue sauce as the tofu grills. Alternatively, you can continue to grill the tofu with the barbecue sauce on the plancha.

7. Transfer the grilled tofu to a platter or plates and serve with the remaining Korean Barbecue Sauce on the side.

NOTE: This makes more sauce than you probably need, but it keeps well and you'll definitely want leftovers.

SHOP: Use extra-firm or firm tofu for grilling (the firmer the better). Another option is to use prebaked tofu (one good brand is Nasoya). Gochujang is a salty, fiery paste of fermented soy beans, rice, and chiles. Look for it at Asian markets, Whole Foods, or Amazon. If unavailable, substitute miso, which will give you a very different, but equally delectable Asian barbecue sauce.

INSIDER TIP: Tofu—even extra firm tofu—is quite soft, with a vexing tendency to stick to the grill grate. A two-step process will help you avoid this: first, press the tofu under a weight to extract some of the excess water. Then sear it on a plancha or in a skillet before grilling it.

DESSERTS AND DRINKS

Sometime between the birth of the s'more (circa 1927, when a magazine called *Tramping and Trailing* listed the first printed recipe for "Some Mores") and 2016, when smoked ice cream appeared on the set of my *Project Smoke* TV show, dessert hit the grill big time. Pineapple slices crusted with cinnamon sugar and caramelized over a screaming hot fire. "Kebabs" of peach and mint grilled on, what else, cinnamon stick skewers. Mango Macadamia Crisp smoke-roasted with fragrant fruitwood. Mexico's quesadilla gets a dessert makeover: stuffed with bananas and dulce de leche before being crisped on the grill. Even chocolate gets the grill treatment with a Salt Slab Chocolate Brownie S'more. And while you're at it, use your grill to take beverages and cocktails to the next level: Check out the Grilled Sangria on page 305. The secret to a spectacular dessert? Fire up your grill.

CINNAMON-GRILLED PEACHES
WITH BOURBON BROWN SUGAR GLAZE

YIELD: Serves 4

METHOD: Direct grilling

PREP TIME: 15 minutes

GRILLING TIME: 8 minutes

GRILL/GEAR: Can be grilled over charcoal, wood, or gas. You also need a chopstick or a metal skewer.

SHOP: This dessert lives or dies by the ripeness of the peaches. You want the sort of fruit you can smell across the kitchen. If your peaches are hard, let them ripen at room temperature. Freestone peaches are easier to cut and skewer than clingstone.

INSIDER TIP: Cinnamon sticks come from the bark of a tropical tree. You have two options: true cinnamon, which comes in shaggy, multi-layer sticks, or cassia, a smooth rolled bark with a cinnamon-like scent. Cassia is easier to find and use, but both work great. For a pleasing salty touch, drape paper-thin slices of *lardo* (Italian cured fatback) over the hot peaches before serving.

Born at Barbecue University, these kebabs have only three ingredients, but they never fail to impress. When you do it right, the ends of the cinnamon sticks burn during grilling, releasing aromatic cinnamon smoke. Meanwhile, the edges of the mint leaves singe, imparting their own refreshing aroma. Then there's the glaze, whose primary ingredients—bourbon, brown sugar, and butter—could make even charcoal taste great.

INGREDIENTS

FOR THE PEACHES

4 large ripe peaches, preferably freestone

8 cinnamon sticks, each at least 3 inches long

8 large fresh mint leaves

FOR THE BOURBON BROWN SUGAR GLAZE

⅓ cup bourbon

4 tablespoons (½ stick) unsalted butter

⅓ cup packed brown sugar, dark or light

Pinch of salt

½ teaspoon pure vanilla extract

Vegetable oil for oiling the grill grate

Peach or vanilla ice cream, for serving

1. Cut the peaches in half lengthwise, running the knife around the crease to the pit. Twist the halves in opposite directions to separate them. Pop out the pit with a spoon and discard. Cut each peach half in half from top to bottom. Using a pointed chopstick or slender metal skewer, make a starter hole in the center of each peach quarter (from the pit side to the outside). Skewer 2 or 3 peach quarters on each cinnamon stick (they should face the same direction), placing a mint leaf between them.

2. Make the glaze: Combine the bourbon, butter, brown sugar, and salt in a saucepan and boil until thick and syrupy, 3 to 5 minutes, whisking steadily. Remove the pan from the heat and whisk in the vanilla extract.

3. Set up your grill for direct grilling and heat to high. Brush or scrape the grill grate clean and oil it well.

4. Grill the peaches until nicely browned on both sides, 3 to 4 minutes per side, basting with the glaze. Meanwhile, spoon the ice cream into bowls or martini glasses. Top each with 2 peach kebabs and drizzle the remaining glaze over them. Awesome.

Direct grill the peach kebabs until sizzling and browned on both sides.

AMARETTI PLANKED PEARS

YIELD: Serves 4 to 8

METHOD: Planking (direct grilling, followed by indirect grilling)

PREP TIME: 20 minutes

GRILLING TIME: 15 to 20 minutes

GRILL/GEAR: Can be grilled over charcoal or gas. You also need a food processor; 2 large cedar or other wood grilling planks; a metal skewer; and a melon baller (optional).

Here's an Italian twist on the traditional baked apple—pears stuffed with almond-flavored amaretti cookie crumbs, brown sugar, and butter, and smoke-roasted on cedar planks. The latter impart a haunting smoke flavor—even if you're working on a gas grill. It's hard to imagine a more satisfying autumn dessert.

INGREDIENTS

16 amaretti cookies (⅔ cup crumbs)

¼ cup packed brown sugar, dark or light, or to taste

½ teaspoon finely grated fresh lemon zest

½ teaspoon ground cinnamon

8 tablespoons (1 stick) unsalted butter, at room temperature

4 fragrant ripe pears

½ lemon

1 cup Smoked Whipped Cream (page 293) or regular whipped cream

1. Make the filling: Place the cookies, brown sugar, lemon zest, and cinnamon in a food processor and grind to coarse crumbs. Add the butter and grind to a coarse paste.

2. Cut each pear in half lengthwise. Using a melon baller or spoon, remove the core and seeds from each half. Rub the cut sides with the lemon half to keep them from browning.

3. Spoon the filling into the hollowed-out pears. The pears can be prepared several hours ahead to this stage and refrigerated.

4. Set up your grill for indirect grilling and heat to medium-high. Brush or scrape the grill grate clean; there's no need to oil it. Place the cedar planks (you can do 2 at a time) directly over the fire (located at opposite sides of the grill). Grill until charred on the bottom, 1 to 2 minutes. Place on a heatproof work surface and let cool.

5. Place 4 pear halves on the charred side of each plank. Return the planks to the grill away from the heat. Close the lid and indirect grill until the pears are soft and the filling is bubbling and browned, 15 to 20 minutes, or as needed. Insert a metal skewer to test for doneness. It should pierce the fruit easily. Serve the pears on their planks, with Smoked Whipped Cream or regular whipped cream on the side.

SHOP: You need ripe pears for this dessert. Let hard pears ripen at room temperature until fragrant and soft. Amaretti are almond-flavored, macaroon-like cookies from Italy. One good and widely available brand is Lazzaroni (recognizable by its bright red tin). In a pinch, you could use graham cracker or cookie crumbs.

INSIDER TIP: As elsewhere in the book, the best way to maximize the smoke flavor from a cedar plank is to char it directly over the fire before you add the pears. This runs counter to the widely accepted practice of soaking the planks in water before grilling, which produces steam, not smoke.

DESSERT "STEAK" SANDWICH
APPLE STEAKS ON GRILLED GINGERBREAD

I usually serve apple "steaks" (grilled apple slices) as a side dish for pork and game. The idea of pairing them with grilled gingerbread came from my *Les Incontournables de Barbecue* ("Musts of Barbecue") TV show in Quebec. The crisp crunch of the apples counterpoints the soft chewy texture of the gingerbread, and grilling endows both with a caramel (burnt sugar) flavor that satisfies long after you've taken the last bite.

YIELD: Serves 4

METHOD: Direct grilling

PREP TIME: 15 minutes

GRILLING TIME: 8 minutes

GRILL/GEAR: Can be grilled over charcoal, wood, or gas.

INGREDIENTS

4 slices gingerbread (each about 3 by 6 inches and ½ inch thick)

6 tablespoons (¾ stick) unsalted butter, melted

2 firm crisp apples, like Honeycrisps

¾ cup granulated sugar

2 teaspoons ground cinnamon

Vegetable oil for oiling the grill grate

Smoked Whipped Cream, for serving (optional; recipe follows)

¼ cup Calvados or apple brandy for flambéing (optional)

1. Set up your grill for direct grilling. Heat one zone to high and one zone to medium-high.

2. Brush the gingerbread slices on both sides with melted butter and set aside.

3. Cut the apples crosswise into ½-inch-thick slices. (Don't worry about the seeds—they add rustic charm.) Brush the apple slices on both sides with melted butter. (The easiest way to do this is on a wire rack set over a sheet pan.) Mix the sugar and cinnamon together in a shallow bowl and place it beside the grill.

4. Brush or scrape the grill grate clean and oil it well. Arrange the gingerbread slices on the medium-high section of the grill and grill until toasted, about 2 minutes per side. Transfer to the wire rack.

5. Dip the buttered apple slices in the cinnamon sugar mixture, turning with tongs to coat both sides. Shake off any excess. Arrange the apple slices over the hottest section of the grill and grill until sizzling and browned, about 2 minutes per side. Give each a quarter turn after 1 minute to lay on a crosshatch of grill marks. Transfer to the wire rack.

6. To serve, spread Smoked Whipped Cream, if using, on each slice of grilled gingerbread. Shingle the grilled apples on top. For a *really* over-the-top dessert, warm the Calvados in a small saucepan (it should be finger-dip warm—do not let it boil). Touch a long match to it to ignite it, taking the precautions for the pineapple in the Note on page 296, then pour it over the apples.

SMOKED WHIPPED CREAM

My first attempt at smoked whipped cream involved a bottle of Laphroaig (a super smoky Scotch whisky). The result was excellent—especially if you like Scotch. I've since graduated to smoking cream in a smokehouse or with a Smoking Gun (you can read about both in *Project Smoke*). But this is a book for grillers as well as smokers, so I want to tell you how to smoke cream in a charcoal grill. (Sorry folks, gas grills just don't put out enough smoke to give you satisfaction.) There are two optional flavorings here to reinforce the smoke flavor: mezcal (a tequila cousin made with smoke-roasted agave cactus hearts) and the aforementioned single malt Scotch.

YIELD: Makes 2 cups whipped cream

GRILLS/GEAR: Can be grilled over charcoal. You also need 1½ cups unsoaked hardwood chips and 2 disposable aluminum foil pans.

INGREDIENTS

1 cup heavy (whipping) cream

3 tablespoons confectioners' sugar

½ teaspoon pure vanilla extract

1 tablespoon mezcal or single malt Scotch whisky (optional)

1. Set up your grill for indirect grilling and heat to medium. Pour the cream into an aluminum foil pan and place it over another foil pan full of ice. Place the pans on the grill grate and add the chips to the coals. Close the lid.

2. Smoke the cream until lightly bronzed with a patina of smoke, 5 to 8 minutes, stirring once or twice to mix the smoke with the cream. Remove the cream from the grill and refrigerate until cold.

3. Beat the cream to soft peaks in a chilled bowl using an electric mixer, handheld beater, or whisk. Add the confectioners' sugar, vanilla, and mezcal (if using), and beat until stiff peaks form. You can also use a whipped cream siphon.

GRILLED "PINA COLADA"
COCONUT PINEAPPLE WITH RUM FLAMBE

Pineapple was the first fruit I ever grilled, and it remains a Raichlendia favorite. Over the years, I've roasted it whole on a rotisserie and charred it, caveman-style, on the embers. I've blasted it with chile powder and salt to make a fiery side dish. And, of course, I've grilled it sliced and crusted with cinnamon sugar to make an irresistible dessert. When you do it right, the high dry heat of the grill brings out smoky caramel flavors you'd never expect of fresh pineapple. This version pays homage to the world's most famous pineapple drink: the piña colada. (And while I'm thinking of that, who among you will try making a piña colada with grilled fresh pineapple?) Coconut cream provides the richness, while shredded coconut supplies the crunch. The key is to grill it over a screaming hot fire so you caramelize the sugars while leaving the fruit raw and juicy in the center.

YIELD: Serves 4 to 6

METHOD: Direct grilling

PREP TIME: 15 minutes

GRILLING TIME: 4 to 6 minutes

GRILL/GEAR: Can be grilled over charcoal, wood, or gas. You also need a basting brush and a wire rack set over a sheet pan.

SHOP: To make your life easier, buy a fresh pineapple that's been peeled and cored. Choose a bright yellow fruit, which tends to be sweeter than a pale straw-colored pineapple. There are two options for coconut liquids: sweetened coconut cream, the base for a piña colada cocktail, or Asian-style coconut milk, which contains no added sugar.

INSIDER TIP: There are two ways you can slice the peeled, cored pineapple for grilling: crosswise into rings or lengthwise into logs. With a little imagination (and perhaps a piña colada or two), the latter look a little like pork tenderloins. Just saying.

INGREDIENTS

1 luscious ripe pineapple, leafy crown removed, peeled, and cored

1 cup granulated sugar

2 teaspoons ground cinnamon

½ teaspoon freshly grated nutmeg

¾ cup (6 ounces) coconut cream, like Coco Lopez, or unsweetened coconut milk

Vegetable oil for oiling the grill grate

1 pint coconut or vanilla ice cream

½ cup toasted sweetened shredded coconut (see box, page 296)

½ cup dark or 151 rum, for serving

1. Cut the pineapple crosswise into ¾-inch-thick slices. Alternatively, cut it lengthwise into 8 strips. Place on a wire rack set over a sheet pan.

2. Place the sugar in a shallow bowl. Add the cinnamon and nutmeg and stir with a fork. Shake the coconut cream well, then pour it into another bowl. Have the coconut cream and spiced sugar next to the grill.

3. Set up a grill for direct grilling and heat to high. Brush or scrape the grill grate clean and oil it well.

4. Brush each pineapple slice on both sides with coconut cream, then dredge it on both sides in the sugar, shaking off any excess.

5. Arrange the pineapple slices over the hot fire and grill until darkly browned (the sugar should start to caramelize) on both sides, 2 to 3 minutes per side. If grilling rounds, give each a quarter turn after 1 minute to lay on a crosshatch of grill marks. If grilling strips, arrange them on the grate on the diagonal, and give each a quarter turn after 1 minute.

6. Scoop the ice cream into serving bowls and arrange the pineapple on top. Sprinkle with toasted coconut. Serve as is, or finish with a rum flambé (see Note).

NOTE: To flambé the pineapple, if using dark rum, warm it in a small saucepan (it should be finger-dip warm—do not let it boil). There's no need to warm 151 rum. Touch a long match to the rum to ignite it, then pour it over the pineapple. For safety's sake, make sure your sleeves are rolled up and there's nothing else but the rum that can catch on fire.

HOW TO TOAST COCONUT

Place the shredded coconut in a dry skillet over medium-high heat. Toast until golden brown, 2 minutes, stirring with a wooden spoon. Transfer the coconut to a bowl and let cool.

MANGO MACADAMIA CRISP

YIELD: Serves 6 to 8

METHOD: Indirect grilling

PREP TIME: 20 minutes

GRILLING TIME: 40 to 60 minutes

The grilled fruit crisp is another longstanding family favorite. With good reason—it's easy to prepare, endlessly versatile, and off-the-charts impressive. It calls for the technique I call smoke-roasting—indirect grilling at high heat with wood smoke. You'll be amazed how the smoke amplifies and transforms the fruit flavor. Over the years, I've made crisps with blueberries, strawberries and rhubarb, peaches, cactus pears (and, of course, regular pears), and apples spiked with bourbon and bacon. Here's a tropical version with a bright, brassy, musky mango filling and a sweet crunchy macadamia nut-coconut crust. Warning: With some people, mango sap produces an allergic reaction similar to that caused by poison ivy. Wear rubber gloves if you have sensitive skin.

GRILL/GEAR: Can be grilled over charcoal or gas. You also need a food processor; a well-seasoned 10-inch cast-iron skillet; and 2 hardwood chunks or 1½ cups unsoaked wood chips.

SHOP: Forgive my partisanship, but the world's best mangoes come from my home state, Florida. Look for Hadens, Keitts, Kents, Tommy Atkinses, or Van Dykes, to name a few of the best-known varieties. Happily, they're in season during the prime barbecue months, June through August. Choose heavy fruits showing some yellow or red on the skin (but Keitts remain green even when ripe). A ripe mango will smell intensely fragrant and feel gently yielding when pressed. If your mangoes aren't there yet, ripen them in a paper bag at room temperature.

INSIDER TIP: The obvious advantage of cooking a fruit crisp on the grill instead of in the oven is that you can smoke it. Smoke has the uncanny power to make familiar dishes taste wondrous and exotic. (I like to think of smoke as the umami of barbecue.) But dessert isn't brisket: You want a light smoke flavor, so use a moderate amount of *unsoaked* wood, preferably fruitwood.

INGREDIENTS

Butter, for greasing the skillet

FOR THE FILLING

5 to 6 ripe mangoes (enough to make 6 cups diced)

¼ cup packed brown sugar, dark or light, or to taste

3 tablespoons all-purpose flour

Grated zest and juice of 1 lime, or to taste

2 tablespoons minced candied ginger

FOR THE TOPPING

1 cup macadamia nuts

¾ cup shredded unsweetened coconut

¼ cup all-purpose flour

¼ cup packed brown sugar, dark or light

1 teaspoon ground cinnamon

Pinch of coarse salt (sea or kosher)

8 tablespoons (1 stick) ice-cold butter, cut into ½-inch dice

Ice cream or Smoked Whipped Cream (page 293)

1. Lightly butter the bottom and sides of a 10-inch cast-iron skillet and set aside.

2. Make the filling: Peel the mangoes and slice the fruit off the pits using long strokes of the knife. (Be careful as mangoes are slippery.) Cut the mangoes into 1-inch dice—you should have 6 cups—and place in a mixing bowl. Stir in the ¼ cup brown sugar, flour, lime zest, lime juice, and candied ginger. Add more sugar or lime juice to taste; the filling should be very flavorful. Spoon the filling into the prepared skillet.

3. Make the topping: Place the macadamia nuts in a food processor. Coarsely chop the nuts, running the processor in short bursts. Add the coconut, flour, brown sugar, cinnamon, salt, and butter. Run the processor

in short bursts until the mixture is coarse and crumbly, 1 to 2 minutes. The butter should form pea-size pieces. Do not overprocess, or the mixture will become gummy. Spoon the topping evenly over the fruit filling in the skillet.

4. Meanwhile, set up the grill for indirect grilling. If using a charcoal grill, heat it to medium-high, then toss all of the wood chunks or chips on the coals. Or, use the gas grill smoking method on page 22.

5. Place the crisp in the center of the grate, away from the heat, and cover the grill. Smoke-roast until the topping is nicely browned and the filling is bubbling, 40 to 60 minutes. Let the crisp cool for a few minutes. Serve with ice cream or with dollops of Smoked Whipped Cream.

Variations

Berry Crisp: Substitute 6 cups of washed berries (one kind or mixed) for the mangoes, and lemon zest and juice for the lime (you'll need 1 lemon). Replace the macadamia nuts with pecans or almonds. Prepare as described on the facing page.

Bacon Brandy Apple Crisp: Substitute 6 cups diced apples for the mangoes, and lemon zest and juice for the lime. Add 1 strip grilled, diced bacon (page 50) and 2 tablespoons of Cognac or brandy. Replace the macadamia nuts with walnuts or pecans. Prepare as described on the facing page.

GRILLED POUND CAKE
WITH STRAWBERRY "SALSA" AND SMOKED WHIPPED CREAM

The grill was the original toaster, and in this dish, you'll use it to make "toast" you can serve for dessert. Grilling gives the pound cake a crusty exterior and the pleasing burnt sugar taste of caramel. To offset the sweetness, serve it with a strawberry "salsa" complete with cilantro and jalapeños. (If that sounds too weird, use fresh mint.)

YIELD: Serves 4 to 8

METHOD: Direct grilling

PREP TIME: 15 minutes

GRILLING TIME: 4 to 8 minutes

GRILL/GEAR: Can be grilled over charcoal, wood, or gas.

SHOP: Being something of a purist, I've tried grilling homemade pound cake. I have to confess: Nothing beats Sara Lee. For an interesting variation, grill slices of angel food cake.

INGREDIENTS

FOR THE STRAWBERRY SALSA

1 quart fresh strawberries, rinsed, stemmed, and quartered

¼ cup slivered fresh cilantro or mint

1 to 2 jalapeño peppers, stemmed, seeded, and minced

3 tablespoons freshly squeezed lime juice, or more to taste

2 tablespoons granulated sugar, or more to taste

FOR THE POUND CAKE

Vegetable oil for oiling the grill grate

8 slices (¾ inch thick) pound cake (see Shop), thawed if frozen

4 tablespoons (½ stick) butter, melted

Smoked Whipped Cream (page 293) or regular whipped cream, for serving

1. Make the strawberry salsa: Place the strawberries, cilantro or mint, jalapeño(s), lime juice, and sugar in a mixing bowl but do not mix. The salsa can be prepared to this stage up to 2 hours ahead and refrigerated.

2. Set up the grill for direct grilling and heat to medium-high. When ready to cook, brush or scrape the grill grate clean and oil it well.

3. Lightly brush the cake slices on both sides with the melted butter. Arrange the slices of cake on the grill at a diagonal to the bars of the grate and grill until lightly browned on both sides, 1 to 2 minutes per side, turning with a spatula. Transfer the grilled cake slices to a platter or plates.

4. Toss the strawberry salsa to mix. Taste for sweetness, adding more sugar and/or lime juice as necessary. Spoon the salsa over the grilled cake. Top each portion with a dollop of Smoked Whipped Cream and serve at once. Serve any extra whipped cream on the side.

INSIDER TIP: On page 293, you'll find instructions for smoking cream on your grill. There's another method that's simple and effective (and essential if you cook on a gas grill): Use a handheld smoker, like a PolyScience Smoking Gun. Place the cream in a bowl and cover with plastic wrap. Pump in the smoke and let the cream infuse for 4 minutes. Repeat 2 or 3 times.

DESSERT QUESADILLAS
BANANA, QUESO FRESCO, AND DULCE DE LECHE

Readers of my books know my enthusiasm for grilled quesadillas. The high dry heat of the grill crisps the tortilla without the greasiness of pan-frying. Well, here's a grilled quesadilla designed to serve for dessert. Dulce de leche and fresh bananas provide the sweetness, with the *queso fresco* (see Shop on page 101) adding a salty cheese note. The cinnamon sugar makes the quesadillas a little more crisp.

YIELD: Serves 2 and can be multiplied as desired

METHOD: Direct grilling

PREP TIME: 15 minutes

GRILLING TIME: 4 to 6 minutes

GRILL/GEAR: Can be grilled over charcoal, wood, or gas. Not that you need one, but there are quesadilla grilling baskets that facilitate turning the quesadillas. Check the Store on barbecuebible.com.

INGREDIENTS

4 flour tortillas (8 inches each)

3 tablespoons unsalted butter, melted

¼ cup cinnamon sugar (optional)

½ cup dulce de leche

1 ripe but firm banana, peeled and thinly sliced crosswise on the diagonal

½ cup coarsely grated or crumbled queso fresco (optional)

Vegetable oil for oiling the grill grate

SHOP: Dulce de leche (a milk caramel originating in South and Central America) is available at Hispanic food markets and most supermarkets or online. Three widely available brands are La Lechera, San Ignacio, and Stonewall Kitchen.

INSIDER TIP: The only remotely challenging part of this recipe is flipping the quesadilla. If you're nervous about your spatula skills, pull the quesadilla off the grate onto a rimless sheet pan. Place a second rimless sheet pan on top to sandwich it, turn that over, then slide the quesadilla back onto the grill. To make cinnamon sugar, stir 1 teaspoon ground cinnamon into ¼ cup granulated sugar.

1. Set up your grill for direct grilling and heat to medium-high.

2. Brush one of the tortillas with melted butter and lightly sprinkle with cinnamon sugar, if using. Place it, butter and sugar side down, on a rimless baking sheet, inverted sheet pan, or pizza peel. Spread the tortilla with a quarter of the dulce de leche. Arrange half the banana slices on top and sprinkle with half the cheese. Spread a second tortilla with a quarter of the dulce de leche and place it, spread side down, on top of the cheese. Brush the top of the tortilla with melted butter and sprinkle it with cinnamon sugar. Assemble the second quesadilla the same way.

3. Brush or scrape the grill grate clean and oil it well.

4. Pulling from one end, gently slide the quesadilla onto the grill grate. Grill until the bottom is browned and the cheese at the edge starts to melt, 2 to 3 minutes. Keep the grill lid closed to hold in the heat.

5. Slide a large spatula under the quesadilla and flip it over (or use the flipping technique outlined in the Insider Tip). Continue grilling until the bottom is browned and the cheese is melted, another 2 minutes. If the tortilla starts to burn, slide it to the unlit part of the grill with a spatula. You'll need 4 to 6 minutes of grilling in all.

6. Transfer the quesadilla to a platter or plate and repeat with the second quesadilla. Cut the quesadillas into wedges for serving.

Spread the bottom tortilla with dulce de leche.

Arrange the banana slices over the dulce de leche.

Arrange the second tortilla, dulce de leche side down, over the bananas and cheese. It's now ready to be brushed with butter and sprinkled with cinnamon sugar.

SALT SLAB CHOCOLATE BROWNIE S'MORES

You didn't think I was going to finish this chapter without the original grilled dessert—the s'more? I won't disappoint you. I give you the richest, awesomest, most decadently chocolaty s'more of all. You start not with graham crackers, but with your favorite chocolate brownie. (Extra points if it's homemade.) You sandwich it with a bar of 70 or 80 percent pure cocoa chocolate—Lindt Excellence, Scharffen Berger, or Valrhona, for example. In the best of all possible worlds, you use fine artisanal marshmallows, preferably that come in rectangles large enough to cover the brownies and in flavors like bourbon or orange (see Shop). If you're feeling *really* ambitious, make your own marshmallows. For extra flavor, you'll add thinly slivered mint leaves or crème de menthe (chocolate has a great affinity for mint). Finally, you smoke-roast the s'mores on a fire-heated salt slab, salt being the secret ingredient used by so many pastry chefs these days to bring out a dessert's sweetness, while paradoxically, not making it taste sugary. Tip o' the hat to the Full of Life pizzeria in Los Alamos, California, where a similar s'more comes sizzling and smoky from a humongous wood-burning oven.

INGREDIENTS

6 excellent chocolate brownies
(each about 3 by 4 inches)

6 fresh mint leaves, rolled and thinly
slivered, or 2 tablespoons crème de
menthe liqueur (optional)

6 squares (each about 2 by 3 inches)
super premium chocolate bar

6 rectangular marshmallows
(each about 2 by 3 inches) or
conventional marshmallows,
cut in half lengthwise

Flaky salt, preferably Maldon,
for serving (optional)

YIELD: Serves 6 and can be multiplied as desired

METHOD: Salt slab grilling/ indirect grilling

PREP TIME: 10 minutes

GRILLING TIME: 6 to 10 minutes

GRILL/GEAR: Can be grilled over charcoal or gas. You also need a salt slab for grilling (see page 29) and 1 cup unsoaked wood chips.

SHOP: A dessert this simple lives or dies by the quality of its ingredients. Sure, you could buy supermarket marshmallows (a brand you remember from your youth), but why ingest tetrasodium pyrophosphate if you don't have to? Instead, splurge on gourmet marshmallows made with natural ingredients, like Plush Puffs (an artisanal company founded by chefs) or bourbon-infused Wondermade marshmallows. Both are available from Amazon.

INSIDER TIP: Warning: Do not make this recipe in cold weather. Hot salt slabs have been known to crack or explode when exposed to cold air.

1. Brush or scrape the grill grate clean; there's no need to oil it. Set up your grill for indirect grilling and heat slowly to medium-high. Gradually heat the salt slab at the same time.

2. Lay the slivered mint leaves atop the brownies or sprinkle the brownies with crème de menthe, if using. Lay a square of chocolate on top, and top with a marshmallow.

3. Arrange the marshmallow-topped brownies on the hot salt slab. Add the wood chips to the coals or to your grill's smoker box and lower the lid. Smoke-roast the s'more brownies until the marshmallows are sizzling and browned, 6 to 10 minutes. Transfer to plates or bowls or serve them right off the salt slab, sprinkled with flaky salt, if using.

GRILLED SANGRIA

Sangria comes from one of the world's great grill cultures, Spain. While I've never seen anyone grill this refreshing wine cooler in the land of paella and *chuletón*, I think you'll find the *Project Fire* version as spectacular to make and serve as it is to drink. In a nutshell, you crust the citrus fruits with sugar, then caramelize them over a hot fire before adding the wine. The resulting smoky burnt sugar flavor takes this sangria into the stratosphere.

INGREDIENTS

Vegetable oil for oiling the grill

1 cup granulated sugar

2 navel or other oranges, cut in half and seeded, if needed

2 lemons, cut in half and seeded

2 limes, cut in half and seeded, if needed

4 cinnamon sticks, each about 3 inches long

½ cup packed brown sugar, dark or light, or to taste

1 cup dark rum

3 cold bottles Prosecco or other sparkling wine, such as Lambrusco (see Shop)

Ice, for serving

Sprigs of fresh mint, for serving

YIELD: Serves 10 to 12

METHOD: Direct grilling

PREP TIME: 15 minutes

GRILLING TIME: 3 to 4 minutes

GRILL/GEAR: Can be grilled over charcoal, wood, or gas. You also need a large punch bowl.

SHOP: In Spain, sangria is rarely carbonated, but here in the United States, many of us grew up on a sort of sweet wine punch made fizzy with citrus soda. I prefer to use sparkling wine: Prosecco to make a white sangria, for example, or Lambrusco (a red sparkling wine from Italy's Lombardy region) to make a red sangria.

INSIDER TIP: True cinnamon has shaggy bark; the smooth-stick spice that often passes for cinnamon is really cassia. Both work great for this sangria: Grilling the cinnamon adds a spicy smoke flavor.

1. Set up your grill for direct grilling and heat to high. Brush or scrape the grill grate clean and oil it well.

2. Place the granulated sugar in a large mixing bowl or punch bowl. Dip the cut sides of the citrus fruits in the sugar, then grill cut sides down until the sugar caramelizes and the fruit is darkly browned, 3 to 4 minutes. (Do not empty the remaining sugar from the bowl.) Grill the cinnamon sticks until lightly toasted. Transfer the fruit and cinnamon to a cutting board and let cool.

3. Dice the fruit into 1-inch pieces. Return to the punch bowl with the remaining granulated sugar. Stir in the cinnamon sticks and brown sugar and muddle with a pestle or wooden spoon. Stir in the rum and let macerate for 10 minutes.

4. Just before serving, stir the cold Prosecco into the fruit mixture. Correct the sweetness, adding sugar to taste. Ladle the sangria into ice-filled glasses and garnish with sprigs of fresh mint.

GRILLED PEACH BELLINIS

YIELD: Serves 4

METHOD: Direct grilling

PREP TIME: 10 minutes

GRILLING TIME: 6 minutes

GRILL/GEAR: Can be grilled over charcoal, wood, or gas. You also need 2 fruitwood chunks or 1½ cups unsoaked wood chips (optional); a food processor; a bamboo skewer; and 4 champagne flutes (optional).

SHOP: Tradition calls for white freestone peaches, but choose ripeness and freshness over color. Prosecco is an Italian sparkling wine.

Born at Harry's Bar in Venice, Italy, in 1948, and named for a Renaissance painter (as was Harry's other masterpiece, carpaccio), the Bellini is the ultimate summer cocktail. Effervescent. Fruity, but not sugary. Served with majesty in a flute, like Champagne. It contains only three ingredients—sparkling wine, sugar, and white peach puree. And it's about to get a lot more interesting, because in the *Project Fire* version—you guessed it—I introduce a smoky caramel flavor by grilling the peaches.

INGREDIENTS

Vegetable oil for the grill grate

2 fragrant ripe peaches, preferably white, peeled, cut in half, and pitted

½ cup granulated sugar, in a shallow bowl

1 bottle cold Prosecco

1. Set up your grill for direct grilling and heat to high. Brush or scrape the grill grate clean and oil it well. Add wood chunks or chips, if using, to the fire, following the instructions on page 21.

2. Dip the peach halves on all sides in the sugar, shaking off the excess. Grill the peaches, starting cut side down, until caramelized (dark brown), 2 to 3 minutes per side, 4 to 6 minutes in all, turning once with tongs.

3. Transfer the peach halves to a plate to cool. Puree 3 halves in a food processor or blender. Cut the remaining half into thin wedges for garnishing the Bellini.

4. Add 2 to 3 tablespoons of peach puree to each of 4 champagne flutes, if using, or wineglasses. Fill each flute with chilled Prosecco and gently stir with a bamboo skewer. Garnish each glass with a peach wedge and serve.

INSIDER TIP: This cocktail lives or dies by the quality of the peaches. Use soft ripe fragrant fruit you can smell across the room and you'll experience the Bellini in all its summer glory. Use the sort of cold stone-hard peaches sold at all-too-many supermarkets and your cocktail will be a pale simulacrum of what a Bellini should be. If that's all you can find, at least let the peach ripen for a few days at room temperature.

CONVERSION TABLES

Please note that all conversions are approximate but close enough to be useful when converting from one system to another.

OVEN TEMPERATURES

FAHRENHEIT	GAS MARK	CELSIUS
250	½	120
275	1	140
300	2	150
325	3	160
350	4	180
375	5	190
400	6	200
425	7	220
450	8	230
475	9	240
500	10	260

NOTE: Reduce the temperature by 20°C (68°F) for fan-assisted ovens.

APPROXIMATE EQUIVALENTS

1 stick butter = 8 tbs = 4 oz = ½ cup = 115 g

1 cup all-purpose presifted flour = 4.7 oz

1 cup granulated sugar = 8 oz = 220 g

1 cup (firmly packed) brown sugar = 6 oz = 220 g to 230 g

1 cup confectioners' sugar = 4½ oz = 115 g

1 cup honey or syrup = 12 oz = 350 g

1 cup grated cheese = 4 oz = 125 g

1 cup dried beans = 6 oz = 175 g

1 large egg = about 2 oz or about 3 tbs

1 egg yolk = about 1 tbs

1 egg white = about 2 tbs

LIQUID CONVERSIONS

US	IMPERIAL	METRIC
2 tbs	1 fl oz	30 ml
3 tbs	1½ fl oz	45 ml
¼ cup	2 fl oz	60 ml
⅓ cup	2½ fl oz	75 ml
⅓ cup + 1 tbs	3 fl oz	90 ml
⅓ cup + 2 tbs	3½ fl oz	100 ml
½ cup	4 fl oz	125 ml
⅔ cup	5 fl oz	150 ml
¾ cup	6 fl oz	175 ml
¾ cup + 2 tbs	7 fl oz	200 ml
1 cup	8 fl oz	250 ml
1 cup + 2 tbs	9 fl oz	275 ml
1¼ cups	10 fl oz	300 ml
1⅓ cups	11 fl oz	325 ml
1½ cups	12 fl oz	350 ml
1⅔ cups	13 fl oz	375 ml
1¾ cups	14 fl oz	400 ml
1¾ cups + 2 tbs	15 fl oz	450 ml
2 cups (1 pint)	16 fl oz	500 ml
2½ cups	20 fl oz (1 pint)	600 ml
3¾ cups	1½ pints	900 ml
4 cups	1¾ pints	1 liter

WEIGHT CONVERSIONS

US/UK	METRIC	US/UK	METRIC
½ oz	15 g	7 oz	200 g
1 oz	30 g	8 oz	250 g
1½ oz	45 g	9 oz	275 g
2 oz	60 g	10 oz	300 g
2½ oz	75 g	11 oz	325 g
3 oz	90 g	12 oz	350 g
3½ oz	100 g	13 oz	375 g
4 oz	125 g	14 oz	400 g
5 oz	150 g	15 oz	450 g
6 oz	175 g	1 lb	500 g

INDEX

inserting thermometer into, 41

internal doneness temperatures, 42, 238

keeping cold before cooking, 44

salmon steaks on a shovel, 239–41, *240*

salt slab–grilled rockfish with mango mint salsa, 251–52

sardines grilled in grape leaves with tomato olive salsa/lemon sesame sauce, 253–55, *254*

whole, spit-roasting, 26

wood-grilled swordfish with butter-fried olives, 242–43

Flare-ups, 40

Flashbacks, 6

Flavoring food, 18–19

Fresh cherry salsa, *216,* 218

Front-loading charcoal grill, 4

Fruit:

amaretti planked pears, 290–91

bacon brandy apple crisp, 299

berry crisp, 299

cinnamon-grilled peaches with bourbon brown sugar glaze, 288–90, *289*

dessert quesadillas (banana, queso fresco, and dulce de leche), *300,* 301–2

dessert "steak" sandwich (apple steaks on grilled gingerbread), 291–92

fresh cherry salsa, *216,* 218

grilled peach Bellinis, 306–7

grilled "piña colada" (coconut pineapple with rum flambé), *294,* 295–96

grilled pineapple and shrimp salad with Vietnamese flavors, 108–10, *109*

grilled pound cake with strawberry "salsa" and smoked whipped cream, 299–301

grilled sangria, 305–6

grilled watermelon salad with arugula and queso fresco, 101–3

mango macadamia crisp, 296–99, *297*

mango mint salsa, 252

planked figs with taleggio cheese and speck, 70–71

"swine-apple" kebabs (pork, pineapple, and jalapeño), 163–64

see also Lemon(s); Orange(s)

G

Game hens, smoke-roasted, with Kentucky fire dip, 209–10

Garlic:

bread, grilled (Texas toast), 84–85

Tuscan bruschetta, 80, *81*

Gas, for grilling, 10–11

Gas gauge, 16

Gas grilling math, 12

Gas grilling tools, 16

Gas grills:

about, 6

adding smoke flavors to, 22

buying, 5

cleaning and maintenance schedule, 47

direct grilling on, 22

fires in, 40

indirect grilling on, 20, 22

lighting, 33

making a smoker pouch for, 23

safety guidelines, 44–45

smoking foods on, 22

spit-roasting on, 25

see also specific types

Gas shutoff, automatic, 16

Gingerbread, grilled, apple steaks on (dessert "steak" sandwich), 291–92

Grate-grabber, 14

Grease fires, 40

Greek grilled cheese (halloumi, honey, and mint), 69–70

Greens:

grilled blt salad, 104–6

grilled watermelon salad with arugula and queso fresco, 101–3

grilled wedge salad with smoked blue cheese dressing, 98–99

Italian cheeseburgers with crispy prosciutto, grilled radicchio, and gorgonzola, 187–88

Thai grilled kale, 274–76, *275*

Green sauce (creamy salsa verde), *200, 203*

Grill basket halibut with maple teriyaki, 249–51, *250*

Grill baskets, 14, 39

Grill cleaner, 18

Grilled asparagus and corn salad with charred lemon vinaigrette, 111–13, *112*

Grilled bacon, 50

Grilled blt salad, 104–6

Grilled chicken breasts with Spanish ham, Manchego cheese, and saffron butter, 206–8, *207*

Grilled clams with linguiça and peppers, 228–29

Grilled eggs with prosciutto and Parmesan, *54,* 55–56

L

Lamb:
  burgers with yogurt and dill,
    188–89
  chop hot pops, 177–78, *179*
  inserting thermometer into, 41
  internal doneness
    temperatures, 42
  kebabs, North African, with
    harissa mayonnaise, 178–81
  leg of, with tandoori seasonings,
    170–72, *171*
  shoulder, Asian-flavored,
    172–75
  sliders, Asian-flavored,
    174, 175
  steaks, grilled, with mint
    chimichurri, 176
Leaf grilling, 30–31
Leg of lamb with tandoori
  seasonings, 170–72, *171*
Lemongrass pork bites, 165–67,
  166
Lemon(s):
  charred, aioli, 263
  charred, vinaigrette, grilled
    asparagus and corn salad
    with, 111–13, *112*
  dill coriander sauce, *240,* 242
  grilled sangria, 305–6
  lamb chop hot pops, 177–78, *179*
  oiling grill grate with, 39
  sesame sauce, *254,* 255
  wood-grilled swordfish with
    butter-fried olives, 242–43
Lettuce:
  grilled blt salad, 104–6
  grilled wedge salad with
    smoked blue cheese dressing,
    98–99
Liquid propane, 10–11

Lobster:
  caveman, with absinthe butter,
    236–38, *237*
  internal doneness
    temperatures, 238
  spit-roasting, 26
Lump charcoal, 9

M

Macadamia mango crisp, 296–99,
  297
Main courses (beef and veal):
  bool kogi beef kebabs, 138–39
  caveman porterhouse with
    pepper hash, 127–30, *128*
  coffee-crusted beef short ribs
    with red-eye barbecue sauce,
    135–37
  dry-brined peppered filets
    mignons with anchovy cream
    or cutting board sauce,
    122–25, *123*
  first-timer's T-bones (how to
    grill the perfect steak),
    116–17
  hanger steaks with mustard
    and caramelized onion sauce,
    126–27
  hedgehog hot dogs, 192–93
  Italian cheeseburgers with
    crispy prosciutto, grilled
    radicchio, and gorgonzola,
    187–88
  the Raichlen "cheesesteak"
    (whole beef tenderloin stuffed
    with grilled poblanos, onions,
    and provolone cheese),
    134–35
  reverse-seared tomahawk
    steaks with blue cheese
    butter, 117–18

  rosemary-smoked veal chops,
    139–41, *140*
  rotisserie prime rib with
    horseradish cream, 130–32,
    133
  triple steak burgers, 184–86,
    185
Main courses (lamb):
  Asian-flavored lamb shoulder,
    172–75
  Asian-flavored lamb sliders,
    174, 175
  grilled lamb steaks with mint
    chimichurri, 176
  lamb burgers with yogurt and
    dill, 188–89
  lamb chop hot pops, 177–78, *179*
  leg of lamb with tandoori
    seasonings, 170–72, *171*
  North African lamb kebabs
    with harissa mayonnaise,
    178–81
Main courses (pork):
  black pepper baby back ribs
    with whiskey vanilla glaze,
    157–58, *159*
  first-timer's pork shoulder
    served with mustard slaw
    and mustard barbecue sauce,
    145–48, *147*
  Italian cheeseburgers with
    crispy prosciutto, grilled
    radicchio, and gorgonzola,
    187–88
  lemongrass pork bites, 165–67,
    166
  mile-long Italian (Italian
    sausage sandwich for a
    crowd), 189–92, *190*
  porchetta pork chops, 153–54
  pork belly steamed buns with
    Chinatown barbecue sauce,
    155–57

Trout, bacon-grilled, with fennel orange salad, 256–57
Truffles or herb butter under the skin, spit-roasted turkey with cognac injector sauce and (the Raichlen butter bird), 220–23, *221*
Tuna:
  albacore, "filets mignons" with peppercorn cream sauce, 244–47, *245*
  internal doneness temperatures, 42
Turkey:
  breast, bourbon-brined smoked, 219–20
  inserting thermometer into, 41
  internal doneness temperatures, 42, 196
  spit-roasted, with cognac injector sauce and herb butter or truffles under the skin (the Raichlen butter bird), 220–23, *221*
Tuscan bruschetta, 80, *81*
Tuscan grill, 16

U

Under-grate smoker box, 16
Upright barrel grills (aka drum grills):
  about, 7–8
  lighting methods, 32–33

V

Veal:
  chops, rosemary-smoked, 139–41, *140*

internal cooking temperatures, 119
internal doneness temperatures, 42
Vegetable(s):
  ember-roasted, salad (escalivada), 99–100
  skins, smoking with, 24
  see also specific vegetables
Venison, internal cooking temperatures, 119
Vietnamese-style wings, 75

W

Walnuts:
  bacon brandy apple crisp, 299
  ember-roasted beet salad with sour cream and dill, *102,* 103–4
  grilled watermelon salad with arugula and queso fresco, 101–3
  grilled wedge salad with smoked blue cheese dressing, 98–99
Watermelon, grilled, salad with arugula and queso fresco, 101–3
Whipped cream, smoked, 293
Whiskey vanilla glaze, black pepper baby back ribs with, 157–58, *159*
Wild rice, cranberries, and pecans, salt slab squash stuffed with, *282,* 283–84
Wine:
  grilled peach Bellinis, 306–7
  grilled sangria, 305–6
Winter grilling, 45

Wire grill brush/wooden grill scraper, 14
Wire racks, 38
Wood:
  alder, 13
  apple, 13
  beech, 13
  cherry, 13
  chunks, 12
  flavoring food with, 11
  hickory and pecan, 13
  logs, 12
  mesquite, 13
  oak, 13
  pellets, 12
  soaking, 34
  typical types used for grilling, 12, 13
Wood-burning grills:
  asado-style, 6
  charcoal method, 34
  how to light, 34
  log cabin method, 34
  pellet grills, 6–7
  tepee method, 34
Wood-burning ovens, 31
Wood-grilled swordfish with butter-fried olives, 242–43
Wood-studded briquettes, 10

Y

Yakitori like they make it in Tokyo, 214–15
Yogurt:
  and dill, lamb burgers with, 188–89
  leg of lamb with tandoori seasonings, 170–72, *171*
  spice-scented, *267, 268*

STEVEN RAICHLEN

Author, journalist, lecturer, and TV host, Steven Raichlen is the man who reinvented modern barbecue. His 30 books include the international blockbusters *The Barbecue! Bible* and *How to Grill*, and the *New York Times* bestselling *Planet Barbecue!* and *Project Smoke* (Workman Publishing). His books have won five James Beard Awards and three IACP–Julia Child Awards and have been translated into 17 languages. An award-winning journalist, Raichlen has written for the *New York Times, Wall Street Journal, Esquire, GQ*, and all the major food magazines. In 2015, he was inducted into the Barbecue Hall of Fame.

Steven Raichlen hosts the popular TV shows *Steven Raichlen's Project Smoke*, *Primal Grill*, and *Barbecue University* on Public Television, and stars in two French language TV shows—*Le Maitre du Grill* and *Les Incontournables de BBQ*. His latest show, *Steven Raichlen Grills Italy*, airs on Gambero Rosso in Italy. Founder of *Barbecue University* at the Broadmoor resort in Colorado Springs, Raichlen has lectured on the history of barbecue at institutions as diverse as Harvard, the Library of Congress, and the Smithsonian. He holds a degree in French literature from Reed College in Portland, Oregon, and researched medieval cooking in Europe on a Thomas J. Watson Foundation Fellowship. He and his wife, Barbara, live in Miami and Martha's Vineyard.